AF601645

GOVERNMENT BUILDING

A BRIEF HISTORY

OF THE

HAWAIIAN PEOPLE

BY

W. D. ALEXANDER

PUBLISHED BY ORDER OF THE BOARD OF EDUCATION OF THE HAWAIIAN ISLANDS

University Press of the Pacific
Honolulu, Hawaii

A Brief History of the Hawaiian People

by
W.D. Alexander

Published by order of the board of Education of the Hawaiian Island

ISBN 0-89875-324-4

Copyright © 2001 by University Press of the Pacific

Reprinted from the 1899 edition

University Press of the Pacific
Honolulu, Hawaii
http://www.universitypressofthepacific.com

All rights reserved, including the right to reproduce this book, or portions thereof, in any form.

In order to make original editions of historical works available to scholars at an economical price, this facsimile of the original edition of 1899 is reproduced from the best available copy and has been digitally enhanced to improve legibility, but the text remains unaltered to retain historical authenticity.

PREFACE

AT the request of the Board of Education, I have endeavored to write a simple and concise history of the Hawaiian people, which, it is hoped, may be useful to the teachers and higher classes in our schools.

As there is, however, no book in existence that covers the whole ground, and as the earlier histories are entirely out of print, it has been deemed best to prepare not merely a school-book, but a history for the benefit of the general public.

This book has been written in the intervals of a laborious occupation, from the stand-point of a patriotic Hawaiian, for the young people of this country rather than for foreign readers. This fact will account for its local coloring, and for the prominence given to certain topics of local interest. Especial pains have been taken to supply the want of a correct account of the ancient civil polity and religion of the Hawaiian race.

This history is not merely a compilation. It is based upon a careful study of the original authorities, the writer having had the use of the principal existing collections of Hawaiian manuscripts, and having examined the early archives of the government, as well as nearly all the existing materials in print. No pains have been spared to arrive at the truth. The principal authorities relied on in the account of Hawaiian antiquities have been David Malo, the historian, the elder Kamakau of Kaawaloa, S. M. Kamakau, the historian, and Haleole, the author of "Laieikawai."

Judge Fornander's "Polynesian Race" has been a storehouse of information for all subsequent writers, and the author can bear witness to his painstaking accuracy, his general fairness and excellent judgment.

Valuable assistance has been received from Mr. J. S. Emerson in regard to the religious belief, as well as the arts and amusements, of the ancient Hawaiians.

A history that aims to be both unsectarian and nonpartisan must necessarily be incomplete. As a general thing, the facts have been stated with but little comment. The dark side of the condition of the people in ancient times and of their intercourse with foreigners had to be in great part ignored.

The extreme brevity that was necessary has compelled the omission of much that is interesting. It is intended to follow this volume by a primary work for younger readers, composed of a series of interesting stories from Hawaiian history, arranged in chronological order.

W. D. Alexander.

Honolulu.

CONTENTS

PART I

PREHISTORIC PERIOD

CHAPTER I

PHYSICAL GEOGRAPHY

CHAPTER II

ORIGIN OF THE HAWAIIAN PEOPLE

CHAPTER III

ANCIENT HAWAIIAN VOYAGES

CHAPTER IV

ANCIENT CIVIL POLITY

CHAPTER V

CIVIL POLITY AND DOMESTIC RELATIONS

CHAPTER VI

OBJECTS OF WORSHIP

CHAPTER VII

IDOLS AND TEMPLES

CHAPTER VIII

CEREMONIAL SYSTEM

CHAPTER IX

DEDICATION OF A TEMPLE AND MAKAHIKI FESTIVAL

CHAPTER X

PRIVATE WORSHIP

CHAPTER XI

SORCERY AND DIVINATION

CHAPTER XII

FUNERAL RITES AND DOCTRINE OF A FUTURE STATE

CHAPTER XIII

ARTS AND MANUFACTURES

CHAPTER XIV

CUSTOMS AND AMUSEMENTS

PART II

TO THE DEATH OF KAMEHAMEHA I.

CHAPTER XV

ANCIENT HISTORY

CHAPTER XVI

DISCOVERY OF THE ISLANDS BY CAPTAIN COOK. 1778-1779

CHAPTER XVII

FROM THE DEATH OF CAPTAIN COOK TO THE ARRIVAL OF PORTLOCK AND DIXON. 1780-1786

CHAPTER XVIII

FROM THE ARRIVAL OF PORTLOCK AND DIXON TO THE DEATH OF KEOUA. 1786-1791

CHAPTER XIX

VANCOUVER'S THREE VISITS AND CONQUEST OF MAUI AND OAHU BY KAMEHAMEHA I. 1791-1795

CHAPTER XX

FROM THE CONQUEST OF OAHU TO THE CESSION OF KAUAI. 1795-1810

CHAPTER XXI

CLOSING YEARS OF THE REIGN OF KAMEHAMEHA I. 1810-1819

PART III

LATER HISTORY

CHAPTER XXII

ABOLITION OF IDOLATRY. 1819

CHAPTER XXIII

COMMENCEMENT OF THE AMERICAN PROTESTANT MISSION. 1820-1823

CHAPTER XXIV

LIHOLIHO'S VOYAGE TO ENGLAND, AND DEATH. 1823-1824

CHAPTER XXV

VISIT OF LORD BYRON AND OUTRAGES BY FOREIGNERS. 1825-1827

CHAPTER XXVI

CLOSING YEARS OF KAAHUMANU'S REGENCY. 1828-1832

CHAPTER XXVII

BEGINNING OF KAMEHAMEHA III.'S REIGN. 1832-1836

CHAPTER XXVIII

TROUBLES WITH FOREIGN POWERS. 1836-1839

CHAPTER XXIX

FIRST CONSTITUTION. DISPUTES WITH CONSULS. 1839-1842

CHAPTER XXX

SUCCESS OF THE EMBASSY IN EUROPE. CESSION TO LORD PAULET. 1843.

CHAPTER XXXI

RECOGNITION OF INDEPENDENCE AND ORGANIZATION OF THE GOVERNMENT. 1843-1847

CHAPTER XXXII

FOREIGN RELATIONS. 1848-1851

CHAPTER XXXIII

CLOSING YEARS OF KAMEHAMEHA III.'S REIGN. 1851-1854

CHAPTER XXXIV

REIGN OF KAMEHAMEHA IV. 1855-1863

CHAPTER XXXV

REIGN OF KAMEHAMEHA V. 1863-1872

CHAPTER XXXVI

LUNALILO, KALAKAUA, LILIUOKALANI. 1873-1891

CHAPTER XXXVII

REVOLUTION AND ANNEXATION. 1892-1898

MAPS.

ILLUSTRATIONS.

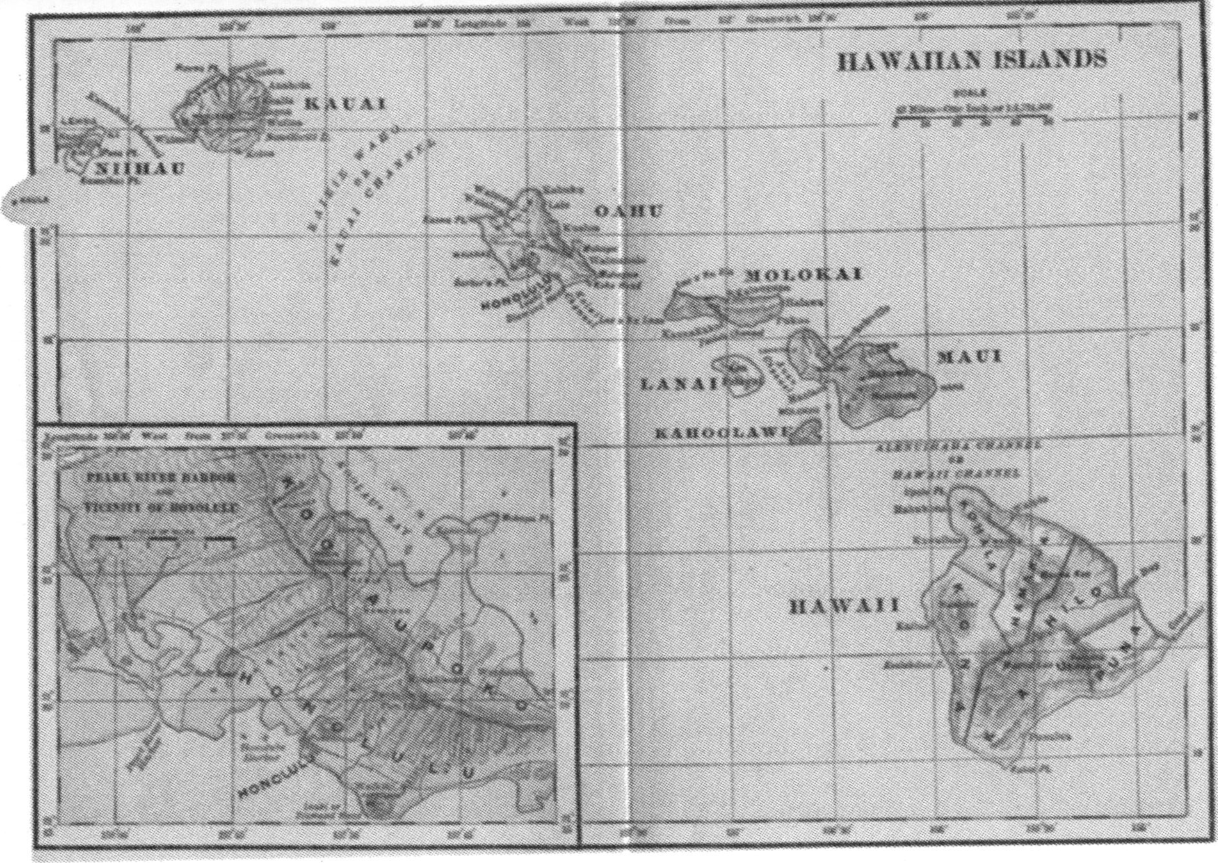
HAWAIIAN ISLANDS
SCALE
KAUAI
NIIHAU
OAHU
HONOLULU
MOLOKAI
MAUI
LANAI
KAHOOLAWE
HAWAII CHANNEL
HAWAII
KOHALA
HILO
PUNA
KONA
PEARL RIVER HARBOR
and
VICINITY OF HONOLULU
HONOLULU

PART I

PREHISTORIC PERIOD

CHAPTER I

PHYSICAL GEOGRAPHY

ALTHOUGH it is true that History has more to do with men and nations than with the countries in which they act their parts, still it is within her province to show how the position, climate, and physical features of a country have influenced the character and fortunes of the people who inhabit it.

Name.—The name *Sandwich Islands* was given to this country by Captain Cook, at the time of its discovery by him, in honor of his patron, the Earl of Sandwich, who was then First Lord of the British Admiralty; but the name *Hawaiian Islands*, derived from that of the largest island in the group, is the official name, used by the people of the islands, and is generally taking the place of the former.

Position.—The Hawaiian Islands lie just within the northern tropic, between 18° 54′ and 22° 15′ north latitude, and between 154° 50′ and 160° 30′ of longitude west of Greenwich.

They occupy a central position in the North Pacific,

about two thousand miles west of North America. This has been in the past one of the most isolated positions in the world, and the one farthest removed from the ancient centers of civilization. Now, however, these islands are directly in the track of commerce between the United States and the Commonwealth of Australia on the one hand, and between the Isthmus of Panama and China on the other. They will necessarily become an important commercial center and resort of shipping in this great ocean.

Extent.—The eight inhabited islands, viz., Hawaii, Maui, Kahoolawe, Lanai, Molokai, Oahu, Kauai, and Niihau, comprise an area of about six thousand seven hundred square miles, of which the largest island, Hawaii, includes nearly two thirds. This island is nearly equal in area to the state of Connecticut, while the whole group is about equal to the principality of Wales or the kingdom of Saxony.

The eight inhabited islands extend from northwest to southeast over a distance of about three hundred and eighty miles. The extent of the group is thus sufficient to develop a spirit of enterprise and skill in navigation among its inhabitants.

Surface.—Few countries comprise a greater variety of surface and of climate. Hawaii contains the highest mountains of any island in the world. In Europe only a few peaks of the Alps are as high as Mauna Loa and Mauna Kea, while Haleakala is about equal to Mt. Etna in extent and elevation. The two largest active volcanoes on the globe (Kilauea and Mauna Loa) are found in Hawaii, while East Maui contains the vast extinct crater of Haleakala, and the other islands abound in sublime and beautiful scenery.

Climate.—The climate of the islands is much cooler than that of other countries in the same latitude. This is due not only to the trade-winds, which blow over a wide extent of ocean, but also to the fact that the ocean itself is cooled by the return current from the region of

CRATER OF KILAUEA
(From a photograph in 1885)

Bering Straits. It is said that the seas surrounding these islands are cooler by ten degrees than those of any other region in the same latitude. The islands are exempt from the destructive cyclones which often prevail in the central part of the Pacific Ocean.

The contrast in climate between the windward and the leeward sides of each island is very striking, the eastern slopes being windy and rainy. and heavily wooded, while the western coast enjoys a warm, dry climate, with a more scanty vegetation; hence the windward side of each island has been cut by the streams into numerous deep and precipitous ravines.

Again, by ascending the mountains, any desirable degree of temperature can be attained, while on the highest summits snow remains during most of the year.

Contrast with Coral Islands.—How favorable the conditions of life are here compared with those of other islands in this ocean, is well shown by the following passage by Professor Dana, referring to the Gilbert Islands:

"How many of the various arts of civilized life could exist in a land where shells are the only cutting instruments; the plants in all but twenty-nine in number; but a single mineral; quadrupeds none, with the exception of foreign mice; fresh water barely enough for household purposes; no streams, or mountains, or hills? How much of the poetry or literature of Europe would be intelligible to persons whose ideas had expanded only to the limits of a coral island; who had never conceived of a surface of land above half a mile in breadth, of a slope higher than a beach, of a change of seasons beyond a variation in the prevalence of the rains?"

Soil.—The soil of these islands, in general, is poor, with the exception perhaps of Kauai, and nature yields but little spontaneously. The valleys, indeed, are fertile and productive, but they are of limited extent. Some of the dry plains, however, can be made fertile by irrigation. In Hawaii and Maui extensive tracts are covered with rugged lava.

Much labor and skill are necessary in order to produce

good crops. This fact tends to render the inhabitants more industrious and hardy than those of some other tropical groups. As there were no metals, the inhabitants were obliged to use the best substitutes they could find.

Animals.—The only quadrupeds existing upon the islands before their discovery by Captain Cook were dogs, swine, and mice, which were probably introduced by the first settlers. These, as well as the domestic fowls, were of the same breeds as are found throughout Polynesia. The sea abounds in fish, for which extensive artificial ponds along the coast have been constructed, which must have cost immense labor.

Plants.—The principal food plants were the taro (*colocasia antiquorum*), which was the Hawaiian "staff of life," the sweet-potato, and the yam. The only fruit-trees in ancient times were the bread-fruit, cocoanut, banana, and *ohia* (the Malay jambo), together with the *ohelo*, wild strawberry, *poha* or Cape gooseberry, and *akala* or raspberry. Many other kinds of fruit have since been introduced. Sugar-cane was indigenous, and grew luxuriantly. The *koa*, *kou*, *lehua*, *kauwila*, and other forest trees supplied abundance of timber for useful and ornamental purposes.

Unfortunately, together with useful animals and plants, many kinds of weeds and noxious vermin, such as mosquitoes, wasps, scorpions, centipedes, and white ants, have been introduced from foreign countries in recent times.

CHAPTER II

ORIGIN OF THE HAWAIIAN PEOPLE

Origin.—The question of the origin of the Hawaiian race is one which can not yet be said to have been fully solved.

As we have seen, the Hawaiian Islands are more than two thousand miles distant from the nearest inhabited land, and the prevailing winds and currents are from the east and northeast to the south and southwest.

Polynesian Affinities.—The affinities, not only of the people, but also of the plants and animals, are with the islands to the south and southwest. The inhabitants of all the groups of islands in the Eastern Pacific, from New Zealand to Hawaii and also to Easter Island, scattered over a distance of four thousand miles, may be considered as one race, which is commonly called the Polynesian race; for they all speak dialects of the same language, have the same physical features, the same manners and customs, the same general system of tabus, and similar traditions and religious rites.*

Again, it has been proved that the Polynesian language is but one member of a widespread family of languages, including those spoken in Micronesia, the Philippine Islands, the Malay Archipelago, and Madagascar.

* For example, the names of the principal gods, the stories told of the demigod Maui, of the origin of fire, about the deluge, and many others, are common to all these islands.

OCEANICA
SCALE OF STATUTE MILES
ASIA
CHINA
JAPAN SEA
JAPAN
JAPAN ISLANDS
Peking
Shanghai
Yokohama
Canton
Hong Kong
Formosa I.
INDO CHINA
SOUTH CHINA SEA
PHILIPPINE ISLANDS
Manila
MALAYSIA
INDIAN ARCHIPELAGO
NEW GUINEA
CORAL SEA
AUSTRALIA
Western Australia
South Australia
New South Wales
Brisbane
Sydney
Perth
Great Australian Bight
Hobart
INDIAN OCEAN
NORTH PACIFIC OCEAN
SOUTH PACIFIC OCEAN
POLYNESIA
HAWAIIAN ISLANDS
CAROLINE ISLANDS
MARSHALL ISLES
GILBERT ISLES
PHOENIX ISLES
AMERICA ISLES
SAMOA
NEW HEBRIDES
FRIENDLY IS.
COOK ISLES
SOCIETY IS.
MARQUESAS ISLES
AUSTRAL IS.
NORFOLK I.
Auckland
NEW ZEALAND
CHATHAM I.
ANTIPODES I.
EQUATOR
TROPIC OF CANCER
TROPIC OF CAPRICORN
San Francisco
NORTH AMERICA
Washington
North Latitude
South Latitude
West Longitude

Malaysian Affinities.—In particular, the brown race in the Moluccas or Spice Islands and Celebes seems to have a close resemblance to the Polynesians, both in language and in physical appearance. Beyond this nothing is certain, although men who have made a special study of the subject have endeavored to prove from their language, traditions, religious rites, customs, etc., that the Polynesians originally came from southwestern Asia.

Savaii, the Center of Dispersion.—As regards the Pacific Ocean, it is pretty well settled that the island of Savaii, in the Samoan group, was the chief center of dispersion for the Polynesian race, to which all their traditions point.*

The traditions of the Marquesans relate that their ancestors came from a Hawaii in the west, stopping on the way at Fiji, Vavau, and Tonga. The dialect of the southern group of the Marquesas is, on the whole, the one most like the Hawaiian, except that it drops the letter *l*.

First Settlement.—It is nearly certain that there were two distinct periods of emigration to these islands. The first settlers must have arrived in very ancient times, as is proved by the discovery of human bones under ancient coral beds and lava flows. Judge Fornander estimates that these islands were inhabited as early as 500 A.D.

These pioneer settlers may have been either expelled from other islands in war, or driven out of their course by storms.†

*The New Zealand natives, or Maoris, who have a very close resemblance to the Hawaiians, have a tradition that their ancestors migrated from *Hawaiki*, which is the same word with *Savaii* and *Hawaii*.

†We know that southerly winds or *konas* sometimes blow here for months at a time. A Japanese fishing-junk, which had been blown out of its course by a typhoon, arrived at Waialua, Oahu, in December, 1832, with four men on board.

Kadu, a native of one of the Caroline Islands, was found by Kotzebue, in 1817, on one of the Marshall Islands, to which he had drifted in a canoe with three companions, a distance of fifteen hundred miles due east. These and other like instances show how migrations have taken place from west to east.

Legend of Hawaii-loa.—There is an ancient tradition about the discovery of these islands by a chief called Hawaii-loa. He is said to have been a famous fisherman and navigator in Kahiki-ku, and by sailing toward the east to have discovered and named Hawaii and Maui. After this he made several trips back and forth, and finally settled in the islands with a large company of retainers. But the truth of this story is very doubtful.

Wakea and Papa.—According to the Hawaiian genealogies, Wakea and Papa, his wife, were the progenitors of the race, or at least founders of the line of chiefs.

It is generally admitted that they did not live in these islands, but in Kahiki, which simply means some foreign country. Wakea is also said to have introduced the tabus.*

Later on we find four consecutive generations of Hawaiian chiefs, which are the same as four in the Maori genealogy, who are said to have lived in their Hawaiki (probably Savaii) before their emigration from thence to New Zealand.

First Period.—Of that first period scarcely any traditions have come down to us. There are no traditions of any voyages to and from other countries for at least thirty generations after Wakea.

Many great works, however, are ascribed to that period, such as the building of certain heiaus, and of the great fish-ponds along the coast of Molokai and in many other places.

Ancient Works.—These are said to have been made by the *menehune* people, a word which in Tahiti is applied to the lowest class of people, sometimes represented in Hawaiian legends as a race of industrious elves or dwarfs.

* Wakea, Atea, or Vatea, is the god of light in the Marquesas and Hervey Islands, while Papa is the earth personified, the Great Mother, which idea is also expressed in the Hawaiian *mele*, Papa-hanau-moku, i. e., mother of islands.

CHAPTER III

ANCIENT HAWAIIAN VOYAGES

Second Period of Migration.—After the Hawaiian people had lived secluded from the rest of the world for many generations, intercourse between them and the islands in the South Pacific seems to have been renewed, and many voyages to have been made, which have been celebrated in song and story.

There seems to have been a general movement throughout Polynesia during the eleventh and twelfth centuries of the Christian era. It was about this time that the Hervey Islands and New Zealand were colonized, according to the traditions of the inhabitants. It is not known what started these migrations, but it may have been the expulsion of Polynesian settlers from the Fiji Islands, and the invasion of Samoa and the Tonga Islands by the refugees.

Voyage of Paao.—The most important emigration was that of Paao (a priest from Upolu in the Samoan Islands) and his followers.*

* He is said to have left Upolu in consequence of a quarrel with his brother, Lonopele, and to have sailed to Hawaii, where he became the high-priest, and built the great heiau of Mookini in Kohala. The office remained in his family down to the time of Hewahewa, who was the last high-priest, in the reign of Kamehameha I. It is said that as he found the island without a king, "on account of the crimes of Kapawa, the chief of Hawaii," he returned to Kahiki, and brought back with him a chief named Pili, whom he established as king, and from whom the Kamehameha dynasty was descended.

Paao is said to have introduced the use of the *puloulou* as the insignia of tabu and to have changed the shape and arrangements of the heiaus.

Voyage of Kaulu.—One of the most famous navigators of this period was Kaulu-a Kalana of Oahu, who visited many foreign islands in company with Luhau-Kapawa, a famous navigator and astronomer of southern birth. In the song of Kaulu it is claimed that he visited Vavau, Upolu, and Kahiki, and many other foreign lands.

Voyage of Paumakua.—Another Oahu chief, called Paumakua, was a famous navigator. He visited the southern islands, and brought back with him several priests, who are described in the traditions as foreigners or haoles of large stature, light complexion, and bright, saucy eyes, from whom several priestly families on Oahu claimed descent.

Voyage of Moikeha.—In the next generation a famous chief named Moikeha, with his brother Olopana, his wife Luukia, and their attendants, left Waipio and sailed to Kahiki, where they became chiefs of a district supposed to have been situated in Raiatea, one of the Society Islands. In this voyage Moikeha took with him as an adopted son a young chief named Laa.

After a long residence in their new domain a family quarrel arose, in consequence of which Moikeha resolved to return to his native land. Under the guidance of his astronomer and navigator, Kamahualele, he set sail in a fleet of canoes, with a goodly company of chiefs and retainers.

When the mountains of Hawaii rose in sight, the prophet chanted a song in which Nuuhiva, Bolabola, and other southern islands are mentioned. After coasting along the shores of the principal islands, they landed at Wailua, Kauai, where the high-chief, Puna, held his court. Here Moikeha married Puna's daughter, and on his death became king of Kauai, where he spent the rest of his life.

In his old age he sent his youngest son, Kila, with a fleet of double canoes, under the guidance of the old astronomer, to bring back his foster-son Laa to Kauai.

Return of Laa-mai-Kahiki.—They took their departure from the southern point of Hawaii, steering by the stars, and arrived safely at Kahiki.*

The young chief, generally known as Laa-mai-Kahiki, immediately returned to these islands, accompanied by a famous sorcerer and prophet, Naula-a-Maihea, and a large train of attendants. On his arrival he introduced the use of the large drum, *kaekeeke*, covered with a shark's skin, with which he astonished the natives. He resided a long time at Kualoa, where he had three sons, from whom the high-chiefs of Oahu and Kauai were descended. After the death of his foster-father he returned to Kahiki, taking his departure from the west end of Kahoolawe (which is still named *Ke-ala-i-Kahiki*, the way to Tahiti), and never returned.

Voyage of Kahai.—A grandson of Moikeha, named Kahai, is said to have made a voyage to Kahiki, and to have brought bread-fruit trees from Upolu in the Samoan group, which he planted at Kualoa, Oahu.

*It is probable that those ancient navigators had large canoes, built up of planks sewed together, and decked over, in part at least, with capacity to hold live-stock and stores for a long voyage, like those of the Paumotu Islands, for example. They were bold and expert seamen, inured to hardship, and had a respectable knowledge of the positions of the principal stars, and of their rising and setting at different times of the year. Even in recent times, instances were not uncommon of persons who had sailed from Hawaii to Kauai out of sight of land, taking their direction from the stars. The fact that they successfully made those voyages is indisputable.

The effect on the ancient Hawaiians of this intercourse with other countries must have been to enlarge their conceptions of the world, to awaken their minds, and to stimulate activity and enterprise. Many priests and sorcerers came from the south at this time, as well as chiefs of high rank, who intermarried with the reigning families here. There seems to have been during this period a great increase of the power of both priests and chiefs, of the severity of the tabus, and of the frequency of human sacrifices.

Cessation of Intercourse.—In the following generation all intercourse with the southern groups seems to have ceased, for there is no further evidence of it in any of the ancient legends, songs, or genealogies for five hundred years. As communication ceased, the ideas of ancient Hawaiians became vague and indistinct, so that Kahiki came to mean any foreign country. It was in their minds a land of mystery and magic, full of marvels, and inhabited by supernatural beings.

CHAPTER IV

CIVIL POLITY

Classes.—The Hawaiian people were divided in ancient times into three classes, viz.:

1. The nobility, *alii*, comprising the kings and chiefs of various grades of rank.

2. The priests, *kahuna*, including priests, sorcerers, and doctors.

3. The common people, *makaainana*, or laboring class.

There was a wide and permanent distinction between the class of chiefs and that of the common people. A common man could never rise to the rank of chief. Nobody conceived of such a thing as possible; nor could a chief be degraded to the rank of a common man or to that of a slave. If conquered in war, he might be slain and offered in sacrifice to the gods, but if his life was spared he was still a chief.

Chiefs.—The reason was that the position of a chief was not merely a political office, but was primarily of a sacred and religious character. The chief was believed to be descended from the gods, and to be in close alliance with the invisible powers, so that he was looked up to with superstitious awe. His birth was announced by thunder and lightning, his coming heralded by rainbows and other signs, and after death he was worshiped as a god. The contrast in stature and appearance as well as in bearing between the chiefs and common people was very striking.*

There were, however, many gradations of rank among the chiefs. The head chief of an island was styled *Moi*, and his position was generally hereditary. Yet, as in Tahiti, "his power over the turbulent district chiefs was neither strong nor permanent, and he could not count on their fidelity." †

Until the reign of Kamehameha I. there were generally at least four separate kingdoms in the group, and sometimes the single island of Hawaii was divided between several independent chiefs.

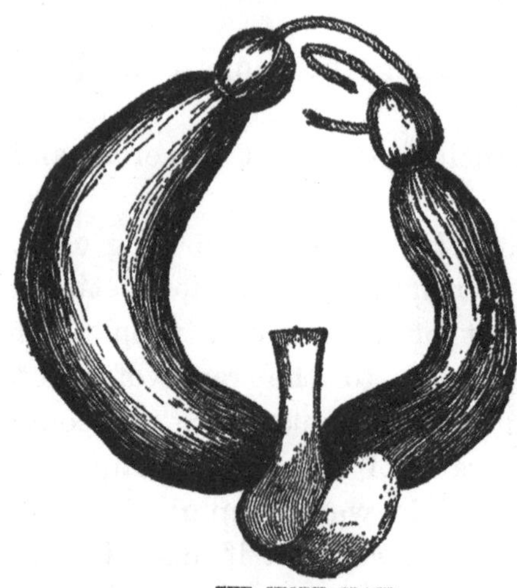
THE IVORY CLASP

Sacred Chiefs.—The highest chiefs were styled *alii kapu*, or sacred chiefs, and almost divine honors were paid to them. When they appeared abroad all the common people prostrated themselves with their faces upon the ground at the warning cry *E moe o!* It is said that certain chiefs were so tabu that they did not show themselves abroad by day.

Death was the penalty for the slightest breach of etiquette. For example, it was death for a common man to

* "No aristocracy," says Jarves, "was ever more distinctly marked by nature." Only a chief had the right to wear the red feather cloak and helmet, or the ivory clasp, *niho palaoa;* his canoe and its sails were painted red, and on state occasions he was attended by men bearing kahilis of various colors.

† Ellis.

remain standing at the mention of the king's name in song, or when the king's food, drinking-water, or clothing was carried past; to put on any article of dress belonging to him; to enter his inclosure without permission; or even to cross his shadow or that of his house. If he entered the dread presence of the sovereign, he must crawl, prone on the ground, *kolokolo,* and leave it in the same manner. The chief's head was especially sacred, and for any one to touch it or occupy a position above it would be treasonable. No subject dared to appear on the deck of a vessel when the king was in the cabin.

Court of a Chief.—The chiefs were surrounded by a throng of attendants, who were generally *kaukaualii,* i.e., noble only on the father's side. One of these had to remain constantly near his master, holding a *kahili,* or fly-brush, another had charge of his spittoon, while another sat ready to *lomilomi,* i.e., to knead and shampoo the royal person whenever desired. There were also in attendance the *aipuupuu,* or chief steward, the *puuku,* or treasurer, the *elele,* or heralds, the *kukini,* or runners, and many others.

Besides these, the court of a great chief comprised priests, diviners, bards, and story-tellers, with dancers, drummers, and buffoons. This crowd of attendants around the chief, supported by him in idleness, were called the *aialo,* i.e., those who eat in his presence.

Land Tenure.—As a general rule the chiefs were the only proprietors. They were supposed to own not only the soil and all that grew upon it, not only the fish of the sea, but also the time and labor of the people. The common people had nothing which they could call absolutely their own.*

* The system of land tenure bore a striking resemblance to that which pre-

Taxes.—There was first the royal tax, which extended over the whole kingdom, each grade of inferiors paying to its superiors, until the whole pile was laid before the king. This tax consisted chiefly of articles of food, such as vegetables, fruit, hogs, dogs, fowls, and fish; kukui-nuts for light; kapas, nets, calabashes, and the red and yellow feathers of certain birds.

Besides this there was a labor-tax, which recurred at certain days in every moon, and which chiefly consisted in cultivating the taro-patches of the chief.

The common people were also liable to be called out for public work, such as building or repairing temples (heiaus), or fish-ponds, or houses for the chiefs. There were various irregular demands made on the people by the chiefs, especially when traveling. For example, the horde of retainers which accompanied Kamehameha I. in his tours, and which usually amounted to a thousand persons, was supported entirely by the contributions of the people. If a sufficient quantity of provisions was not forthcoming, the king's servants would plunder the people of pigs, provisions, etc., often leaving them entirely destitute; and in like manner each petty chief taxed his dependents according to his power or inclination.*

vailed in Europe in former times, and which is called the feudal system. All the lands were considered to be the property of the king, and were held of him by the high-chiefs in fief, i. e., on condition of tribute and military service. On these great landlords he relied to carry out his plans, promote his interests, and fight his battles.

Each of the district chiefs divided up his territory among an inferior order of petty chiefs, who owed to him the same service and obedience that he owed to the king. In this way the land was subdivided again and again, down to the miserable serfs who tilled the soil. It is estimated that the common laborers did not receive on an average more than one third of the avails of their industry, while the other two thirds were divided between the chiefs of different grades and the king.

* There were, however, some restraints on the arbitrary power of the chief. His tenants could leave him and enter the service of a more popular chief, and

The common people were not fixed to the soil, as in some countries, but could and often did remove from one land to another. They were merely tenants at will, liable to be dispossessed at any time. At the death of any chief all his estates reverted to the king, by whom they were again assigned to new landlords.

Again, at the accession of a new king it was an ancient custom to redivide and distribute all the lands of an island among the adherents of the new sovereign, which often caused a civil war.

Besides, there were ancient customs which had come to have the force of unwritten law, and ancient proverbs handed down from the wise men of old. This kind of customary law, for instance, regulated the irrigation of lands, fixing the proportion of water to which each land was entitled.

Crimes such as theft were punished by private revenge, unless the injured party was too weak, when he either had recourse to sorcery or appealed to the chief, who dispensed a rude kind of justice. Executions were generally secret. The chief's *ilamuku* or executioner often did his work at the dead of night, when his victim was asleep.

the frequent wars obliged him to pay some regard to those upon whom he would have to depend in the day of battle.

CHAPTER V

CIVIL POLITY AND DOMESTIC RELATIONS

Priests.— The priests or kahunas proper were divided into several orders, which were hereditary. As before stated, the highest of these was founded by the foreigner Paao.

The regular priests had lands set apart for their support, and had great influence, due to their being the medium of communication with the gods, and having the power of selecting victims for the human sacrifices.

It was their special duty to commit to memory and teach to their children the long prayers used in the temple service. In general, they were the learned class, and kept alive whatever knowledge of astronomy, history, medicine, etc., had been handed down.

A much lower class of kahunas were the diviners, *kilokilo*, the sorcerers, *kahuna anaana*, who prayed people to death, and the doctors, *kahuna lapaau*, who depended more on charms and incantations than upon medicines.

Common People.—Even among the common people, *makaainana*, there were different grades. Those who were skilled in some art, as canoe-building, etc., and famous fishermen, enjoyed more consideration than other members of their class.

Slaves.—There were also bond-slaves, *kauwa*, lower even than the common people, who were probably made so in war. The opprobrious epithets *laepuni* and *maka-*

wela applied to them imply that they were marked in the forehead.

Wars.—There was no separate military caste or standing army, but most of the people, especially those employed around the chiefs, were trained in the use of weapons, and occasionally drilled in large bodies in sham fights.

Weapons.—Their weapons were simple, and consisted of long spears, *pololu;* javelins or short spears, *ihe;* daggers, *pahoa;* and clubs made of hard wood, *newa*, and *laau palau*. They never used the bow in war, but only in sport for shooting rats. Slings, however, made of cocoanut fiber or human hair, were extensively employed. The sling-stones were smooth round pebbles, and by long practice they learned to throw them with great force and precision. They used no shields, but became wonderfully expert in catching or warding off spears thrown at them.* The elegant feather helmets and cloaks of the chiefs were worn for ornament and not for defense.

Forts.—They often had fortresses, *pakaua*, either natural or artificial, to which they could retreat if defeated, such as the hill of Kauwiki at Hana.

Battles.—Their battles, however, were generally fought in the open field without much strategy, and they seldom practiced lying in ambush as most savages do. Idols were carried in the ranks, and the priests used to rush forward, making hideous faces and uttering diabolical yells, to strike terror into the enemy.

The first man killed on either side was called a *lehua*, and his body was immediately dragged to the priest, who offered it to his god. The wives of the warriors often

* Vancouver relates that in a sham fight he saw six spears cast at once at Kamehameha I., of which he caught three, parried two, and avoided the sixth by a quick movement of his body.

followed in the rear, carrying water and food. They were frequently killed.

Sea Fights.—Sometimes they engaged in sea fights in fleets numbering upwards of a hundred canoes on each side, but this rarely happened.

Generally no quarter was given, and no mercy was shown to the vanquished. They were hunted out of their hiding-places and beaten to death, and their bodies were often mutilated and left unburied. Cannibalism, however, was regarded with horror and detestation.

The bones and teeth of slain enemies were sometimes preserved as trophies of victory.

Treaties.—Branches of the *ti* plant and of young banana-trees were used as flags of truce. Treaties of peace were ratified in the temples by sacrificing swine and depositing wreaths of *maile* woven jointly by the leaders on both sides, after which heralds were sent to proclaim the news far and wide.*

Marriage as Affecting Rank.—Marriages were contracted with very little ceremony except among chiefs. It is said that in rare cases children were betrothed, *hoopalau*, when quite young, and then strictly watched over till marriage. Among the chiefs it was an important matter of state policy to marry the women of the highest rank, because rank descended chiefly from the mother.

Thus the son of a queen would be considered a noble, even though his father should be of low origin; but if a chief should marry a common woman, her children would hold an inferior position, and could not succeed to his rank.

In the reigning families, brothers and sisters sometimes married each other from state policy, in order to

* Ellis.

have children of the highest possible rank, *alii niaupio,* as they were called.

Among the better class of people the consent of the relatives, particularly of the brothers of the bride, was obtained, and presents were exchanged. But offers of marriage were made as frequently by the women as by the men.

Wedding Ceremonies.—As in most countries, they often made a feast to celebrate the event. Sometimes when chiefs of high rank were married they came in state with their attendants and joined noses, *honi,* before the assembly, amid loud shouts of *hoao na'lii e!* "the chiefs are married!" But the principal ceremony more often consisted in the bridegroom's casting a piece of tapa over the bride in the presence of her relatives, or their friends throwing it over both. Several instances of this are mentioned in Hawaiian chronicles.

The marriage tie was loose, and the husband could dismiss his wife without any ceremony. Polygamy was allowed in all ranks, but practiced mostly by the chiefs, who could best afford it.*

Infanticide.—Infanticide was fearfully prevalent, and there were few of the older women at the date of the abolition of idolatry who had not been guilty of it. It was the opinion of those best informed that two thirds of all the children born were destroyed in infancy by their parents. They were generally buried alive, in many cases in the very houses occupied by their unnatural parents. On all the islands the number of males was much greater than that of females, in consequence of the

* The state of society will not bear description in this work. The ideas and sentiments connected with the home and family in Christian countries could not be said to exist.

girls being more frequently destroyed than the boys. The principal reason given for it was laziness,—unwillingness to take the trouble of rearing children.

It was a very common practice for parents to give away their children to any friends who were willing to adopt them.

No regular parental discipline was maintained, and the children were too often left to follow their own inclinations, and to become familiar with the lowest vices.

Neglect of the Helpless.—Among the common people old age was despised. The sick and those who had become helpless from age were sometimes abandoned to die or put to death. Insane people were also sometimes stoned to death.

CHAPTER VI

OBJECTS OF WORSHIP

Deification of the Powers of Nature.—The ancient Hawaiians had innumerable objects of worship.

To them the earth, the air, and the sea were filled with invisible beings or *akuas*. In the mind of the savage all the powers of nature, especially those that are mysterious and terrible, are living and spiritual beings like man himself. To the ancient Hawaiian the volcano, the thunder, the whirlwind, the meteor, the shark, above all, the mysterious and dreaded disease, were each either the work or the actual embodiment of a malicious spirit. It is remarkable, however, that no worship was paid to the sun, moon, or stars.

Local and Tutelar Deities.—There were some deities that haunted particular localities, especially lonely or dangerous places; others that presided over different trades or professions; and others that watched over particular families, etc. One large class of divinities were the deified spirits of the dead.

The Four Great Gods.—The four great gods that were worshiped throughout all Polynesia were Kane, Kanaloa, Ku, and Lono.* These four deities were believed to have existed *mai ka po mai*, i.e., since the period of primeval chaos or night. They were conceived of as power-

*It may be remarked that the Hawaiians were accustomed to count by fours.

ful, invisible beings, dwelling in or above the clouds, but also appearing on earth in human form.

Kane.—The most ancient and powerful of these was Kane. Tane was also the chief god of Raiatea in the Society Islands. Some of the prayers in his honor seem to be fragments of a simpler and grander creed, and speak of him as father of men and founder of the world, Kane-makua and Kane-kumu-honua. He was imagined to be less malicious and cruel than the other deities.

Kanaloa and Kaneapua.—Kanaloa is always associated with him as his younger brother. They were said to have once resided at Waipio, Hawaii, and to have created springs of water in many places during their tours around the islands. Other legends give them the credit of having introduced banana-trees and other useful plants from Kahiki. Another younger brother, Kaneapua, was an inferior deity, worshiped by fishermen.

Ku.—Ku appears to have been feared as a dark and malevolent being, delighting in the sufferings and immolation of human victims.

Lono.—Lono had a separate order of priests, and temples of a lower grade, in which human sacrifices were never offered. The New-Year games were held in his honor, and he was specially invoked for rain and on certain family occasions.*

Multiplication of Deities.—As time went on there was a strong tendency to multiply divinities, and each of these four gods was worshiped under various special attributes or functions, which afterwards came to be regarded as different persons.

* Traditions connected with the ancient kings Lonokawai and Lono-i-ka-makahiki seem to have been mixed up with those belonging to the primeval god Lono.

Thus we have Kane-makua, the special god of certain fishermen; Kane-puaa, the god of agriculture; Kane-nui-akea, who inspired prophets; etc., etc.

In the same way there were many varieties of Ku, and several of Lono.

Local Gods.—There were a great many gods of different localities, such as Kane-hoa-lani, god of the sky; Kane-huli-koa, god of the sea; gods of the cardinal points; Poli-ahu, goddess of Mauna Kea; Lilinoe, goddess of Haleakala; and many others. There were many places where travelers always made offerings of tapa or leaves or flowers, generally before a sacred stone, as at Nuuanu Pali, Kaliuwaa Valley, etc.

Laamaomao, an ancient deified chief, was the god of the winds, and Kane-wahi-lani was the god of the lightning, attended by a troup of hunch-backed *akuas*.

Gods of Professions.—Of the professional gods some have already been mentioned.

Fishermen adored Ku-ula and his wife, Hina-hele, Moku-halii, a shark god, and many others. Ku-kaili-moku, also called Kaili, was the god of war.

Kapa beaters venerated Lauhuki, a deified chiefess, who was changed into the *wauke* or paper-mulberry tree. Sorcerers worshiped Uli, as well as other lesser deities. Necromancers employed a number of petty demons on errands of mischief, such as Kuamu, Pua, Kapo, etc., *akua noho*. Hula dancers worshiped Laka, robbers and murderers Kuialua, and poisoners Kalaipahoa, while thieves and gamblers also had their patron gods.

Deified Animals.—A large class of *akuas* were incarnated in certain animals, which were feared or believed to have an uncanny or supernatural character. For example, there were several shark gods, which were worshiped by fishermen, and sometimes possessed or inspired their devotee or *kahu.*

There was a class of *moo*, or lizard gods, such as Kihawahine, a deified chiefess much employed by necromancers. Lizards were regarded with superstitious awe, as in New Zealand, and there were many traditions about gigantic reptiles, which were probably reminiscences of the crocodiles of the East Indian Archipelago.

The owl had a sacred character, and its appearance in time of danger was a good omen. The god of owls was Kukauahi. The *alae* bird was also worshiped by some. Its cry was an omen of death.

Pele and Her Family.—Pele, the goddess of volcanoes, and her numerous family formed a class of deities by themselves. She with her six sisters, Hiiaka, her brother, Kamohoalii, and others, was said to have emigrated from Kahiki (Samoa) in ancient times. They were said to have first lived at Moanalua in Oahu, then to have moved their residence to Kalaupapa, Molokai, then to Haleakala, and finally to have settled on Hawaii.

Their headquarters were in the Hale mau-mau, in the crater of Kilauea, but they also caused the eruptions of Mauna Loa and Hualalai. In southern Hawaii Pele was feared more than any other deity, and no one dared to approach her abode without making her an offering of the ohelo-berries that grow in the neighborhood. Whenever an eruption took place great quantities of hogs and other articles of property were thrown into the lava stream in order to appease her anger.*

* Mr. Ellis says: "The conical craters were said to be their houses, where they frequently amused themselves by playing draughts, *konane;* the roaring of the furnaces and the crackling of the flames were the music of their dance, and the red fiery surge was the surf in which they played."

Pele was identical with the Samoan fire goddess Fee. Her sister, Hiiaka-i-ka-poli-o-Pele, was much employed by sorcerers.

Aumakuas.—The *aumakuas* were tutelar deities, attached to particular families, and were generally, but not always, deified ancestors. They were identical with the Tahitian *oromatuas*, but were not so malignant.*

Sickness and misfortune were generally caused by the displeasure of these deities, who had to be propitiated by prayers and offerings, which were different with different aumakuas. The most unpardonable sin in their eyes was the neglect to perform a vow, *hoohiki*.†

Kini akua.—The *kini akua* were multitudinous little elves inhabiting the woods, whose favor it was best to gain.

Kupuas.—The *kupuas*, or demi-gods, were men possessed of preternatural powers, or mighty magicians like Maui, Kana, or Kamapuaa.

Maui.—Maui was celebrated in all the islands of Polynesia for his exploits of obtaining fire for men, of drawing up islands from the bottom of the sea with his magic hook, *manaiakalana*, and of lassoing the sun, and compelling him to move more slowly. His hook was preserved at Tonga in the last century.

* If, as was often the case, they resided in particular species of animals, as the shark, owl, eel, etc., then that animal was tabu to the family, and could not be injured without fatal consequences. If the family *aumakua* resided in certain stones, then it would be tabu for members of the family to sit on those stones.

† Fabulous stories were told of deliverances wrought by *aumakuas*. For instance, one man was rescued from drowning by his shark-god, and another, taken captive in war, and tied up to be roasted in an oven, was set free by his guardian owl-god.

People sometimes gave the bodies of their relatives to sharks in order that their spirits might enter into the sharks, or threw them into the crater of Kilauea, that they might join the company of the volcanic deities, and afterward befriend the family.

Kamapuaa.—Kamapuaa was a *kupua* or demi-god, who had the power of assuming the form of a man or that of a gigantic hog, as suited his caprice. There are many legends about his war with his uncle Olopana, the chief of Koolau, Oahu. He was the local deity of the Kaliuwaa valley in Koolau.

LAVA FLOW

Other legends relate his contest with the goddess Pele, whose fires he nearly extinguished by pouring sea-water into her crater.*

* According to one version of the story, the volcanic deities succeeded in drying up the water, and in driving the monster to the sea, amidst a shower of red-hot stones. Another account, however, states that he gained the day, and that he finally married Pele; in consequence of which no more extensive volcanic eruptions took place, and no new islands were formed

CHAPTER VII

IDOLS AND TEMPLES

Idols.—The Hawaiians usually worshiped their gods by means of idols, believing that by the performance of certain ceremonies power, *mana*, was imparted to the idols so that they became a means of communication with the unseen divinities. They imagined that a spirit resided in or conveyed influence through the image representing it.

ANCIENT IDOL

The principal gods which stood in the great heiaus were of *ohia* wood, and were purposely made hideous in order to inspire fear. Another class of gods, such as Kukaili-moku, Koloewa, etc., was represented by images of wicker-work, covered with red feathers, with eyes made of mother-of-pearl, and wide gaping mouths armed with sharks' teeth.

The common people also had small idols for private worship, which they carried to the heiaus on great occasions. The pebbles from the beach of Ninole, Kau, were sought after as idols, and were supposed to have the power of self-propagation. Sometimes worship was paid to shapeless stones, which were supposed to be the shrine or residence of a deity.

Temples.—There were two principal orders of temples and also of the priests who officiated in them, viz., those of Ku and those of Lono.

The former were of higher rank, and far more severe and exclusive in their tabus and ritual than the latter.

The name *luakini* was applied to the chief heiaus or temples of the former class, which belonged to the *Moi* or highest chief of the island. It was only at these heiaus that human sacrifices could be offered, and hence they were called *heiau pookanaka.*

The *luakinis* were commonly erected upon hills near the sea, and formed conspicuous objects in the landscape.

A few of the most famous ones were those of Mookini in Kohala, of Puukohola at Kawaihae, of Pakaalana in Waipio, Hawaii, and of Kawaluna in Waolani, Nuuanu. They were, in general, extensive stone platforms or terraces, surrounded by stone walls. All the houses built within the inclosure had to be of *ohia* wood, and thatched with the *uki* or Dianella. On the other hand, in the smaller temples dedicated to Lono (*mapele*) the *lama* was the only kind of wood allowed, and the houses had to be thatched with the *ti* leaf. These last could be built by chiefs of inferior rank, and their consecration required only three days, if no delay occurred, while the dedication of a *luakini* occupied from ten to fourteen days of protracted rites of the severest kind.

Temple of Puukohola.—There was a good deal of variety in the plan of these structures, but the great heiau of Puukoholá, built by Kamehameha I. in 1791, is a good example of them.

According to Ellis, it is an irregular parallelogram two hundred and twenty-four feet long and one hundred feet wide, with walls twelve feet thick at the base, and varying in height from eight feet on the upper side to twenty feet on the lower side. The entrance was a narrow passage between two high walls, and the interior was divided into terraces paved with smooth, flat stones. At the south end was an inner court where the principal idol used to stand, surrounded by a number of images of inferior deities.

Oracle.—In the center of the court stood the *lananuu*, a lofty frame of wicker-work, in shape something like an obelisk, hollow, and four or five feet square at the base. This was the oracle, in which the priest stood as a medium of communication with his god, when the king came to inquire of him.

Altar.—Near the entrance to the inner court was the *lele* or altar, a sort of scaffolding supported by posts, on which offerings were laid and left to moulder away.

Sacred Houses.—About the center of the terrace was a sacred house, in which the king resided during the periods of tabu, and at the northern end stood the houses of the priests.

The outer walls were crowned with hideous wooden idols of all shapes and sizes. From native writers we learn that in front of the *lele* was the *hale pahu* or drum-house, with the door facing the *lele*. Beyond this was the principal house, called *mana*, with the door toward the *lele*. At the end of the *mana* stood a small house called *Waiea*, in which certain prayers called the *aha* were recited.

At the other end of the *mana* was a long house called *hale umu*, in which the fire of the heiau was lighted and certain offerings cooked. Somewhere in the heiau was a pit called *luapau*, which was probably a receptacle for the bones of the victims.

In the outer court stood a house called the *Hale o Papa*, set apart for female deities, under a priest of its own, to which the female chiefs came on certain occasions. Women in general were excluded from the interior of the heiaus.*

Almost every headland had its altar or *unu*, dedicated to Ku-ula or Kinilau, or to the shark-god Mooalii, the patron of fishermen.

Sacred Rocks.—There were numerous sacred rocks, from one to six feet high, called the *pohaku o Kane*, which the common people used as family shrines, before which they made offerings and prayers.

Ipu o Lono.—In time of drought small heiaus called *ipu o Lono* were built for rain. But the term was generally applied to a sacred calabash, kept in private houses, in which offerings were made to the tutelar gods of the family.

Puuhonuas.—The *puuhonua* was a place of refuge, an inviolable sanctuary in time of war. "Hither," says Ellis, "the man-slayer, the man who had broken a tabu, the thief, and even the murderer, fled from his pursuers, and was safe." The gates were always open, and as soon as he had entered he repaired to the presence of the idol and made a short address of thanksgiving. In war time a white flag was unfurled from the top of a tall spear at each end of the inclosure, a short distance outside of the walls.

* Inferior chiefs had smaller chapels, according to their rank and wealth.

The priests and their attendants would immediately put to death any one who should follow or molest those who were within the pale of the *pahu tabu*. After remaining several days in the *puuhonua* they could return home under the protection of the gods. In the island of Hawaii were three famous *puuhonuas*, one at Honaunau, ad-

HEIAU (TEMPLE) AT WAIMEA, KAUAI

joining the *Hale o Keawe*, one at Waipio, the heiau of Pakaalana, containing the *Hale o Liloa*, and one in the little islet of Mokuola in Hilo Bay.

In the island of Lanai the land of Kealia Kapu was a famous asylum; and in Oahu the land of Kualoa was sacred. All canoes had to lower their masts on passing it from Makawai to Kaaawa. The heiau at Waolani in Nuuanu was sacred to fugitives and the sick.

On Kauai there was a *puuhonua* at Wailua, and another at Waimea.

The most celebrated *puuhonua* was the one at Honaunau, which measures seven hundred and fifteen feet by four hundred and four, containing about seven acres, and is surrounded by a massive wall, twelve feet high and fifteen feet thick. Formerly large wooden images stood

HALE (HOUSE) O KEAWE

on the walls, about four feet apart. Within this inclosure were three heiaus, built of very large stones.

Hale o Keawe.—The *Hale o Keawe* was in fact a tomb or sacred depository of the bones of the chiefs, erected by Kanuha, a son of Keawe II., about the year 1690 A.D. It was built of *kauila* timber, thatched with *ti* leaves, and surrounded by a strong paling, with a paved court at each end. Numerous idols stood on the fence at intervals all around, and twelve were set on pillars arranged in a semicircle at the southeast end of the inclosure, before which offerings were formerly placed.*

* Many other images were kept in the house, some of wood and some of wicker-work, covered with red feathers. Under their powerful protection were kept the bones of Keawe and other ancient chiefs, wrapped up in bundles, and carefully bound with cinet made of cocoanut fibers, together with red feathers and other valuable articles. They are now deposited in the Royal mausoleum in Honolulu.

CHAPTER VIII

CEREMONIAL SYSTEM

The Tabu.—The tabu system, which is characteristic of the Polynesian race, was perhaps most fully developed in the Hawaiian Islands. It was a complicated system, which covered the entire daily life of the people with a vast net-work of regulations and penalties. These were not merely laws but religious ordinances, and the violation of them was not merely a crime, but a sin, which would bring down the vengeance of the gods.

Some tabus were permanent, and others special and temporary. Of the former kind were those relating to the chiefs or to the idols or temples, while others belonged to particular times or were imposed by the king.

Special Tabus Relating to Women.—The most oppressive of these regulations were those relating to the sexes. It was tabu for men and women to eat together or even to have their food cooked in the same oven. A complete domestic establishment comprised at least six houses: 1st, a chapel for the family idols; 2d, the *mua*, or men's eating-house, which was tabu to females; 3d, the *hale noa*, or common sleeping-house; 4th, the *hale aina*, or women's eating-house; 5th, the *hale kua*, or house for beating tapa; and 6th, the *hale pea* for the women during certain tabu periods. The first two houses were tabu to the women on pain of death.

Several kinds of food were forbidden to the women on pain of death, viz., pork, bananas, cocoanuts, turtles, and certain kinds of fish, as the *ulua*, the *humu*, the shark, the *hihimanu* or sting-ray, etc. The men of the poorer class often formed a sort of eating-club apart from their wives. These laws were rigorously enforced.

For example, at Honaunau, Hawaii, two young girls of the highest rank, Kapiolani and Keoua, having been detected in the act of eating a banana, their *kahu*, or tutor, was held responsible, and put to death by drowning. Shortly before the abolition of the tabus, a little child had one of her eyes scooped out for the same offense. About the same time a woman was put to death for entering the eating-house of her husband, although she was tipsy at the time. There were many tabus that related to ceremonial purity, especially in connection with their funeral rites, of which more hereafter. There were many occasions when no canoe could be launched, no fire lighted, no tapa beaten or poi pounded, and no sound could be uttered on pain of death; when even the dogs had to be muzzled, and the fowls were shut up in calabashes for twenty-four hours at a time.

Calendar.—Their ritual was so closely connected with their division of time that it seems necessary to consider the latter in this place. The Hawaiians, like all other Polynesians, reckoned time by lunar months containing either twenty-nine or thirty days alternately. As twelve of these months fell eleven days short of the true year, they had discovered the deficiency, and occasionally inserted an intercalary month. The Polynesian year began with the month Makalii about November 20th, when the Pleiades rise at sunset. The reckoning on Kauai and Oahu, however, is said to have differed two months from that of Maui and Hawaii.

During four months, beginning with Ikuwa, which corresponds to our October, the regular religious services were suspended, and special services and games held in honor of Lono.

New Year's.—The great *makahiki* or New Year's festival was held about the end of Welehu, which nearly corresponded to November. The five months beginning with Kaelo, our January, were war-months, but during the remaining seven months there could be no war.

Lunar Month.—Each night of the lunar month had its appropriate name. During each month there were four tabu periods of two nights and one day each, dedicated severally to each of the four great gods. All their religious rites, as well as their fishing, planting, etc., were regulated by the moon.

Prayers.—Their temple service was most elaborate and complicated. The numerous prayers were known by special names, and had been handed down by word of mouth for many generations. They were in a very ancient style, and understood only by a few, and often occupied several hours in their recital. They were not merely prayers in the proper sense of the word, but magical incantations, and in order to secure the desired effect it was necessary to repeat them without the slightest mistake.

During the most important class of prayers, called *ahas*, it was necessary that absolute silence should be observed, as the least noise would break the spell and destroy the whole effect of the charm.

In some services there were responses made by the

people or by a company of priests, the assembly rising and sitting at given signals, or holding their hands toward heaven for half an hour at a time. The service always closed with the words "*Amama! ua noa. Lele aku la.*" At a great heiau there were numerous priests, who divided the different parts of the service between them, and each had his specialty. It should be observed, however, that the king was the head of the church, that he presented the human sacrifices on great occasions, and pronounced the concluding *amama.*

Human Sacrifice.—The human sacrifice was the crowning act of the ancient worship, only offered on the most important occasions, and at the heiaus of the highest class. The victims were either prisoners taken in war or persons accused of a violation of some of the numberless regulations of the tabu, *poe lawehala.* The female sex seems to have been exempt from sacrifice.

The mode of execution was generally that of secret assassination, the victim being stunned by a blow with a club from behind. Whenever a temple was to be dedicated, a new house built for the chief, or a new war-canoe launched, many people fled to the mountains and lay hid till the danger had passed.

The Mu.—The person employed to procure victims was known as the *Mu;* this word inspired peculiar terror, even long after the abolition of idolatry. The corpses were dragged to the heiau, presented to the idol, and laid face down upon the *lele,* together with hogs, etc., where the mass was left to putrefy in the sun.*

Monthly Tabus.—As was stated above, there were four

* Thus in 1807 four men were sacrificed in the heiau at the foot of Diamond Head, because the queen, Keopuolani, was dangerously ill.

tabu periods during each moon, viz.: 1st, that of Ku, from the third to the sixth night; 2d, that of Hua, at full moon, including the fourteenth and fifteenth nights; 3d, that of Kaloa or Kanaloa, the twenty-fourth and twenty-fifth nights; and 4th, that of Kane, the twenty-seventh and twenty-eighth nights.

During these tabu periods a devout king generally spent the time in the heiau, and no person could pass its limits on pain of death.*

Women were forbidden to enter canoes, or to have any intercourse with the other sex as long as the tabu lasted.

The Aku and Opelu Tabu.—Two kinds of fish, the *aku* or bonito and the *opelu*, had a sacred character, and were tabu by turns, for six months at a time. At the *kapu hua*, i.e., the 13th day of Kaelo, in January, a human sacrifice was offered, together with the fish *aku*, at which it is said that the *Kahoalii*, a man personifying the god, plucked out and ate an eye of each. By this ceremony the tabu was taken off from the *aku*, and the *opelu* became tabu for the next six months, not to be eaten on pain of death.

In the month of Hinaiaeleele, or July, the tabu was taken off the *opelu* and reimposed on the *aku*. The first night, Hilo, of this month was *kapu loa*. No fire could be kindled, and no sound of man or beast or fowl must be heard.

Toward morning the high-priest, accompanied by another priest, went to the *opelu* house of Ku-ula, the god

* "This time," says an eye-witness, Archibald Campbell, "was spent in prayer, in sacrificing pigs, in eating the sacrifices, and in conversation. The priest continued praying for three hours at a time, during which the most profound silence was observed. The congregation stood with arms uplifted for about three quarters of an hour at the beginning and end of the prayer."

of fishermen, where he sacrificed a pig, and recited the great *aha* as during a dedication. Afterward the congregation was arranged in four rows, and long prayers recited, the people rising up and sitting down at the recurrence of certain words in the service, while a man was sent to the woods for *pala* fern.

Next morning the head fisherman, wearing a white malo, took the *pala* and a new net in his canoe, and put to sea.

Meanwhile a strict tabu was observed on shore; no fire could be lighted, and no canoe launched, on pain of death, nor could any canoe from abroad land on that day.

The fisherman, after praying to his *aumakuas* and to Ku, proceeded to cast his net. If he and his crew made a haul of *opelu*, they paddled at once for the shore with loud shouts of joy. The head fisherman then took seven of the fish to the priest, who sent some of them to the king, and placed the rest on the *lele* in the temple.

The chief also proceeded to the heiau, where he offered his *opelu* to the gods, plucking out and eating the right eye of the fish. Next day the sea was free, and the *opelu* was *noa*, or free to all, but the *aku* in its turn was tabu for the next six months.

CHAPTER IX

CEREMONIAL DEDICATION OF A TEMPLE

Dedication.—The consecration of a temple, or *luakini*, which was often performed just before a war in order to insure victory, was the most important as well as the most laborious of their religious services. Nine priests conducted different parts of the ceremonies, which occupied ten or more days. The proper time for the dedication was in the spring (in the months of Nana, Welo, or Ikiiki).

Purification.—About twelve days were occupied by preliminary rites of purification. A religious procession made the circuit of the island or district, consisting of the *akua alaea*, i.e., a man personating the god, with a peculiar head-dress of human hair, girt with white kapa, and carrying spears, accompanied by a priest bearing a calabash of red ocher, *alaea*, and other attendants, preceded and followed by men bearing white flags. When they arrived at the *ahu*, or pile of stones which marked the boundary of a land, on which an image of a hog made of kukui wood had been placed, the priest smeared the image with the red ocher, and offered a prayer. At the same time, the tenants of the land brought contributions of pigs, kapas, feathers, etc., after which the procession moved to the next land.

After this tour had been completed, on the evening before the new moon a responsive service was held at the heiau, to which the whole population was summoned, during which the priest sprinkled the people with holy water, i.e., salt water mixed with a little turmeric and *limu kala* moss, with a bunch of *pala*, a sacred fern.

Bringing Down of the Idol.—The next thing in order was to bring down the principal idol, called the *hakuohia*, from the forest. A great procession was formed, consisting of the king, the *hakuohia* priest, and a crowd of attendants carrying idols and various offerings, and leading a human victim. The tree had been selected and the ax consecrated the day before. On arriving at the tree the priest recited the appropriate *aha* amid dead silence, after which the king pronounced the *amama*, and killed the hog with a single blow.

The priest inquired whether any sound of man or beast or bird or cricket had been heard during the *aha*, and if not it was a good omen. The doomed man was then brought forward, and offered to the god by the king, after which his body was buried at the foot of the tree. The consecrated hog was baked in an oven on the spot, while the tree was cut down, trimmed, and covered with *ieie* vines.

After the company had feasted, a procession was formed with the feather-gods in front, followed by the chiefs and people with *pala* fern, ohia-branches, etc., and others carrying the new idol, uttering fearful yells. The inhabitants of the village remained indoors, for it was death to meet the procession, and all fires were strictly forbidden. The images were finally carried to the heiau, where they were deposited with shoutings and beating of drums.

Kauila Ceremony.—The remaining services at the heiau

occupied seven or eight days. Before the houses could be thatched, the *kauila* ceremony was performed, at which the whole population had to assist. The multitude was seated in eight rows in the outer court. The keepers of the portable sacred images brought them forth, and formed in line together with *Kahoalii*, a naked man personating a god or deified chief. The high-priest came forward with a bunch of *pala* or *ieie* in his hand, girded with white kapa, and attended by a man bearing a skull filled with holy water. He then intoned a long prayer, at certain passages of which the image-bearers rose and went through various evolutions, marching and counter-marching in perfect time, with *Kahoalii* at their head. At other passages, the congregation rose and sat down eight times, and joined in the closing responses, "*Ola, ola o Ku!*" Toward evening the *hakuohia* idol was brought to its place in front of the *lananuu*, near the altar, where a hole had been dug for its pedestal. Then another human victim was sacrificed and buried in the hole, after which the image was planted over the dead body, while the *aha popouana* was recited.

The Great Aha.—That night was the most solemn and critical of all. The omens were carefully observed, and prayers were offered in every house for the success of the coming *aha*, and for auspicious weather, that there might be no wind or rain, no thunder or lightning, no high surf, and no sound of man or beast to mar the ceremonies. If the sky was clear and every thing favorable, between midnight and morning the king and high-priest entered into the small house called *Waiea* to perform the great *aha* (*hulahula*), while the congregation sat in front of the *mana* house, listening and watching in profound silence. The king stood listening intently and holding a pig, while the high-priest, clad in white kapa, and holding a *lama* rod wound with *oloa* (white kapa), recited the long prayer. At its close the king killed the pig with a single blow, and offered it up with a short prayer to the four great gods. The priests then asked the king whether the *aha* was perfect, and whether he had heard the voice of man or dog or mouse or fowl, or any thing else during the prayer. If not, he tapped the large drum as a signal that it was over, and they both went out to question the assembly outside. If no one had heard a sound during the ceremony, the high-priest congratulated the king, and predicted for him victory and long life. The people then raised loud shouts of "*Lele wale ka aha e!*" which were repeated by all who heard them, and so the news traveled far and wide.

Kuili Ceremonies.—During the next three nights the *Kuili* ceremonies were performed.*

During each day great numbers of hogs were cooked and feasted on by priests and people.

On the fourth night another great *aha* (*hoowilimoo*) was performed by the king and the priest of Lono, while another priest, with a large company of fishermen, put to sea to fish for *ulua*.

Offering of the Ulua.—The idols were now invested with white kapa and received their several names, the principal one being called *Moi;* and a great sacrifice was made of hogs, bananas, cocoanuts, red fish and white kapa, besides several more human victims, which were placed on the *lele*. If the fishermen failed to catch any *ulua* that night they killed a man in the village, and dragged

* The houses in the heiau were lighted up with torches all night, and there were noisy prayers and chantings by the priests divided into sections, with much gesticulation and clapping of hands.

his body to the heiau with a hook in his mouth, as a substitute for the fish.

As the *ulua* priest approached, chanting an incantation and carrying his hook and line, everybody fled, and even the priests retired within the drum-house. When he had finished chanting his *aha* behind the *lananuu*, he reported to the king the omens which he had observed, and the fish was offered up to the god. If he had broken his rod or line, or if the bait had all been eaten, it was a bad omen.

The Hono Ceremony.—On the next day more sacrifices were offered, and all the people, priests, and chiefs repaired to the sea to bathe, after which the *hono* ceremony took place. The congregation was all seated in rows in front of the drum-house, and the *hono* priest took his place with a sacred *lama* wand in his hand, and recited his prayer, at one passage of which all had to hold up their hands toward heaven, and remain in that position for a long time, motionless, on pain of death.

Closing Ceremonies.—On the last day, the priest of Papa presided. The wives of the king, clad in white wrappers, brought a long white girdle as an offering to the *Hale o Papa.* Many dogs and fowls were also offered, as being lawful for women to eat. The priest of Papa recited the prescribed prayer, and the queen prayed for children. The devotees of various female deities also presented themselves at the same place with offerings. Then the congregation was ranged in rows, and the priests of Papa made the concluding prayer, the laity joining in the closing responses, and ending the whole ceremony with loud shouts of "*noa honua!*"

Such were some of the principal ceremonies held at the dedication of a *luakini* or temple.

Makahiki Months.—As has been stated above, the religious services were suspended during the four *makahiki* months, commencing near the beginning of October. During this period pork could not be eaten by the chiefs, not having been consecrated by sacrifice to the gods. The great festival took place in the latter part of November.

On the 23d day of the moon of Welehu, the image of Lono makua, the Makahiki god, was decorated.*

Purification.—The next night fires were lighted on the shore all around the island, and the people all went to bathe in the sea, warming themselves at the fires. This was a rite of purification, after which they all put on new *malos* and *paus*.

Tabu Days.—The next morning the festival began, and for four days no work, no fishing, no bathing, no pounding of kapa, no beating of drums or blowing of conchs was permitted. Land and sky and sea were tabu to Lono, and only feasting and games were allowed. The high-priest was blindfolded, and remained in seclusion for five days.

Collection of Taxes.—Meanwhile all the konohikis on the island had been getting ready the taxes of their respective lands, in anticipation of a visit from the long god, who now made a tour of the island. The long god was preceded by a man carrying two long rods, which he set up in the ground on arriving at the boundary of a

*This idol was like a round pole, twelve feet long and three or four inches in diameter, with a head carved at one end. A cross-stick was fastened to its neck, at right angles to the pole, and about six feet long, to which were attached feather wreaths, and an imitation of a sea-bird, the *kaupu*, was perched upon it. A long white kapa like a sail was fastened at the top to the cross-piece, and left loose at the bottom. A short idol was also made, called the *akua paani* (god of sport), and *makawahine*, because it was set up at the boxing-matches and other games.

land. The land was then under a tabu or interdict, and no one could leave it until the tax was fully paid. The taxes were brought to the *ahu*, and when the tax-collector was satisfied, the priest chanted a prayer to Lono, the crowd joining in the responses, closing with the shout, "*Aulu e Lono!*" when the land became *noa* or free, and the long idol moved on to the next land. When the procession arrived at the chief's house, the inmates called out, "*E weli ia oe, Lono, ea!*" "Welcome to thee, Lono!" to which the bearers of the idol responded, "*Nauane.*"

This was twice repeated before they entered the house, where they were feasted on the choicest dishes the country could produce. The food had to be put into their mouths, because their hands were tabued by contact with the idol. Then the wife of the chief bound a fine white kapa girdle on the idol, while her husband fastened an ivory clasp, *niho palaoa*, around his neck.

Games.—As evening came on, the people assembled from the surrounding country to see the boxing-matches, etc., under the immediate patronage of the short god. For the next two days, all kinds of games were carried on, such as boxing, wrestling, sliding down hill, throwing the *maika*, foot-races, etc., attended with general gambling and revelry. On the fifth day, called *Lono*, the bandage was taken off the high-priest's eyes, and canoes were allowed to go a-fishing for that day. The tabu was then put on again until the long idol returned, i.e., for about twenty days.

Kalii Ceremony.—On that evening the *Kalii* ceremony was performed as follows: The king went a-fishing with a numerous company, taking the long idol with him. On his return he was accompanied by a warrior, expert in the spear exercise. As the king leaped on shore a man rushed forward with two spears bound with white kapa, and hurled one at him, which was parried, after which he simply touched the king with the other spear, and the ceremony was over.* This was followed by sham fights, until the king put a stop to them, and repaired to the heiau to pay his devotions to Lono.

The next day the long idol was stripped of its ornaments, which were packed up and deposited in the temple for use another year, and a white canoe, called "Lono's canoe to return to Kahiki in," was sent out to sea, after which all restrictions on fishing and farming were taken off, *noa ka makahiki.*

* Kamehameha, however, always caught the spear himself.

CHAPTER X

PRIVATE WORSHIP

Family Worship.—Besides the public worship in the heiaus, almost every act of the ancient Hawaiian was attended with prayers and offerings to the tutelar deities. This private and family worship of the common people was in great part addressed to an inferior class of divinities. Every avocation had its patron gods, who had to be propitiated, besides the ancestral *aumakuas*, and there were also innumerable omens to be observed.*

Fishermen.—Fishermen had many tabus peculiar to themselves, and formed almost a distinct community. Their small heiaus, often called *ku-ulas*, stood on every promontory. A fisherman could not use a new net or fishing-rod without prayer and sacrifice to his patron god. Especially had the shark-god to be propitiated. Besides, there were countless minute regulations, which varied in different islands and districts.

House-building.—In building a house, the professional advice of a *kilokilo* or diviner had to be taken as to the position and direction of the house, and even the arrangement of the sticks composing the framework, or sickness and death would ensue. If it were a chief's house, human

* Mr. Dibble states that "the people were in the habit of praying every morning to the gods, clapping their hands as they muttered a set form of words in a sing-song tone. This was practiced by the chiefs and many of the people."

sacrifices would be required, so that many people fled to the mountains at such times from fear of the mysterious *Mu*. When the door was to be finished, a priest was sent for to offer the *kuwa* prayer, and to cut the thatch over the door.

Again, before the house was occupied, offerings and prayers had to be made both to the great gods and to the *aumakuas*, and it was usual to employ a priest to sleep alone in the house one or two nights before the owner moved into it.

Canoe-building.—The building of a canoe was a very serious business, almost equal to bringing down an idol for the heiau. The whole operation had to be superintended by a *kahuna kalaiwaa*. The choice of the tree was of the utmost importance. The *kahuna* paid great attention to the actions of birds, particularly of the little *elepaio*, and used to pass a night in the heiau, in order to receive directions from his *aumakuas* through dreams. Before the tree was cut down, offerings were made of a hog, red fish, cocoanuts, and *awa*, and prayers were addressed to Ku-pulupulu and other gods. The gods were again invoked before the canoe was dragged down to the shore. After it was finished and ready for launching, a final sacrifice was offered, called the *lolo*, and an *aha* was recited by the priest, standing with the owner at the bow of the canoe. In this prayer the names of Tahiti, Vavau, Upolu, and other islands of the South Pacific are mentioned. If the silence was broken by any noise or by any one's coming, it was a fatal omen, foreboding death and disaster, but if not, the canoe was safe.

Agriculture.—Those engaged in agriculture were very careful to plant on certain days of the moon. The *oo* or digger had to be fashioned with prayers addressed to

Ku-pulupulu or Ku-moku-halii, to insure good luck. Then there were prayers to be repeated when planting, and at different stages of the growth of the crop, addressed to Kane-puaa, and prayers for rain addressed to Lono or Ku. When the crop was ripe, the first fruits were offered to the family gods on the proper day of the moon.

Some of the food was cooked together with red fish. The family idol was brought, together with the *ipu o Lono* or sacred calabash, part of the food was offered to the god, and the rest was consumed by the company. After this, the field or taro-patch was *noa* or free.

The *hale kua*, where the women beat kapa, was tabu, and the whole manufacture was under the patronage of the goddess Lauhuki. The *hula* dance was regarded as an act of service to the obscene deity, Laka.

Again, there were appropriate ceremonies for several different periods of a child's life.

Rites at a Child's Birth.—When a male child was born, he was taken to the heiau, where offerings were made to the idols, and prayers offered by the priest, after which the father prayed to the four great gods to grant his son long life and prosperity.

Rites at a Boy's Promotion.—When a boy was four or five years old he was removed from the *hale noa* to the *hale mua*, where he could partake of tabu food, such as pork, and was henceforth forbidden to eat with women. On this important occasion a hog was baked for the gods, its head cut off and laid upon the *kuahu* or altar before the idol, and one ear placed in the *ipu o Lono*, which was attached to the idol's neck. Then bananas, cocoanuts, and *awa* were offered, and the boy's father, holding the *awa*, recited a long prayer, chiefly addressed to Lono. He then chewed a little of the *awa* and of the fish, and pronounced the concluding *amama*, after which the assembled worshipers feasted on the consecrated pork, and the boy was promoted to be an *ai kapu.* *

It is a significant fact that while every other act in life was accompanied with prayers and sacrifices to the gods, there were no religious ceremonies connected with marriage. Not even the favor of the *aumakuas* was invoked. It was entered upon with less ceremony than fishing or planting.

* Circumcision was attended with similar rites.

CHAPTER XI

SORCERY AND DIVINATION

THERE was another and darker part of the ancient religion which filled a larger place in the minds of the common people than the regular services in the heiaus, and had a more debasing influence upon them. This class of superstitions was common to all the Polynesian tribes. The basis of it was their belief that nearly all forms of sickness and disease were caused by evil spirits, with whom communication could be held through *kahunas* or sorcerers, of whom there were many different schools.

1. Kahuna Lapaau or Medicine Men.—Ordinary cases of illness were believed to be caused by the displeasure of the *aumakuas*, who were supposed to be jealously watching for any infringement of the tabus, and especially any neglect to fulfill a vow. If a chief was ill, offerings and prayers were made in the heiau, and chapels were built for the gods Lonopuha and Koleamoku. If his illness was severe, human sacrifices were offered to the tutelar god of the family. In ordinary cases a *kahuna lapaau* was called in, whose chief function was to propitiate the invisible powers who caused the malady. It is true that certain vegetable remedies were used, but their efficacy depended entirely on the good-will of the *aumakuas*. The medicine seems to have been considered more as the vehicle or medium through which the spirit would act, than as having any power in itself to cure the disease.

The tutelar gods of this class of practitioners were Maiola and Koleamoku. There were many omens, too numerous to mention, by which the *kahuna* judged whether the patient would recover or not. After prayer and sacrifices he would go to sleep, in order to receive intimations from his *akua* by dreams or visions as to the cause and remedy of the disease. If it did not rain during the night, on the following morning a fire was kindled and a fowl was baked for the *aumakuas*, a dog for the men's eating-house, and another for the women, five kapas being used to cover each oven. These offerings were afterward eaten by the relatives of the patient, and prayers offered to the *aumakuas* and the gods of medicine. Sometimes the patient was treated to a steam bath by being seated upon a pile of heated stones strewed over with wet leaves, while enveloped in kapas, after which he was dipped in the sea. If he did not improve, some squid, *hee*, was spread out all night and baked in the morning. The *kahuna* then repeated the *pule hee* prayer, while some of the squid was fed to the sick man. If this did not relieve him it was evident that something uncommon was at work, some malevolent *akua* sent by a sorcerer to destroy him. The next thing to be done was either to propitiate the demon, and send him back to his employer, or to employ a more powerful spirit to expel him. In such a case it was usual to employ sorcerers who had "familiar spirits" in their service. Of these there were many different schools, which had different patron deities, and used different kinds of incantations. They may, however, be reduced to two classes, of which the first may be called:

2. **Necromancers or Mediums.**—There were several varieties of these, which were styled *kahuna hoonohonoho*, *hoounauna*. *hookomokomo*. and *hooleilei*. but in the main

their methods were the same. As has been already stated, the chief god of sorcery was Uli, but there was an inferior order of demons, mostly females, who were sent on errands of mischief, *akua noho*, viz., Pua, Kapo, Kuamu, Kiha-wahine, a reptile goddess, etc. The goddess Hiiaka-i-ka-poli-o-Pele was also much employed by this class of *kahunas*. Certain shark-gods may be added to the list.

Unihipili.—Sometimes a necromancer employed as his agent for evil the departed spirit of some relative, which he had retained in his service as an *unihipili* by preserving his bones, and by the unremitting use of incantations and offerings at every meal. If, however, he or his heir and successor should neglect these rites for a single day, this evil power would be turned against him to his own destruction.

Kahuna hoonoho.—The practices of the *kahuna hoonoho* strongly resembled those of modern spiritism. The medium was called the *kahu* or *ipu* of the spirit, which was often called a *makani* or wind. Sometimes the spirit descended upon the *kahu*, and sometimes it spoke from the roof of the hut.* The necromancer always demanded *awa* before commencing operations. "*E inu i ka awa i ikaika ka makani.*" After drinking the *awa* the wind descended upon the *kahuna*, and showed him the cause of the sickness, whether the patient had been bewitched by a sorcerer, and by whom. The same practitioners were employed in cases of theft to recover stolen goods, and to detect the thief.

Kahuna hoounauna.—The *kahuna hoounauna*, etc., had the power of sending familiar spirits on errands. In cases where a patient had been bewitched, if the *kahuna* called

* Probably some of these *kahunas* were ventriloquists.

in by his friends possessed more powerful incantations or had a more powerful demon in his service than the hostile sorcerer, he could compel the evil spirit not only to confess by whom he was sent, but even to return and destroy his own *kahu*.

3. Sorcerers.—There was another class of sorcerers, still more feared and hated than the former, who were regarded, as Dibble says, "more like evil spirits than human beings," and were sometimes stoned to death or beheaded by the order of a chief.

Of this class the principal divisions were the *anaana*, the *kuni*, the *hoopiopio*, and *pahiuhiu*, and the *apo leo*. Uli was the chief deity invoked by them all.

Anaana.—The ceremonies of the *anaana* and the *kuni* were very similar. The *anaana* sorcerer always performed his incantations in secret, and generally at night. In order to effect his purpose it was absolutely necessary for him to secure something connected with the person of the intended victim, as the parings of the nails, a lock of the hair, the saliva from the mouth, etc., which was termed the *maunu* or bait. For this reason the chiefs always kept their most faithful servants around them, who carefully buried or burned every thing of the kind or sunk it out at sea.

After the requisite imprecations and offerings had been made, the *maunu* was either buried or burned. It is probable that the sorcerer sometimes used poison to accomplish his ends, but the power of imagination and of superstitious fear was often sufficient to make the victim give up all hope and pine away till he died. The *kahuna* was sometimes moved by revenge, but he more often exercised his black art for hire. The greater the number of his victims, the higher his reputation and the larger his fees.

Kuni.—The *kuni* ceremonies were always performed in public and in the daytime. They were employed at the death of a person to discover and destroy the sorcerer who was supposed to have caused his death, or to detect and kill a thief. The name *kuni* (i.e., to burn) refers to the fireplace, which was always connected with the ceremony. A preliminary offering of a pig was given to the *kahuna* as a retainer, *alana*, and a prayer was made to Uli.* After this, the speedy death of the thief was certain. No power could save him.

If the object was to avenge the death of a person who had been anaana'd, some of the hair of the deceased was burned, or pieces of the liver were fed to dogs and fowls, which were immediately burned to ashes, while the fire-prayer was chanted.†

Next morning the *kahuna* asserted that he had seen the *hoaka* or wraith of the guilty wizard, with his eyes shut and head down, which was a sign that he would surely die.

Hoopiopio and Pahiuhiu.—The *hoopiopio* and *pahiuhiu* forms of sorcery were substantially the same. In the former method the *kahuna* took his place in the road over which his intended victim was sure to pass, and made a magic mark across the road, at the same time muttering an imprecation or prayer to Uli. In the latter, he drew a square with his finger, dividing it into four

* A fireplace was then made, and four sticks with flags of white kapa set up at the corners, surrounded by the plant called *auhuhu*, fish-poison, and green gourds. A fire was kindled by rubbing the fire-stick *aulima* on a stick of *akia*, a poisonous shrub, and a large quantity of wood was burned. If his object was to punish a thief, the *kahuna* took several kukui-nuts and threw the oily kernels one after another into the fire, chanting the "fire-prayer" or imprecation in the name of Uli.

† In either case the ashes, kukui-nuts, etc., at the fireplace, were afterwards collected and thrown into the sea.

equal squares, and placed a small stone on the center of the figure. He then addressed a prayer to Kane Pohakaa, the *aumakua* in the stone, for the death of his victim. When the unsuspecting victim came along and stepped on the fatal spot, a spell would come upon him from which he was sure to die, generally in a few days.

Apo Leo.—*Apo leo* was the art of depriving a person of the power of articulate speech. In order to do this, the *kahuna* prayed at night to Uli and Hiiaka, presenting them with the usual offerings of *awa*, etc. The next day he sought out his intended victim and entered into conversation with him, during which (as was believed) he caught and took away his voice, or paralyzed his vocal organs, so that he could never speak again. He might linger a long time in this wretched condition, or die in a few days if the sorcerer so willed.

4. **Kalaipahoa** was the name of a famous poison-god, whose worship was of comparatively recent origin. According to the legend, one Kaneakama, living on West Molokai, had a dream in which his tutelar deity showed him a poison-tree on Mauna Loa, and directed him to cut it down and make an idol of it, by means of which he could cause any one's death. It was believed to be the only existing tree of its kind, and to be so poisonous that the least particle of it mixed with any one's food and drink, and accompanied with the proper incantations, was sure to cause his death. It was eagerly sought after, and several pieces of it were in the possession of different chiefs, who used it to get rid of persons who were obnoxious to them, both high and low. Kamehameha I. is said to have kept the principal image always near his person. Kaahumanu collected and burned all the fragments of

it that could be found. It is still a disputed question whether it was really poisonous or not.

5. **Kilokilo or Diviners.**—There was a numerous class of diviners or fortune-tellers called *kilokilo*, who lived on the credulity of the people, and were divided into several distinct branches.

The worst of these were the *kilokilo uhane*, who reported on the condition of the soul, *uhane*, and interpreted dreams.

The ancient Hawaiians believed that each individual had two souls, one of which occasionally left the body, as in trances, dreams, etc., and returned to it again. The diviners took advantage of this belief to extort from the people whatever they coveted. For instance, a *kilokilo* would gravely inform his neighbor that he had seen his double or wraith in a dream or vision, wandering naked, with his eyes shut, tongue hanging out, etc. (which was a sign that his *aumakuas* were offended with him), and that he was in danger of losing his double entirely. The owner of this wandering soul would be terrified, and willing to do any thing that the soothsayer required. The latter generally ordered certain kinds of fish, white dogs, white chickens, *awa*, and ten kapas to cover the oven with. The *kilokilo* then recited prayers while kindling the fire by friction.

When the offerings were cooked, he offered the *pule kala* or prayer for pardon, after which they were eaten by the assembled company, and he pronounced absolution. For this service he received a liberal fee.

Po'i-uhane.—The *po'i-uhane*, who worshiped Hiiaka, had the faculty of not only seeing the souls of living persons, *kakaola*, but of catching them with the hand, *po'i*, and of either squeezing them to death or imprisoning them in a water-calabash. The sorcerer then had the owner of the soul in his power, and could levy blackmail on him as he pleased, for if he killed his *kakaola* he would go into a decline and soon die.

Astrologers.—The *kilokilo hoku* or astrologers were a more respectable class, and helped to keep alive the knowledge of astronomy possessed by the ancient navigators. They were continually studying the heavens, and based their predictions on the positions of the moon and planets in relation to certain fixed stars and constellations, which were associated with the fortunes of particular families of chiefs.

Nana-Uli.—The *nana-uli* or soothsayers predicted not only changes in the weather, but also future events, such as the death of chiefs, wars, etc., from appearances in the sky, tidal waves, the arrival of shoals of certain kinds of fish, etc.

Prophets.—The *kaula* and *makaula* (prophets) were comparatively harmless persons, who lived solitary lives, and believed themselves to be at times inspired by Kane-nui-akea. They were often attached to the high-chiefs as counselors.

CHAPTER XII

FUNERAL RITES; DOCTRINES OF A FUTURE STATE

Burial of Chiefs.—Several different modes of burial were practiced, and the funeral rites of a high-chief differed widely from those of the common people. At the death of the king, the whole district was considered polluted for ten days, so that the heir to the throne was obliged to remove to another district and remain there during this tabu period.

The *kuni* sorcerers were first set to work to avenge the chief's death, if there was any suspicion that it had been caused by sorcery.

Human Sacrifice.—A human sacrifice, called the *moepuu*, was then offered, in order that the king might enter the other world with attendance suitable to his rank. Many people fled to the mountains from fear of the *mu ai kanaka* (the man-eating *mu*), and remained there in hiding-places till the tabu period was past. The corpse was enveloped in banana and taro leaves, and buried in a shallow grave about a foot deep. A fire was kept burning over it to hasten decomposition, while certain prayers were continually repeated (the *pule hui*). This was kept up for ten days. The corpse was then disinterred, and the flesh stripped from the bones, which were collected in a bundle, tied up with cinet, and covered with kapa and red feathers. This was called an *unihipili*.

The *uko* (hog), which had been already baked, was now offered, and worship was paid to the bones of the deceased, who was thus deified. This ceremony removed the pollution of the district, and the heir to the throne could now return.

Mourning Customs.—Meanwhile the most extraordinary mourning ceremonies, *kumakena*, took place. Besides the universal and long-continued wailing, the people generally knocked out one or more of their front teeth, and cut their hair in the most grotesque shapes, sometimes bald on both sides, while leaving it long on the top of the head, etc. Some tattooed their tongues, and others burned semicircles on their bodies in different places with blazing bark.*

Concealment of Bones.—The deified bones of the chiefs were generally carefully concealed in the most secret and inaccessible caves. Before death they made their most trusty attendants swear to conceal their bones so that no one could ever find them. "I do not wish," said a dying chief, "that my bones should be made into arrows to shoot mice with, or into fish-hooks." This practice was called *hunakele*. In some cases, however, the bones were deposited in a temple as objects of worship. Thus the bones of many ancient chiefs of Hawaii were deposited in the *Hale o Keawe* at Honaunau, and those of Liloa at the heiau in Waipio Valley. Those of many ancient kings were deposited in a cave at the head of the Iao Valley, Wailuku,

* At the same time, the people generally threw off for the time all clothing and all restraints of decency, and appeared "more like demons than human beings." Houses were often burned, property was plundered, revenge taken for old forgotten injuries, and a state of anarchy prevailed, according to the testimony of eye-witnesses. Even as late as 1823, at Keopuolani's death, many natives fled to the mountains, while others "carried their effects into the missionaries' inclosure and begged permission to remain there, hoping to find a sanctuary within their premises amidst the general devastation which they expected would follow her decease."

and some were thrown into the crater of Kilauea, "under the impression that the spirits of the deceased would be admitted into the society of the volcanic deities."

Burial of Priests, Etc.—The bodies of priests and chiefs of inferior rank were laid out straight, wrapped in many folds of kapa, and buried in that posture, the priests sometimes within the precincts of the temple in which they had officiated. A pile of stones, and frequently a circle of high poles around the grave, marked the place of their interment. As soon as death had taken place, all except the immediate relatives had to leave the house, which became ceremonially polluted. Other friends might wail outside, but it was tabu for them to enter, or touch, or eat with those within.

Burial of Common People.—Sometimes the body was partially embalmed by being salted and dried (*ialoa*). The lower class of people generally raised the upper part of the body immediately after death, and bent the face forward to the knees, after which the head, hands, and knees were bound together with cinet or cord. The body was afterward wrapped in a coarse mat, and buried the first or second day after death, with great secrecy by night.

They preferred to deposit their dead in caves or subterranean caverns, with calabashes of water and poi, sugarcane, etc., by their sides; but they also often buried them in a sitting posture in small pits near their houses or in the sand. No prayer was offered at the grave except occasionally by the people of Oahu.

Purification.—The morning after the burial the rite of purification was performed as follows: The persons defiled by the dead went and bathed in fresh water and on their return seated themselves in a row at the door of the house. Then the priest came with a calabash-lid containing holy water, and pronounced the form prescribed for purification, (beginning *Leleuli*, etc.), the audience uttering the regular responses, and closing with the shout "*Noa honua!*" after which he sprinkled them with the holy water, and they were clean.

Doctrine of a Future State.—The conceptions which the ancient Hawaiians had of the future state were vague and inconsistent.

Lolupe was the name of a deity invoked in funeral ceremonies, who conducted the spirits of the chiefs to their final abode after death, and assisted them in the journey. According to some traditions and dirges, Ka-onohi-o-ka-la (the eye-ball of the sun) conducted the souls of heroes to a heaven in or beyond the clouds. According to others, they went to Kane, to the *aina huna o Kane* or hidden land of Kane, which seems to have been a sort of Fata Morgana or fairy island in the West. It was said that mariners sometimes saw in the distance a beautiful island abounding in cocoanut trees, but it was all unsubstantial and ghostly, and receded before them like the mirage of the desert; but the great majority of the dead, after a delay of a few days, went to a subterranean Hades.*

Leaping-places.—There were several precipices from the verge of which the unhappy ghosts were supposed to leap into the lower world.†

* During the first few days after death ghosts generally haunted the place of sepulture, and endeavored to strangle their enemies, but kept growing weaker and weaker day by day.

They were distinguished by the peculiar squeaking or whistling sound, *muki*, which they produced, like the ghosts which did "squeak and gibber in the Roman streets." In rare cases a departing soul would be met by a friendly *aumakua* or *unihipili*, who compelled it to go home and re-enter the body. This was their way of accounting for cases of catalepsy or trance.

† According to Mr. Dibble, one of these was at the northern point of Hawaii,

Wakea.—The lower world was divided into two distinct kingdoms, the upper one ruled by Wakea, and the lower by Milu. The region of Wakea, the ancestor of the race, was a quiet and peaceful realm of comparative comfort, reserved for the select few. Wakea was possessed of higher tabus and greater power than Milu, and only admitted those who had been scrupulous in observing the religious rites and tabus during life.

Milu.—Milu was said to have been an ancient chief of Hamakua, Hawaii, notorious for his wickedness during life, who afterwards became king of a realm of darkness and misery below that of Wakea, to which the great majority of the dead were destined. Their food consisted of lizards and butterflies, but there were streams of water of which they could drink, and spreading *kou* trees beneath which they reclined.

Milu's province was also said to be a noisy and disorderly place, where lawless *akuas* kept up wild games all night.* In both New Zealand and Mangaia, Miru was the goddess of hell, who devoured the souls of cowards.

Ghosts.—The Hawaiians were exceedingly superstitious about ghosts and haunted places. There were certain places, especially old battle-fields, which it was un-

one at the west end of Maui, and the third at the southern point of Oahu. Near the northwest point of Oahu is a rock called the Leina ka-uhane, where the souls of the dead descended to Sheol. The same term, *reinga* or leaping-place, is applied in New Zealand to their place of descent to the *po* or Inferno, at the North Cape. According to another account the entrance to the *lua* or pit of Milu was situated at the mouth of the great valley of Waipio, Hawaii, at a place called *ke one* (the sand), where the sands have long since covered it up and concealed it from mortal sight.

* The hero Hiku was fabled to have descended by means of an immensely long rope of *koali* vines (Convolvulus, or rather Ipomea) into the abyss of Milu, and to have brought back his bride Kawelu. Almost the same legend was told in New Zealand of the lovers Hutu and Pare.

safe to pass at night. The feeling of *incubus* or nightmare was ascribed to a ghost sitting upon the sufferer. A *lapu* was a malicious and dangerous specter. The term *oio* was applied to a procession of ghosts, which it was death to meet. There were persons in Waipio who affirmed that they had seen Kamehameha I., the conqueror, with his chiefs, warriors, and attendants, marching past in ghostly procession. In Honokahau Valley in Maui an *oio* was said to have been seen led by the headless specter of Kanihonui, a chief beheaded by Kamehameha for adultery.

Such an *oio* in that valley was said to have left several men dead in its track.

CHAPTER XIII

ARTS AND MANUFACTURES

The arts and manufactures of the ancient Hawaiians were similar to those of the other Polynesian tribes, and particularly to those of the Society Islands.

Tools.—When we consider that they were destitute of metals and of the cereal grains, as well as of cotton, flax, and wool, we must admit that the Hawaiians made as much progress as could well have been expected of them. Their cutting tools were made of stone, or sharks' teeth, or bamboo. Their axes were chiefly made of a hard, compact kind of lava, found on the summits of Mauna Kea and Haleakala. The art of making them was handed down from father to son.

The principal tool used in cultivating the soil was the *o-o*, which was then simply a stick of hard wood, either pointed or shaped into a flat blade at the end.

With these rude tools extensive works were carried out, such as building terraces, leveling and embanking their taro-patches, and constructing irrigation-ditches, often miles in length.

Agriculture.—The principal crop was the taro or *kalo*, but sweet potatoes were chiefly raised in the dry and stony districts, and yams in Kauai and Niihau. They also cultivated the sugar-cane, bananas, calabash-gourds, the *wauke* or paper-mulberry for its bark, and the *awa* (Piper methysticum) for its narcotic roots.

The subsistence of the common people was, on the whole, poor and scanty.

Fishing.—Fishing was next to agriculture in importance, and was carried on with great ingenuity and skill. The ancient fishermen had a most intimate knowledge of all the different kinds of fish frequenting the seas, and of their habits and feeding-grounds. All the shoals and hidden rocks for several miles out to sea were well known to them, as well as the different kinds of fish frequenting each. There were many modes of fishing—by spearing, by baskets, by hook and line, and with nets. The spearing was chiefly practiced by divers under water, or at night by torchlight in shallow water.

Hooks.—Their hooks were made of bone, of mother-of-pearl, of whales' teeth, and of tortoise-shell, and were of many styles, adapted to different kinds of fish. A showy variety of cowry was used to attract the *hee* or squid.

Nets.—Their nets were made of twine spun from the strong and durable fiber of the *olona* (Touchardia latifolia), and were of many different patterns and sizes, which may be divided into two classes—long nets, sometimes over one hundred fathoms in length, and bag-nets. The long nets were often drawn into large circles, so as to inclose shoals of fish, and sometimes ropes hundreds of fathoms in length, having dry *ki* leaves braided to them by the stems and hanging down in the water, were used to sweep around and drive the fish into the net, thus inclosing thousands at one haul. The numerous artificial fish-ponds, already referred to, are not found in southern Polynesia.

Fish-poison.—Another method of catching fish was by the use of a poisonous plant, the *auhuhu* or *hola* (Tephrosia piscatoria), which was bruised and placed by divers beneath the stones in places frequented by the fish. The poison was so powerful that the fish were soon overcome by it and floated to the surface, where they were collected.

Canoes.—In the mechanical arts the Hawaiians accomplished some creditable work, considering the tools at their command.

Their canoes were not built up of planks, as in Fiji, but each one was hollowed out of a single tree. Strips of hard wood, however, were sewed on the upper edge of the canoe on each side, closing over the top at both stem and stern. Their model was finer than that of the Tahitian canoes, and they were faster sailers. As in other Polynesian groups, the canoes were steadied by an outrigger, *ama*, a slender log of light wood parallel to the canoe and fastened to it by curved cross-pieces, *iako*. They also had large double canoes, sometimes from fifty to a hundred feet long, with a raised platform or *pola* in the middle, for passengers of rank. The ancient sails were made of mats, triangular in shape, and broad at the top. Their skill in navigation has been referred to in Chapter III. In the management of canoes in the surf they were unsurpassed.

Houses.—House-building was a laborious undertaking in the olden time. After cutting down the trees in the mountains they had to drag or carry them several miles to the shore, braid the cord, and collect the *pili* grass, *hala* leaves, or ferns for thatching, etc.

The houses were oblong, with low sides and steep roofs to shed the rain. There were professional builders, who were expert in framing the timbers and in thatching the corners and ridge-pole of the house. There were many technical names for different sticks of the frame, and many minute rules to be followed in the work. Very few houses had any windows, and the doors were low and narrow. Some of the chiefs' houses were from forty to seventy feet long and twenty feet wide. They were not as elaborately ornamented as in some other groups. Those of the lower class were mere hovels, ten feet long by six feet wide, and four feet high, and were entered by a small hole in the side.

Furniture.—Their furniture consisted chiefly of calabashes for water, poi, and valuables, wooden dishes, and stone utensils of various kinds, fish-baskets, and mats. The large gourd (Cucurbita maxima) was not known in any other group in the Pacific. The bottle-gourd (Lagenaria vulgaris) was used for water-containers and for *hula* drums. With their stone adzes they made circular dishes of *koa* and *kou* wood, holding from a pint to five gallons, as neatly as if they had been turned in a lathe.*

Mats.—The common floor-mats, made by the women, were formed of the leaves of the pandanus or *hala* tree. Generally a platform or *hikiee*, raised two or three feet above the floor, extended across one end of the house. This was spread with a layer of rushes, and covered with sleeping-mats. A superior quality of mats was made on Kauai and Niihau of a fine rush called *makaloa*. These mats were of great size and dyed in various patterns.

Lights.—For lights at night they used the nuts of the *kukui* tree (Aleurites moluccana). These were baked in an oven and shelled, after which the kernels were strung on a split of bamboo or the thin stock of a cocoanut-leaf, and used as candles, beginning at the top. Each nut would burn about four minutes, when the one below it

* The art of pottery was unknown in Polynesia.

took light and the burned-out nut was broken off. They also used stone lamps with kapa wicks, and *kukui* or fish-oil.

Clothing.—Their cloth or kapa was made of the bark of the paper-mulberry or *wauke* (Broussonetia papyrifera) and of the *mamake* (Pipturus albidus), which were cultivated with much care. Its manufacture was left entirely to the women, who peeled off strips of the bark and scraped off the outer coat with shells. After being soaked a while in water each strip was laid upon a smooth log and beaten with a square grooved mallet of hard wood until it resembled thick flexible paper. The strips were united by overlaying the edges and beating them together. There were several qualities of kapa, some so fine as to resemble muslin, and other kinds very thick and tough, which appeared like wash-leather. It was bleached white or stained with vegetable or mineral dyes, impressed with bamboo stamps in a great variety of patterns and colors, and glazed with a kind of gum or resin. Nothing like a loom was known in Polynesia.

Dress.—The dress of the women consisted of the *pa-ú*, a wrapper composed of five thicknesses of kapa, about four yards long and three or four feet wide, passed several times around the waist and extending below the knee, while that of the men was the *malo* or girdle, which was about a foot wide and three or four yards long.

The *kihei* or mantle, about six feet square, was occasionally worn by both sexes. It was worn by the men by tying two corners of the same side together, so that the knot rested on one shoulder, and by the women as a long shawl. In general, this paper cloth would not bear washing, and lasted only a few weeks.

The *kapa moe* or sleeping kapa was made of five layers

of common kapa, three or four yards square. The outside piece (*kilohana*) was stained or painted with vegetable dyes.

Ornaments.—The Hawaiians have always been noted for their fondness for flowers and other ornaments. The *ilima* (Sida fallax) was formerly much cultivated on account of its yellow flowers, of which wreaths or leis were made for the head and neck. Then, as now, the fragrant orange-colored fruit of the pandanus was often made into necklaces. Feather leis were worn both as coronets and necklaces.* Their bracelets, *kupee*, consisted of shell or ivory ornaments fastened on the back of the wrist by a small cord.

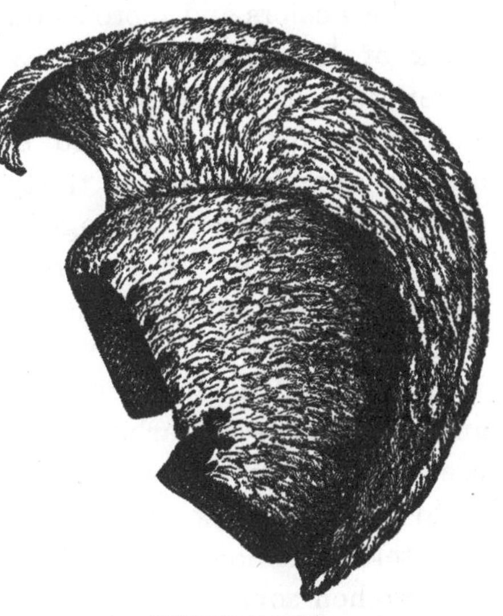

FEATHER HELMET

Helmets.—The elegant feather helmets worn by the chiefs on state occasions were made of wicker-work, covered with the golden-yellow or the scarlet feathers of certain birds—the *o-o*, the *mamo*, and the *iiwi*.

Feather Cloaks.—The feather cloaks or robes of state, called *mamo*, were magnificent and costly insignia of rank. Their ground-work was a fine netting of *olona* or native

* An ornament for the neck formerly much worn by the chiefs was the *niho palaoa*, which consisted of a hooked ornament made from the tooth of a sperm whale or walrus, suspended in front by a large number of braids of human hair. Necklaces were also made of ivory beads (*lei poo*).

hemp, to which small delicate feathers of a bright yellow color were attached so as to overlap each other, forming a perfectly smooth surface. The birds which produced these feathers were caught by means of branches smeared with sticky *papala* gum, and well baited with their favorite flowers.* These choice yellow feathers were reserved for royalty alone. Inferior chiefs had smaller capes and cloaks of various colors and more common feathers. The feather cloak of Kamehameha I. is said to have occupied nine generations of kings in its construction.

The kahilis or feathered staffs carried on state occasions were from ten to thirty feet in height, and were composed of feathers arranged on branches attached to the staff, so as to form colored cylinders fifteen or eighteen inches in diameter, the handles being covered with rings of tortoise-shell or ivory.

Tattooing.—The ancient Hawaiian tattooed but little, and in a perfectly arbitrary style. Tattooing was not used here as elsewhere to serve the purpose of costume, or to indicate rank or lineage. It was sometimes done as a token of mourning at the death of a friend or chief. The women sometimes had the back of the hand marked so as to resemble an open-worked glove.

It was the fashion among the women to wear the hair short in front and on the sides of the head, and to turn up the edges on the forehead and temples with a wash made of lime or white clay.

* These birds were honey-suckers, living on the nectar of the flowers of the ohia, the banana, and the large lobelias. The yellow feathers were taken from two species of birds, viz.: the *o-o* (Acrulocercus nobilis), which has one little tuft of yellow feathers under each wing, and the still rarer *mamo* (Drepanis pacifica), which has also larger golden-yellow feathers on its back. The latter species is nearly extinct. The scarlet feathers were obtained from the *iiwi* (Vestiaria coccinea), a song-bird with gorgeous scarlet coat and black wings; and from the *akakane* (Fringilla coccinea).

CHAPTER XIV

CUSTOMS AND AMUSEMENTS

Cooking.—In ancient times, as now, the Hawaiians practiced the well-known Polynesian method of steaming their food in the *umu* or under-ground oven with heated stones. The labor of cooking and of pounding the poi on a large wooden tray with a stone pestle was performed entirely by the men. Fire was produced by friction, by rapidly rubbing a pointed stick (the *aulima*) in a groove made in another stick (the *aunaki*) until the heap of fine powder collected at the end of the groove took fire. The wood of the *olomea* or *hau* tree was generally preferred for this purpose.

Salt was manufactured from sea-water, and also collected from the salt lake of Aliapaakai and elsewhere. It was much used in salting fish and pork, and seasoning their food, which does not seem to have been practiced by other Polynesians.

Awa Drinking.—Neither fermented nor distilled liquors were used by the Hawaiians, but in common with all the Pacific islanders they drank an infusion of the roots of the *awa* plant, elsewhere called *kava.* It was first chewed, after which the masticated morsels were placed in a wooden bowl, and water poured upon them. The infusion was strained through a mesh of *ehuawa* (cyperus) fibers, and was then ready for drinking. Its effects were narcotic and stupefying. Although *awa* drinking was not attended here with as much ceremony as in Tonga and Fiji, still it was mainly restricted to the chiefs and priests.

Barter.—There was no circulating medium which served the purpose of money, and all trade was conducted by barter. Certain districts were noted for the superiority of certain products, such as stone axes, kapas, mats, canoes, etc., which they exchanged with other districts, and thus a small commerce was carried on.*

Games.—The ancient Hawaiians had a great variety of games, both for children and adults. The *makahiki* festival in the latter part of the month of Welehu was devoted to sports and general gambling. In fact, most of these games were resorted to chiefly for the purpose of betting, to which they were excessively addicted. Both men and women of all ranks were eager to stake every article they possessed on the success of their favorite players, and the games seldom ended without fierce brawls between the different parties.

Boxing.—Among their athletic sports that of *mokomoko* or boxing was the favorite national game. It was regulated by fixed rules, and presided over by umpires. The champions generally belonged to different chiefs or districts, and were attended by crowds of partisans. As many as ten thousand spectators were present on these occasions. A knock-down or blood-starting blow was followed by deafening yells, dancing, and beating of drums by the surrounding multitude. The elated victor strutted around the ring, challenging others to the contest, until he met his match. It was not uncommon for several to be left

* It is said that there were periodical fairs held at various places, of which the banks of the Wailuku River at Hilo were the most famous, according to Ellis.

dead in the arena during one of these games. Less fatal in their results were the games of *hakoko*, wrestling, and *kukini*, foot races, which were very popular.

Maika.—A favorite amusement, the *maika*, consisted in bowling a circular, highly-polished stone disk called an *ulu*, three or four inches in diameter and an inch or more thick, swelling with a slight convexity from the edges to the center. A *kahua* or level track about three feet wide and half a mile in length was made smooth and hard. In this track two short sticks were fixed in the ground only a few inches apart, at a distance of thirty or forty yards. The game consisted in either sending the stone between these sticks, or in seeing which party could bowl it farthest. It is said that one of their best players would bowl the stone upwards of a hundred rods.

Pahee.—The *pahee* was a similar game, in which short blunted darts of highly polished hard wood from two to four feet in length were thrown or rather glanced along the level track between two darts laid down at a certain distance.

The game called *kea pua*, which was played chiefly by children, was similar to the *pahee*, but the darts used were the dried flower-stalks of the sugar-cane.

Holua.—Another popular sport was the *holua*, which consisted in sliding down hill on a long narrow sledge called a *papa holua*. The runners were from twelve to fourteen feet long and three inches deep, made of hard red wood, highly polished, and curving upward at the forward end. They were set about four inches apart, and fastened together by ten or more cross-pieces, on which two long, tough sticks were fastened and connected by wicker-work.

A smooth track was made down the side of a steep hill, extending to a great distance over the adjoining plain, and covered with dry *pili* grass. The player, grasping the sledge about the middle with his right hand, ran a few yards to the starting-place, and then threw himself with all his strength upon it, and shot head-foremost down the hill. Sometimes they were carried half a mile before stopping.

Surf-Swimming.—The most popular of all their pastimes with all ranks and ages was surf-swimming or *hee nalu*, still practiced. In this sport the players use a light board made of the wood of the koa tree or sometimes of the *wiliwili* (Erythrina), about eight feet long and eighteen inches broad, stained black and highly polished. With this they swim out to sea, diving under the rollers which they meet, until they reach the outer line of breakers; then, lying flat on their boards, they balance themselves upon the forward slope of the highest breaker, and ride them with the speed of a race-horse toward the shore.

Other ancient sports were the *lele kawa*, or leaping from a precipice into the deep water below; *lele kowali*, or swinging on a long rope suspended from a lofty cocoanut tree; *koheoheo*, or the children's game of jumping the rope; and flying kites, *lupe*.

Konane.—The *konane* was a complicated game of checkers, played with black and white pebbles upon a board divided into numerous squares.

Puhenehene.—In the favorite game of *puhenehene*, five bundles of kapa, *puu*, were placed between the two parties. Under one of these a player was to hide a stone called the *no'a*, after which the other side were to point out the *puu* under which they guessed it to be concealed, striking it with a rod tipped with feathers. The side that guessed right the greater number of times won the game. The games called *kilu* and *ume* were always played at night, in an inclosure made for the purpose, and were connected with many vile associations.*

Shooting mice with bow and arrows, *pana iole*, was a game played only by chiefs, and connected with religious ceremonies. Cock-fighting, too, was much practiced in ancient times. Few of the games mentioned above were ever played without a wager.

The children had many games with strings, called *hei*, similar to the English cat's-cradle. They also played at walking on stilts, and at tossing and catching pebbles, *kimo*, and at spinning tops made out of little gourds, *hu*.

Music — the Ukeke.—The ancient Hawaiian instruments of music were very few and simple. The *ukeke* was a strip of flexible wood or bamboo, mounted with two or three strings of *olona* or of cocoanut fiber, which are said to have been tuned to the intervals of a second or fourth, and may be regarded as a primitive guitar.

Kiokio.—The *kiokio* was a small gourd pierced with three holes: one to put against the nose to blow through, the other two for the fingers. The nose-flute, another form of it, was made of a joint of bamboo, with the nose-hole on one side, and two finger-holes near the other end.

Drums.—There were also several kinds of drums, as the *kaekeeke*, made of a section of the hollowed trunk of a cocoanut tree, with one end covered with shark-skin; smaller drums made of cocoanut-shells, *puniu*, covered

*The *kilu* itself was a small gourd of a peculiar shape, which was thrown at a stick set up at a distance.

in the same manner; and *hòkeo* made of two gourds, placed one upon the other, which were used with the *hula*. The drums were chiefly used to mark time as an accompaniment to dancing or chanting. The other instruments had a range of only one or two notes, and their singing was a monotonous chanting on one, two, or three notes, but in very accurate time.

Dancing.—The *hulahula* was not so much dancing in the usual sense of the term as acting out by gestures and movements the ideas expressed by the songs which they accompanied.

Different kinds of dances were sometimes named from the nature of the accompaniment, as the *pai umauma*, in which they struck their breasts in time, the *paipu*, in which the accompaniment was the calabash or *hokeo*, the *ka-laau*, in which the tune was marked by striking on sticks, the *hula pahu*, accompanied by drums, etc. Some dances were in honor of the gods, or in praise of the chiefs, as the *alaapa-apa*. But the greater part were intended for the gratification of the baser instincts, and were accompanied by songs unfit to be mentioned.

The dancers were generally women, and wore a decorated *pa-u* with wreaths on the head, dogs'-teeth buskins on the ankles, hogs'-teeth bracelets, *hulili*, on the wrists, and the whale's-tooth ornament, *niho palaoa*, or *lei palaoa*, on the neck. Children sometimes engaged in the less objectionable dances, and men sometimes performed as buffoons between the acts. Certain dances were performed by large companies of women drawn up in solid squares and moving in perfect time. The dancers generally remained stationary in one place, and moved the arms and body in keeping with the sentiment of the accompanying chant.

As has been stated, the professional *hula* dancers were devotees of the foul goddess *Laka.*

A shrine was fitted up for her worship, consisting of a *kuahu* or wooden shelf, on which was a stick of *halapepe* or Dracaena aurea, wrapped in kapa, and surrounded with green wreaths of *maile*, *ieie*, ferns, and other foliage. Prayers and offerings were frequently made before the shrine, and certain tabus strictly observed during the whole period of the training, at the close of which the final sacrifice or *ailolo* hog was offered.

Poetry.—The Hawaiians were always passionately fond of poetry. Their poems (*mele*) had no rhyme or meter in the European sense. They consisted of short musical sentences or lines, divided into bars or measures, with great attention to the accent and cadence of the concluding word. Sometimes they were divided into stanzas, each stanza ending in a refrain or chorus. The sound of the letter *t* was "universally and invariably used" in poetry instead of *k*. The style and diction of poetry was quite different from that of prose. It was highly figurative, abounding in lists of names, and in allusions to their mythology, to places, to local winds and rains, and favorite flowers, as the *lehua.*

Some of the principal classes of meles* were the following:

1. Religious chants, prayers, and prophecies.

2. Inoas or name-songs, composed at the birth of a chief in his honor, recounting the exploits of his ancestors, etc.

* Many meles, some of which were several hundred lines in length, were handed down for centuries, by oral tradition. In the same way the genealogies of the chiefs and historical traditions, as well as numerous legends and romances, *kaao*, were preserved by professional bards and story-tellers, who were attached to the retinues of the high-chiefs.

3. Kanikaus, dirges or lamentations for the dead.
4. Ipos, or love-songs.

The following is a passage in a dirge, preserved by Mr. Ellis, which was in memory of Keeaumoku:

Auwe, auwe, ua mate tuu Alii,	Alas, alas, dead is my chief,
Ua mate tuu hatu, tuu hoa,	Dead is my lord and my friend;
Tuu hoa i ta wa o ta wi,	My friend in the season of famine,
Tuu hoa i paa ta aina,	My friend in the time of drought,
Tuu hoa i tuu ilihune,	My friend in my poverty,
Tuu hoa i ta ua me ta matani,	My friend in the rain and the wind,
Tuu hoa i ta wela o ta la,	My friend in the heat and the sun,
Tuu hoa i ta anu o ta mauna,	My friend in the cold from the mountain,
Tuu hoa i ta ino,	My friend in the storm,
Tuu hoa i ta malie,	My friend in the calm,
Tuu hoa i na tai ewalu,	My friend in the eight seas.
Auwe, auwe, ua hala tuu hoa,	Alas, alas, gone is my friend,
Aohe e hoi mai!	And no more will return.

PART II

TO THE DEATH OF KAMEHAMEHA I.

CHAPTER XV

ANCIENT HISTORY

First Period.—The first two hundred and fifty years after the departure of Laa-mai-kahiki, mentioned in Chapter III., appears to have been a period of comparative peace and prosperity, during which few inter-island wars took place, and each island kingdom seems generally to have attended to its own affairs. It was during this period that extensive works of irrigation, etc., were executed, and the population multiplied under such wise chiefs as Manokalanipo of Kauai, Mailekukahi of Oahu, and Liloa of Hawaii.

Kalaunuiohua.—About the end of the thirteenth century, however, it is said that Kalaunuiohua, a warlike and ambitious *Moi* of Hawaii, undertook to subdue the whole group. He collected a fleet and an army and invaded Maui, where he defeated and captured the leading chief of that island. Elated by this success, he proceeded first to Molokai, where he was again victorious, and then to Oahu, where he defeated and captured the chief of Ewa and Waianae. With the three captive chiefs in his train he set sail for Kauai, and landed near Koloa, where he was met by Kukona at the head of the warriors of Kauai, and totally defeated, his fleet being taken and his army destroyed. In fact, the island of Kauai appears to have ever afterward maintained its independence until the nineteenth century.*

Luukoa.—About a century later three high-chiefs of Hawaii, together with Luukoa, a Maui chief, invaded Oahu, landing at the Ewa lagoon. Marching inland, they were defeated by Mailekukahi at the Kipapa ravine, which is said to have received that name from its having been paved, *kipapa*, with the corpses of the slain.

Second Period.—Of this last period, extending from about 1450 A.D. to the conquest of the group by Kamehameha I., Judge Fornander has justly said:

"It was an era of strife, dynastic ambitions, internal and external wars on each island, with all their deteriorating consequences of anarchy, depopulation, social and intellectual degradation, loss of liberty, loss of knowledge, loss of arts."

Wars became more frequent and more cruel, while the common people became more and more degraded and oppressed, and were probably decreasing in numbers here as well as in Tahiti before the end of the eighteenth century.

Story of Umi.—The most famous chief during this period was Umi, who reigned over the island of Hawaii

* It was about this time that a vessel called "Mamala" in the tradition arrived at Kahului, Maui. The captain and crew are said to have been foreigners of light complexion, with bright eyes, who intermarried with the natives and became progenitors of a light-colored stock. As there were no Europeans in the Pacific Ocean in the thirteenth century, it is most probable, as Judge Fornander has suggested, that these foreigners were the crew of some Japanese junk, driven out of its course by a typhoon, and drifted to these shores, as has twice happened in recent times.

about 1500 A.D. He was the son of Liloa, a celebrated king of Hawaii, and Akahiakuleana, a woman of low rank, who lived in East Hamakua. Umi was brought up in ignorance of his rank until he was about sixteen years old. His mother then revealed to him the secret, and invested him with the red malo, the yellow-feather wreath, and the whale's-tooth ornament, which Liloa had left with her as pledges and tokens of her son's royal birth.

With these credentials he went to Waipio, boldly entered the tabu inclosure, and in spite of warning shouts and cries of death forced his way into the presence of the aged king. "Who art thou?" said Liloa. "I am Umi, thy son," replied the young man, displaying the tokens which his mother had given him. Liloa recognized them at once, and publicly acknowledged him as his son, second only to Hakau, his heir.

Umi excelled in all manly exercises, and soon became popular with all classes. Hakau, on his accession to the throne, proved to be a cruel, rapacious, and treacherous tyrant. He deposed and outraged the old counselors of his father, two of whom took refuge with Umi, who had retired to Laupahoehoe. By their advice Umi suddenly marched to Waipio at the head of a large force, slew the tyrant, and was proclaimed *Moi* of Hawaii amid general rejoicing. His reign was a long and prosperous one. He removed his court from Waipio to the Kona district, which has ever since been the favorite residence of Hawaiian kings. He built a remarkable temple on the tableland between Mauna Loa and Hualalai, now known as Ahua-a-Umi, which he is said to have occupied as his head-quarters. Around this heiau he caused six pyramids of stone fifteen or twenty feet high to be erected—

one by each district of the island, besides one for himself.

To strengthen his position he married Piikea, the daughter of Piilani, king of Maui, who sent a large fleet of double canoes to escort her to Hawaii, as became her rank. Soon afterward Piilani died, and was succeeded by his eldest son Lono-a-pii, a surly and avaricious chief, who soon drove his younger brother to seek refuge with Umi at Waipio.

Their sister Piikea persuaded Umi to espouse the cause of the exiled chief Kiha-a-Piilani. Accordingly he collected the best warriors from every district of Hawaii, and an immense fleet of war-canoes, with which he crossed the channel to Hana, Maui.

He first besieged and took a fort on the top of the hill called Kauwiki, which was considered almost impregnable in those days, and then proceeded to Waihee, where he defeated and killed Lono-a-pii. Kiha-a-Piilani, who thus succeeded his brother in the government of Maui, was an able and prosperous chief, and deserves to be remembered for the paved road which he caused to be made around East Maui, the remains of which are still to be seen.

Discovery of the Islands by the Spaniards.—Umi was succeeded by his eldest son Kealiiokaloa, who was succeeded in turn by his youngest brother Keawe-nui-a-Umi. During the reign of the former, a foreign vessel was wrecked at Keei, in South Kona, Hawaii. The tradition relates that only the captain and his sister reached the shore in safety, and that they knelt down on the beach, remaining a long time in that posture, whence the place was called Kulou, as it is at this day.

Unlike the Fijians, the people received them kindly and set food before them. The strangers intermarried with the natives, and became the progenitors of certain well-known families of chiefs, such as that of Kaikioewa, former governor of Kauai.

In reckoning by generations, and allowing thirty years on an average to a generation, we find that Kealiiokaloa was born about A.D. 1500, and probably came to the throne about A.D. 1525–30.

Now we learn from Spanish historians that Cortez, the conqueror of Mexico, fitted out several exploring expeditions on the western coast about this time. The first squadron, consisting of three vessels, commanded by Alvarado de Saavedra, sailed from Zacatula for the Moluccas or Spice Islands, October 31, 1527. These ships sailed in company, but when they were a thousand leagues from port they were scattered by a severe storm. The two smaller vessels were never heard from, but Saavedra pursued the voyage alone in the "Florida" to the Moluccas, touching at the Ladrone Islands on the way.*

No white people except the Spaniards were navigating the Pacific Ocean at that early period, and it seems to be certain that the foreign vessel which was wrecked about this time on the Kona coast must have been one of Saavedra's missing ships.

There is also little doubt that these islands were discovered by the Spanish navigator Juan Gaetano, in the year 1555.†

* As has been shown by Judge Fornander, this storm was probably a Kona gale from the southwest, which would have driven the vessel directly toward Hawaii.

† He had previously crossed the Pacific Ocean as pilot for Ruy Lopez de Villalobo in 1542, on which voyage they discovered the Caroline Islands (Islas del Rey). The account of his second voyage has never been published, but there is an ancient manuscript chart in the Spanish archives on which a group of islands is laid down in the same latitude as the Hawaiian Islands, but over ten degrees of longitude too far east, with a note stating the name of the discoverer and the date of the discovery.

The southernmost and largest island was named La Mesa, "the table," which points to Hawaii, with its high table-land. North of it was La Desgraciada, "the unfortunate," or Maui, and three small islands called Los Monjes, "the monks," which were probably Kahoolawe, Lanai, and Molokai.

In June, 1743, the British ship of war "Centurion," under Lord Anson, after a bloody engagement captured the Spanish galleon from Acapulco near the Philippine Islands, on her way to Manila. A manuscript chart was found on board, containing all the discoveries which had been made in the navigation between Mexico and the Philippine Islands. In this chart the above-mentioned group of islands is laid down in the same position as in the old chart in the Spanish archives. A copy of it is to be seen in the account of Lord Anson's voyage which was published in London in 1748. These islands did not lie in the track of the Spanish galleons, for on leaving Acapulco they steered southwesterly so as to pass far to the south of them, and on their return voyage they sailed northward till they reached thirty degrees of latitude, and then ran before the westerly winds till they approached the coast of North America. This was fortunate for the Hawaiians, who thus escaped the sad fate of the natives of the Ladrone or Marianne Islands.

The error in longitude need not surprise us when we consider that chronometers were not yet invented, and that Spanish navigators depended entirely on "dead reckoning" for their longitude.

Later History of Hawaii.—Keawe-nui-a-Umi was succeeded by his son Lono-i-ka-Makahiki, who instituted the games which were celebrated during the *makahiki* festival. The rest of the history of this period is taken up with traditions of frequent and bloody wars, especially between the kings of Hawaii and Maui for the possession of the district of Hana. The warlike kings of Oahu also repeatedly invaded Molokai, for which they contended with the chiefs of the Windward Islands. It was during one of these inter-island wars that Kamehameha I. was born, on a stormy November night in the year 1736, at Halawa, in Kohala, Hawaii.

Alapainui.—At that time Alapainui, who had made himself *Moi* of Hawaii by force of arms, was collecting a fleet and army from all the districts of the island for the invasion of Maui.

He took with him two young princes, viz., Keoua, the father of Kamehameha I., and his half-brother Kalaniopuu, who afterward became king. On his arrival in Kaupo, Maui, he learned that his adversary Kekaulike, king of Maui, had just died; that his bones had been deposited in the cave at the head of the Iao Valley; and that his own nephew, Kamehamehanui, had succeeded him as king of Maui. Accordingly he made peace with the young king, and joined his forces with those of Maui for the relief of Molokai.

Battle of Kawela.—The king of Oahu had invaded that island, and was ravaging it without mercy, having driven its chiefs to take refuge in their mountain fastnesses. Obstinate and bloody battles, which lasted several days, were fought in the vicinity of Kawela. At last the Oahu army was completely routed, and their king, Kapiiohokalani, slain on the field.*

Alapai then invaded Oahu, but without success, and returned to Hawaii.

* To this day the sands of Kawela are full of half-buried human bones and skulls, which bear witness to the ferocity of the struggle.

Battle of Keawawa.—In the following year (about 1738) he again landed on Maui with a large army, for those days, to support the cause of his young nephew against his half-brother Kauhi, who had usurped the sovereignty. On the other side, Kauhi was aided by Peleioholani, king of Oahu. There was desperate fighting for two days, north of Lahaina, during which the pretender Kauhi was taken prisoner and put to death.

The kings of Hawaii and Oahu then met and made a treaty of peace, by which Kamehamehanui was recognized as *Moi* of Maui, after which they returned to their respective islands, Molokai being left to the king of Oahu.

Accession of Kalaniopuu.—At the death of Alapainui, about 1754, a bloody civil war followed, as usual, the result of which was that Alapai's son Keaweopala was killed, and Kalaniopuu, descended from the old dynasty, became king of Hawaii. He was a restless and warlike chief, and signalized his reign by bloody wars with the kings of Maui for the possession of the eastern districts of that island. Although often defeated, he managed to hold the famous fort of Kauiki in Hana for more than twenty years. It was retaken at last by Kahekili, brother of Kamehamehanui, by cutting off the water-supply of the garrison, who were forced to surrender at discretion. They were put to death without mercy, and their bodies baked in ovens by way of insult.

A few years before this, in 1775, Kalaniopuu on invading the district of Kaupo had been routed and driven back to his canoes.

He returned to Hawaii and spent a whole year in collecting and organizing an army, which was divided into nine brigades, each known by an individual name. But

Kahekili had not been idle, and had received reinforcements from Oahu.

Battle of the Sand-hills.—Landing at Maalaea Bay, Kalaniopuu sent his favorite regiment, called the Alapa, comprising the flower of his army, in advance. It was attacked in flank among the sand-hills near Wailuku, and hardly a man escaped to tell the tale.

The next day he advanced again with his whole force, but was completely defeated and driven back to Maalaea. He then sent his son Kiwalao to humbly sue for peace, which was granted, but did not last very long, as he soon renewed his cruel raids on the people of Maui and Lanai.

The young prince Kamehameha I. distinguished himself in these campaigns as a brave and skillful warrior.

The war was still going on in the district of Koolau, Maui, when Captain Cook discovered these islands.

CHAPTER XVI

1778–1779

THE DISCOVERY OF THE ISLANDS BY CAPTAIN COOK

THE discovery of these islands by Captain James Cook was the turning-point in their history. It brought them into connection with the rest of the world, and ushered in a new era of unexampled progress.

The great navigator had already made two voyages of discovery around the globe, and was then making a third voyage to find, if possible, a northern passage from the Pacific to the Atlantic Ocean.

On the 8th of December, 1777, with his two armed ships, the "Resolution" and the "Discovery," he sailed from Bolabola, one of the Society Islands, for the northwest coast of America.

Sailing nearly due north, on Sunday morning, the 18th of January, 1778, he discovered the island of Oahu, bearing northeast by east, and soon after saw the island of Kauai directly ahead.

The next morning, the 19th, he stood for Kauai, and soon made out a third island, Niihau, bearing northwest.

As he approached the southeastern side of Kauai a party of native fishermen came alongside, and bartered fish and vegetables for nails and bits of iron, but they were afraid to venture on board. He was agreeably surprised to find that they spoke a language differing but little from that of the Society Islands.

As the ships proceeded slowly along the leeward side of the island there was great excitement on land, the people crowding to the shore, and collecting on the heights to view the novel sight.

After standing off and on during the night, Captain Cook again approached the land on the morning of the 20th, and met several canoes filled with people, some of whom took courage and came on board.

Three armed boats were then sent under command of Lieutenant Williamson to look for a watering-place. About noon he returned and reported that he had found a good watering-place, but that on attempting to land in another place, "the natives had pressed so thick upon him, trying to take away the oars, muskets, and every thing else they could lay hold of, that he was obliged to fire, by which one man was killed."

Landing at Waimea.—The ships soon afterward anchored in Waimea Bay, and between three and four o'clock P.M. Captain Cook went ashore with three armed boats and twelve marines. The moment he leaped ashore, the natives all fell flat upon their faces, and remained so until he had made signs to them to rise. They then brought a great many pigs, which they offered to him with plantain trees, while a long prayer was recited by a priest. Captain Cook gave them presents in return for theirs. The next morning trading was commenced for hogs, fowls, and vegetables in exchange for nails and pieces of iron,* and the natives willingly assisted in filling and rolling the water-casks.

*They were amazed and delighted to see so much iron, which was to them a precious metal.

Several feather cloaks and helmets were offered for sale, besides great numbers of skins of red birds, the *iwipolena*.

Meanwhile Captain Cook, accompanied by the surgeon and the artist of the expedition, and a numerous train of natives, took a walk up the valley, and visited a heiau, of which he gives a description and a drawing.

On the 22d a southerly storm with rain set in; and the next day, as Captain Cook endeavored to change his anchorage, his ship was driven out to sea. Being unable to regain the Waimea roadstead, he ran down to Niihau, and after cruising around for several days anchored off the west coast of that island on the 29th. After he had left Kauai, a young chief of high rank, together with his wife, came off in a double canoe to visit Captain Clerke of the "Discovery," and exchanged presents with him.

Visit to Niihau.—The two ships remained off Niihau, collecting water and provisions till February 1st, 1778, when they landed three goats, a boar, and a sow pig of English breed. They also brought on shore seeds of melons, pumpkins, and onions. On account of the stormy weather and high surf, Lieutenant Gore and twenty men had been detained on shore for two nights, where they were hospitably treated by the natives. The next day, February 2d, both the ships sailed to the northward in prosecution of their voyage. They left behind them diseases, unknown before, which spread through the group, causing misery and death to the people.

Effect on the Minds of the Natives.—The Hawaiians were left in a state of the utmost wonder and perplexity in regard to the character of their strange visitors.*

*The majority of them looked upon Captain Cook as an incarnation of their god Lono, who, as they supposed, had now returned in fulfillment of an ancient

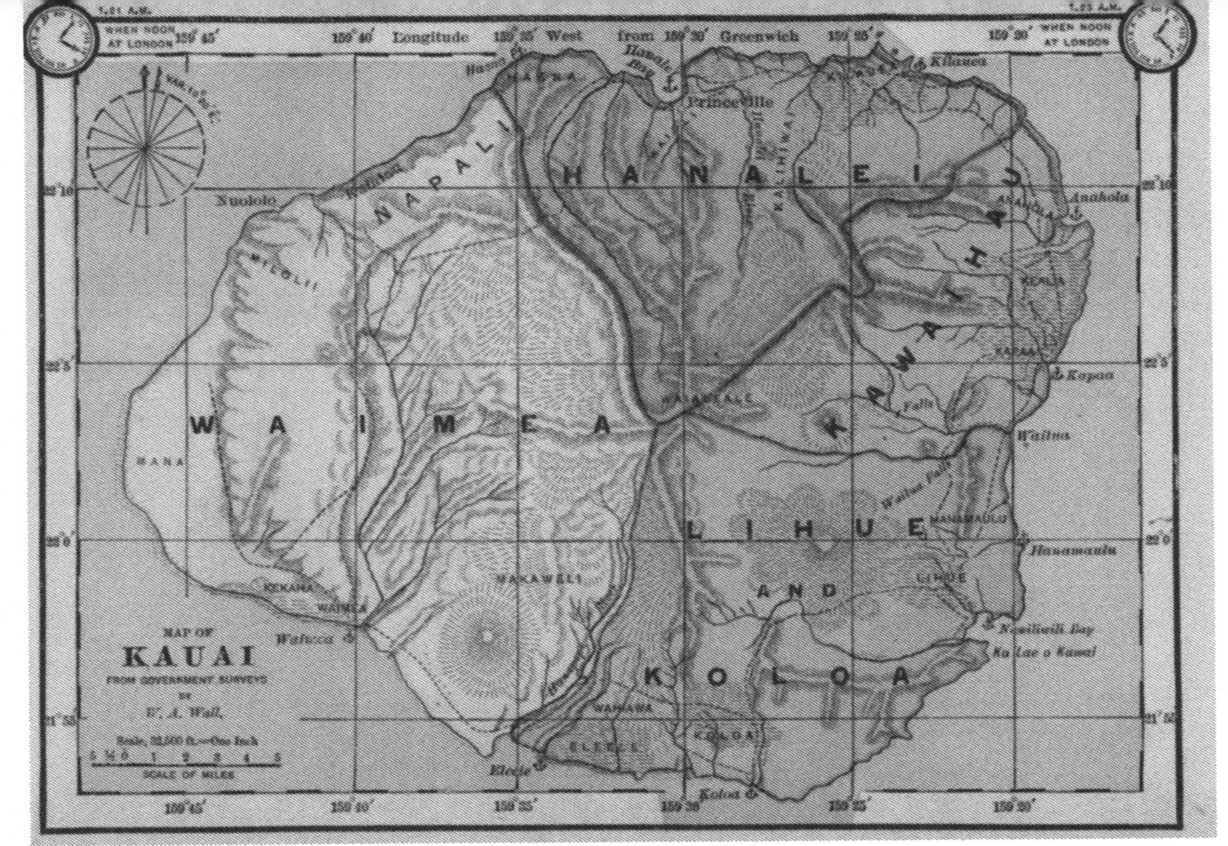
MAP OF
KAUAI
FROM GOVERNMENT SURVEYS
BY
W. A. Wall.
Scale, 32,500 ft.=One Inch
SCALE OF MILES
Longitude West from Greenwich
WHEN NOON AT LONDON
1.21 A.M.
1.23 A.M.
159°45′
159°40′
159°35′
159°30′
159°25′
159°20′
22°10′
22°5′
22°0′
21°55′
WAIMEA
NAPALI
HANALEI
KAWAIHAU
LIHUE AND KOLOA
Nuololo
Hanalei Bay
Princeville
Kilauea
Anahola
Kapaa
Wailua
Hanamaulu
Nawiliwili Bay
Ka Lae o Kamai
Koloa
Eleele
Waimea
MANA
KEKAHA
MAKAWELI
WAHIAWA
LIHUE

Messengers were sent to Oahu and Maui to inform the chiefs there of the arrival of these wonderful beings. The messengers said: "The men are white; their skin is loose and folding; their heads are angular; fire and smoke issue from their mouths; they have openings in the sides of their bodies into which they thrust their hands, and draw out iron, beads, nails, and other treasures; and their speech is unintelligible. This is the way they speak: 'a hikapalale, hikapalale, hioluai, oalaki, walawalaki, poha,' etc."

Second Visit of Captain Cook.—Having explored the coast of Alaska, Bering's Straits, and the Arctic Ocean until he was stopped by the ice-fields, Captain Cook returned to spend the winter in the sunny isles which he had discovered at the beginning of the year. He arrived off the northeast coast of Maui on the 26th of November, and beat to windward around the east end of the island.

Kalaniopuu, the aged king of Hawaii, was then at Wailua in Koolau, engaged in war with Kahekili. Attended by several of his chiefs, he visited the ships, and his nephew, Kamehameha, spent the night on board of the "Resolution," returning in his double canoe in the morning.

Captain Cook then approached Kukuipahu in Kohala, where he lay off and on for a time, trading for provisions. When the natives saw the sailors smoking and eating watermelons, they exclaimed: "Gods indeed! They eat the flesh of men, and the fire burns in their mouths!"

Captain Cook spent the month of December beating around the eastern and southern sides of Hawaii, and

prophecy, and upon his crew as supernatural beings. Others pronounced them to be foreigners, *haoles*, from Kahiki or other mysterious lands to the south.

finally anchored in Kealakekua Bay January 17th, 1779. Immense crowds of people collected there from the rest of the island, and the bay presented an extraordinary sight. During the king's absence the chiefs Palea and Kanaina kept order among the people.

AN OFFERING BEFORE CAPTAIN COOK

Worship of Captain Cook.—An aged priest named Koa came on board with them, and saluted Captain Cook with the utmost veneration. He then threw a piece of red kapa over his shoulders, and stepping back made an offering of a pig, while he recited a long prayer. The same afternoon Captain Cook, with two of his officers, accompanied the priest on shore, where the people retired or prostrated themselves at his approach. On landing he was conducted to the heiau of Lono, near a pond north of the village of Napoopoo, where various ceremonies took place, the object of which was to solemnly acknowledge and install Captain Cook as an incarnation of the god Lono. He was first stationed in front of the sacred images, where he was robed with red kapa, and long prayers were addressed to him by two priests, while a dead hog was offered to him. Similar ceremonies were repeated on other parts of the heiau, after which he was anointed with the chewed kernel of a cocoanut wrapped in a cloth, and regaled with *awa*, baked pork, etc.

A few days later, when he visited the priests' residence at Napoopoo, they conducted him to the Hale o Lono, or house of Lono, where he was worshiped with nearly the same ceremonies as before. Whenever he went on shore one of the priests accompanied him with a wand in his hand, ordering all people to prostrate themselves, and sacrifices were offered to him.*

A site for an observatory was selected near the heiau, where tents were set up and instruments erected, and the priests effectually tabued the place by setting up white rods around it. The party on shore received from the priests every day a liberal supply of hogs and vegetables, while several canoe-loads of provisions were daily sent to the ships, for which no return was ever made or asked.

On the 24th Kalaniopuu arrived from Maui, and a strict tabu was immediately put upon the bay, no canoes being allowed to leave the shore.

Kalaniopuu's Visit to Captain Cook.—On the 26th the king made a grand ceremonial visit to the ships, with three large canoes, attended by chiefs wearing their feather cloaks

* As Jarves says, "He moved among them an earthly deity, observed, feared, and worshiped."

and helmets, and armed with spears and daggers, and by priests bearing gigantic idols of wicker-work, covered with red feathers, with eyes made of mother-of-pearl and mouths set with double rows of sharks' teeth.

After paddling around the ships, chanting prayers or hymns, they went toward the observatory, where Captain Cook landed to receive them. On entering the tent the king placed his own magnificent feather cloak upon Captain Cook's shoulders, and a feather helmet on his head, and laid five or six other beautiful cloaks at his feet. He also presented him with a number of large hogs and a large quantity of cocoanuts and bread-fruit, after which the priests made offerings and prayers to their supposed patron divinity.

In return Captain Cook took the royal party on board of the "Resolution," and presented the king with a linen shirt and a cutlass. The English officers were afterward feasted on shore, and entertained with boxing and wrestling matches. On his part, Captain Cook gave an exhibition of fire-works, which the natives took for flying spirits.

Quarrels with the Natives.—After the first ten days, the natives began to tire of their guests, and to show them less respect. Their violations of tabu and their abandoned conduct were such as to disgust even heathens, while the lavish contributions levied upon the people for their support began to be felt as a heavy burden.*

On the 2d of February Captain Cook, being in want of fuel, concluded to take the fence around his heiau, and offered the priests first two and then three hatchets for

* On the 28th one of the seamen died and was buried in the heiau with both Christian and pagan funeral rites. This was enough to show the natives that the strangers were mortal like themselves.

it, which they declined to accept. His men, however, carried off not only the railing of the temple but even the twelve idols within it, upon which the chief priest meekly requested that at least the central image should be restored. About this time an affray took place between the natives and a party from the "Resolution," who had been sent to bring off the rudder. Quarrels in trade and thefts became more and more common.

On the 3d of February, the day previous to the departure of the ships, Kalaniopuu presented Captain Cook with an immense quantity of vegetables, a large herd of swine, and an extensive collection of kapas and red and yellow feathers. Captain King says: "We were astonished at the value and magnitude of this present, which far surpassed any thing of the kind we had seen at either the Friendly or Society Islands."

They finally sailed February 4th, but the joy of the people over their departure was unfortunately to be of short duration.

Return of Captain Cook.—Captain Cook's intention was to survey the Leeward Islands, and to lay in a supply of water before sailing for the Arctic. But off Kawaihae the ships encountered a violent gale, in which the "Resolution" sprang her foremast. It was therefore decided to put back to Kealakekua Bay, in order to repair it on shore. They arrived at their old anchorage on the morning of Thursday, February 11th.

"An ominous silence everywhere prevailed, and not a canoe was to be seen." A boat which had been sent ashore brought back word that Kalaniopuu was absent, and had left the bay under tabu. Toward night a few canoes came off with provisions, but the behavior of the natives plainly showed that their former friendship was at an end. Almost the only articles in demand were iron daggers, which Captain Cook had ordered to be made for barter.

The next day (Friday) the damaged masts and sails and the astronomical instruments were landed at the former camp, and the friendly priests tabued the place as before. On Saturday afternoon, matters rapidly went from bad to worse. At length some of Palea's retainers stole a pair of tongs and a chisel from the armorer of the "Discovery," leaped into their canoe, and paddled with all haste to the shore. Several muskets were fired after them in vain, and a boat was sent in chase.

Palea, who was on board, offered to recover the stolen articles, and followed in another canoe. The thieves reached the shore first, beached their canoe, and fled inland. Mr. Edgar, the officer of the boat, undertook to seize this canoe, which belonged to Palea, who refused to give it up, protesting his innocence of the theft. A scuffle ensued between them, in which Edgar was worsted, when a sailor knocked Palea down by a heavy blow on the head with an oar. Upon this the whole crowd of natives looking on immediately attacked the unarmed seamen with stones, and forced them to swim off to a rock at some distance. Palea, however, soon recovered from the blow, dispersed the mob, called back the sailors, and restored the missing articles as far as he could.

The following night the large cutter of the "Discovery" was stolen by Palea's people, taken two miles north, and broken up for the sake of the iron in it.

Landing of Captain Cook.—Captain Cook then determined to bring the king on board of the "Resolution," and to keep him a prisoner until the stolen boat should be returned,—a plan which he had tried more than once with success in the South Seas. Accordingly, on Sunday morning, the 14th, he landed with a lieutenant and nine marines, proceeded to Kalaniopuu's house, and invited him to come on board and spend the day with him.

Blockade of the Bay.—At the same time a blockade was placed upon the bay, three boats, well armed and manned, being stationed at equal distances across the entrance to cut off any communication by water.

While Captain Cook was trying to decoy the aged king on board, a canoe came from Keei with two high-chiefs, viz., Kekuhaupio, a famous warrior, and Kalimu, Palea's brother, who knew nothing of the blockade. They were fired upon from the boats, and Kalimu was killed, upon which Kekuhaupio made all haste with the sad news to the king, who was on his way to the shore. An immense crowd had collected, many of whom now armed themselves with spears and daggers. The leading chiefs held the old man back, and refused to let him go any farther.

Affray and Death of Cook.—One warrior approached Captain Cook with a dagger, saying that the foreigners had killed his brother, and he would be revenged. Captain Cook fired at him, but without effect, and ordered Lieutenant Phillips to withdraw the marines to the shore. The instant they began to retreat he was hit by a stone, and perceiving the man who had thrown it, shot him dead. The marines and the people in the boats then opened fire, upon which the chiefs rushed in before they had time to reload, and killed four of the marines. The rest escaped by swimming to the boats. Meanwhile Captain Cook turned for a moment, and waved his hat to the men in the boats to cease firing and pull in, when a chief from behind stabbed him in the back with an iron dagger, which passed quite through his body. The captain fell forward with his face into the water and expired. Lieutenant Phillips then drew his sword, and engaging the chief whom he saw kill Captain Cook, soon dispatched him, after which he swam off to the boats. Lieutenant Gore, of the "Resolution," perceiving with his glass what was going on, fired several round shot into the middle of the crowd, and both the thunder of the cannon and the effect of the shot caused a sudden retreat from the shore to the hills. Seventeen natives, five of whom were chiefs, including Kanaina, were killed in this affray. There is reason to believe that Kamehameha took an active part in it. The camp on the other side of the bay was also attacked, but the guards took their station on the heiau, and kept the natives at bay until they were reinforced from the ships.

About noon the "Resolution's" foremast, with the tents, sails, and astronomical instruments, was safely brought on board. Afterwards, Lieutenant King was sent to demand the bodies of Captain Cook and the marines.

The body of Captain Cook, however, was carried to a small heiau above the *pali* or precipice, where the regular funeral rites were performed that night; the flesh was removed from the bones and burned, and the bones were tied up with red feathers and deified.*

Recovery of Part of Captain Cook's Remains.—On Monday night two friendly priests secretly brought off part of Captain Cook's body, which had been allotted to Kau, the head-priest of Lono. On Wednesday a watering party from the ships was attacked by the natives and another fight took place, in which six natives were killed,

*Part of the bones were kept in the temple of Lono, on the east side of Hawaii, and worshiped by the people until 1819, when they were concealed in some secret place.

and deplorable acts of cruelty were perpetrated by the sailors. The "Discovery" fired round and grape shot into the village of Napoopoo, and a cocoanut-tree was lately standing near the landing-place, with a hole through it made by one of the cannon-balls fired on this occasion. The sailors set fire to the village, and the houses of the friendly priests, with all their effects, were consumed. On Thurs-

COOK'S MONUMENT

day a high-chief, "Eappo," was sent by Kalaniopuu to sue for peace, and on Saturday he delivered up part of the bones of Captain Cook. A tabu was laid upon the bay, and on Sunday, the 22d, the remains of the late commander were committed to the deep with military honors.

The ships finally sailed on the 23d, passing to the

leeward of Lanai and along the windward side of Oahu. They anchored one day off Waialua, and then proceeded to their former station at Waimea, Kauai. Here they procured a supply of water, not without annoyance from the natives, and called at Niihau for yams, finally leaving the group for Kamchatka and the Arctic Ocean on the 25th of February, 1779.

CHAPTER XVII

1780–1786

FROM THE DEATH OF CAPTAIN COOK TO THE ARRIVAL OF PORTLOCK AND DIXON

SUCH was the impression made on the civilized world by the tragical death of Captain Cook, that no foreign vessel touched at the islands for over seven years. During this period Hawaii was rent into three independent petty kingdoms, while all the other islands were brought under the sway of Kahekili and his brother Kaeo.

Dissensions on Hawaii.—The dissensions which led to the breaking up of the kingdom of Kalaniopuu seem to have begun before the close of his reign. About the year 1780 he held a great council of the highest chiefs of Hawaii in the valley of Waipio to settle the succession, at which Kauikeaouli Kiwalao, his son by the tabu Maui princess Kalola, sister of Kahekili, was proclaimed heir to the throne, or to the title of "Moi." The second place in the kingdom was awarded to his nephew Kamehameha, together with the charge of the ancestral war-god Kukailimoku, and of his heiaus.*

*Some months later, as Kiwalao was about to offer up the corpse of Imakakoloa, a rebel chief, to this war-god, Kamehameha interfered and performed the ceremony himself. This bold assertion of his prerogative excited such hostile feeling that the old king advised him to leave the court in Kau, and retire to his hereditary estates. Accordingly he returned to Kohala, where he spent more

Death of Kalaniopuu.—Kalaniopuu died at Wai-o-Ahukini, near the south point of Kau, in the spring of 1782. After the period of mourning had expired, about the month of July, Kiwalao, with his half-brother, Keoua Kuahuula, his uncle, Keawe-mauhili, and other chiefs, prepared to bring the bones of his father to be deposited in the famous *Hale o Keawe* in Honaunau, South Kona.

It had long been the custom after the death of a *Moi* to redistribute the lands of the island in a grand council of chiefs, a custom which had often led to civil war. Kalaniopuu and Alapai had each gained the throne by successful rebellion.

At this time the western side of Hawaii (Kona) was held by four powerful chieftains, who were closely allied. These were the twin brothers Kameeiamoku and Kamanawa, their half-brother Keeaumoku, and Keawe-a-Heulu. In view of the weak and irresolute character of the young king, the grasping and overbearing disposition of his uncle, and the fiery ambition of his brother Keoua, they had good reason to be alarmed for the security of their possessions. Accordingly they sent Kekuhaupio of Keei, the greatest warrior of his time, to persuade Kamehameha to leave his retirement and put himself at their head. Convinced by his arguments, Kamehameha quickly assembled his retainers, and accompanied him back to Kaawaloa.

Meanwhile Kiwalao had sailed for Honaunau in his double canoe, with the remains of the late king lying in state on another double canoe, attended by a large num-

than two years in quietly cultivating and improving his lands, building canoes, and fishing. Several of his public works are still to be seen, such as a tunnel by which a water-course is carried through a ridge in Niulii, besides a canoe-landing in Halaula, a fish-pond, etc. He was at this time forty-five years of age.

ber of chiefs and armed warriors. Each party distrusted the other, but neither wished to go to war. The conflict was brought on at length by the mad rashness of Keoua.

On arriving at Honaunau, the young king crossed the bay and called on Kamehameha, who received him with all due respect and courtesy. After the usual wailing was over, Kiwalao frankly said, "Where are you? It is possible that we two may die. Here is our aged uncle pushing us on to war. Perhaps you and I only may be slain. Alas for us two!"

On the next day, after the funeral ceremonies were over, Kiwalao came out on a platform adjoining the *Hale o Keawe*, and declared the last will and testament of his father, which simply confirmed the decision of the council held at Waipio, but did not suit the Kona chiefs. During the next few days the important business of dividing the lands of the kingdom was taken in hand, in which Keawemauhili of Hilo and his favorites received the lion's share.

Battle of Mokuohai.—Keoua was entirely neglected, and was told that he must be contented with the lands he already possessed.

Upon this he went off in a rage, armed his retainers, and proceeded to "run amuck," as it were. They first went to Keomo and cut down cocoanut-trees (which was a challenge to war), and then to Keei, where they picked a quarrel and killed some of Kamehameha's people. Their bodies were taken to Honaunau and offered in sacrifice by Kiwalao, who thus assumed the responsibility of the war and put himself in the wrong.

For several days there was desultory skirmishing, while the two parties were mustering their forces, and finally a pitched battle was fought, called the battle of Mokuohai.

The "City of Refuge" at Honaunau was crowded with the women and children of both parties. During the hottest of the fight Keeaumoku was tripped up by a long spear, and severely stabbed by his enemies. Kiwalao, seeing it, called out to them to save his ivory neck-ornament, *niho palaoa*, from being smeared with blood. At this critical moment Kamanawa came to his rescue, and Kiwalao himself was struck down by a sling-stone. When Keeaumoku saw him fall he crawled up to him and cut his throat with a dagger armed with sharks' teeth. The king's party was completely routed. Keoua fled to his canoes and embarked for Kau, where the people acknowledged him as successor to his brother. Keawe-mauhili was taken prisoner, but escaped during the night and crossed the mountains to his own district of Hilo.

QUEEN KAAHUMANU IN 1816

Invasions of Hilo.— After making extensive preparations by sea and land, Kamehameha renewed the war against the two allied chiefs, who held the windward side of the island. Landing in Puna, he marched first to the crater of Kilauea (in order to prevent a junction of his enemies), and thence to Waiakea, where he encountered Keawe-mauhili's force, aided by a body of warriors from Maui. Kamehameha's forces were totally routed and forced to flee to their canoes, after which he retired to Laupahoehoe. This is known as the *kaua awa*, the bitter war. He next made a raid along the coast of Puna, where he had a skirmish with a party of fishermen, in which he was beaten over the head with a paddle, and narrowly escaped with his life. After this he returned to Kohala, and devoted himself for a considerable time to peaceful pursuits.

In 1785 he again invaded Hilo, but without success (the war of Hapuu). It was about this time that he married Kaahumanu, the daughter of Keeaumoku.

Invasion of Kipahulu.—In 1786, taking advantage of Kahekili's absence on Oahu, he sent an expedition under the command of his younger brother, Kalani-malokuloku, to retake the districts of Hana and Kipahulu, Maui, which had been conquered by Kahekili four or five years before. He met with little resistance at first, and by his kind treatment of the people gained the surname of "Kelii maikai," the good chief, by which he was ever after known. Kamohomoho, a younger brother of Kahekili, was speedily sent with a force to drive out the invaders. He found them in Kipahulu, and after much hard fighting utterly defeated them, and forced the remnant that escaped to flee back to Kohala. Keliimaikai himself was obliged to lie hidden until nightfall, when he obtained a passage over to Hawaii.*

Conquest of Oahu by Kahekili.—Kahekili, who had ruled over Maui and Lanai since the death of his brother Kamehamehanui in 1765, was a master of intrigue, stern

* Thus far Kamehameha had fought his battles with only the rude weapons of ancient times, and had met with no great success since the battle of Mokuohai. At a later period he was enabled to enter upon a new career of conquest by the assistance of foreigners and by the possession of fire-arms.

and taciturn in manner, and crafty and cruel in disposition. He made himself peculiar by having one side of his body tattooed so as to appear almost black, while the other side was left its natural color. He had thus far successfully resisted the attacks of both Kalaniopuu and Kamehameha.

Peleioholani, the great king of Oahu who subdued Molokai, was succeeded by an incompetent son, Kumuhana, who was deposed by his chiefs, and returned to Kauai about 1773. They then elected Kahahana, a young chief who had been brought up at the court of Kahekili, and had married his half-sister. Kahekili consented to their going to Oahu on condition that the sacred land of Kualoa in Koolau and the *palaoa pae* (the whalebone and ivory drifted ashore) should be ceded to him.

After Kahahana's installation the council of Oahu chiefs refused to ratify this cession of the national emblems of sovereignty to Kahekili. This latter, however, dissembled his resentment, for he was only too glad to receive their help in his sanguinary wars with Kalaniopuu. Meanwhile he labored to poison the mind of Kahahana against his wisest counselor, the priest Kaopulupulu, whom he secretly accused of having offered the throne of Oahu to himself (Kahekili). The weak and credulous prince believed the slander, and caused Kaopulupulu to be treacherously assassinated at Puuloa. He was already unpopular, and this murder still further alienated the minds of both chiefs and people from him.

Kahekili then considered that his time had come, and recalled the auxiliary troops he had sent to Hilo. In the year 1783 he mustered all his forces at Lahaina, and without warning sailed for Oahu, landing at Waikiki. A decisive battle was fought in Nuuanu Valley, in which

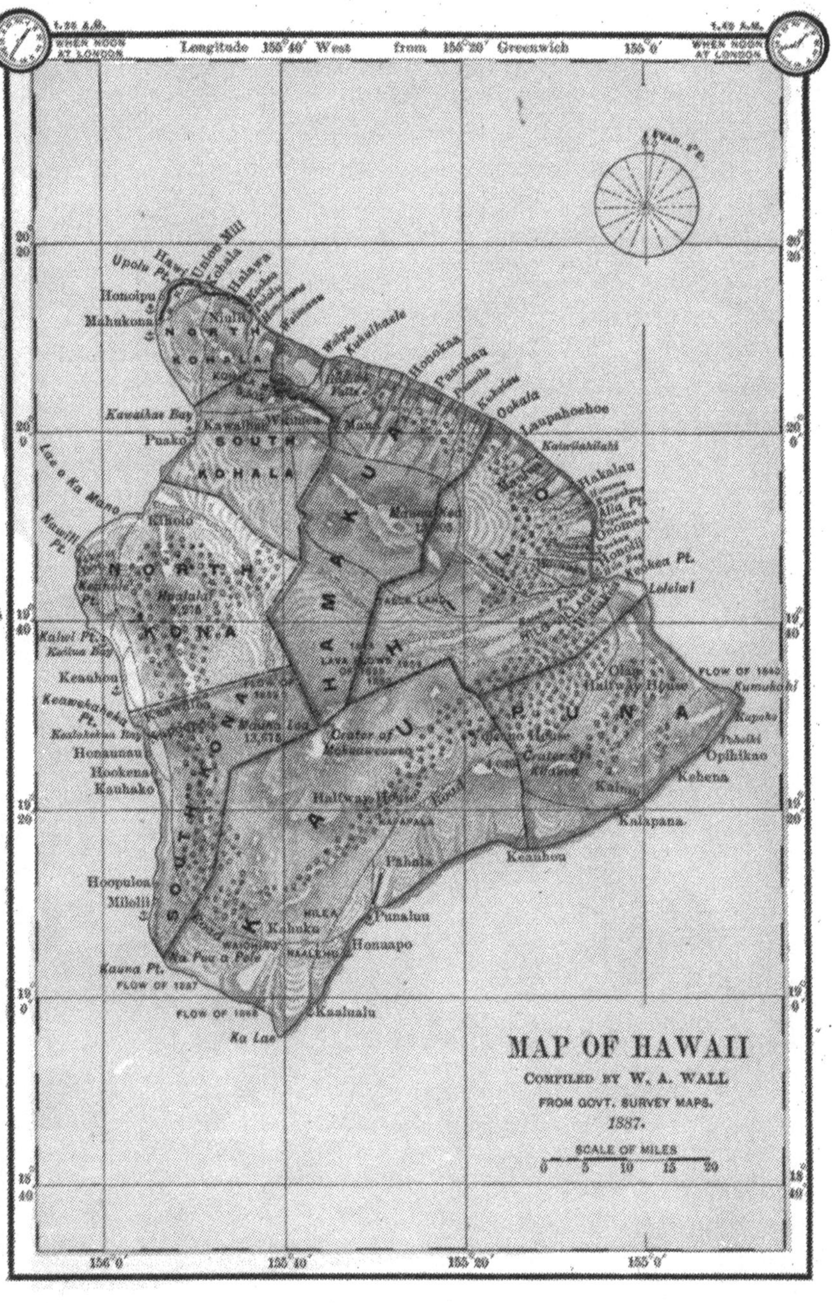

MAP OF HAWAII
COMPILED BY W. A. WALL
FROM GOVT. SURVEY MAPS.
1887.
SCALE OF MILES
0 5 10 15 20
Longitude 155° 40′ West from 155° 20′ Greenwich 155° 0′
WHEN NOON AT LONDON
NORTH KOHALA
SOUTH KOHALA
NORTH KONA
SOUTH KONA
HAMAKUA
HILO
PUNA
KAU
Upolu Pt.
Honoipu
Mahukona
Kawaihae Bay
Puako
Keauhou
Honaunau
Hookena
Kauhako
Hoopuloa
Milolii
Kauna Pt.
FLOW OF 1887
FLOW OF 1868
Ka Lae
Kaalualu
Honuapo
Punaluu
Kahuku
Pahala
Keauhou
Kalapana
Kehena
Opihikao
Kumukahi
FLOW OF 1840
Laupahoehoe
Ookala
Crater of Mokuaweoweo
Mauna Loa 13,675
Halfway House

Kahahana's army was routed, and he and his wife fled to the mountains. After hiding for a year, he was betrayed by his wife's brother Kekuamanoha, and his body was sent from Ewa to Waikiki for sacrifice.

Molokai and Oahu were now subject to Kahekili, who used his power without mercy. His cruel and rapacious conduct caused an extensive conspiracy of the people of Oahu, aided by several Maui chiefs, who sympathized with the unfortunate queen or were dissatisfied with the division of the lands. Their plan was to kill Kahekili and his principal chiefs on one and the same night in the different districts of Oahu. The secret, however, leaked out in time to save all except Hueu, who was massacred with all his retinue at Waialua.*

Soon after this, disturbances broke out in Kula, Maui, and Kahekili sent his son Kalanikupule with some of his best warriors to settle them. They were just in time to repel the invasion of Maui already mentioned (p. 121).

*Kahekili's vengeance was terrible. The native Oahu chiefs were nearly all exterminated. He ravaged the Kona and Ewa districts, massacring men, women, and children. The streams of Niuhelewai in Palama and of Hoaeae in Ewa are said to have been choked up with the corpses of the slain. A house was built of human bones in Moanalua. Kaiana and a few other chiefs escaped to Kauai in 1785.

CHAPTER XVIII

1786-1791

FROM THE ARRIVAL OF PORTLOCK AND DIXON TO THE DEATH OF KEOUA

The Fur Trade of the Northwest Coast.—The narrative of Captain Cook's last voyage showed what profits might be made by purchasing furs from the Indians of the northwest coast of America with pieces of iron, beads, blankets, etc., and selling them for cash in the Canton market.

Accordingly several expeditions were fitted out in England, America, India, and China to engage in this profitable trade. Nootka Sound in Vancouver Island became the general rendezvous of the fur-traders on the coast. After disposing of their furs in China, they often took cargoes of tea for England or for the United States.

Arrival of Portlock and Dixon.—The first ships that visited the islands after the death of Captain Cook were the "King George," commanded by Captain Portlock, and the "Queen Charlotte," under Captain Dixon, which sailed together from London, and arrived off the coast of Hawaii May 24th, 1786. Both of these commanders had served under Captain Cook in his last voyage. They touched at Kealakekua Bay on the 26th day of May, but as the natives became insolent and troublesome, they left for Oahu and anchored in Waialae Bay June 3d.*

*Here they remained four days, buying fresh water, at the rate of a sixpenny nail for a two-gallon calabash full. Captain Portlock noticed that nearly

About the same time, May 28th, 1786, La Pérouse, the famous French explorer, with his two frigates, anchored off Honuaula, East Maui, where he spent one day in friendly intercourse with the people, and sailed for Alaska.

DIAMOND HEAD

Portlock and Dixon again visited the islands in November, 1786, and spent the winter, mostly at Waialae, Oahu, and at Waimea, Kauai, where they laid in ample supplies of provisions, wood, and water, in exchange for nails, beads, and pieces of iron hoop. They touched at these places again the following year on their way to China.

all of the iron daggers sold by Captain Cook at Hawaii were now in the hands of Kahekili's warriors, having probably been captured in war. They next touched at Niihau for yams, and proceeded thence on their way to the Northwest Coast.

Many other vessels engaged in the fur trade followed their example and visited the islands, generally in the winter season, or on their way to China.

Kaiana's Visit to China and his Return.—Among the first of these was Captain Meares, who arrived at Waimea, Kauai, in August, 1787, in the snow "Nootka," and spent about a month there. He took the famous chief Kaiana as a passenger to Canton, where he remained three months, and received the greatest kindness from the English residents.

KAIANA

Captain Meares then fitted out two vessels, the "Felice" and the "Iphigenia," for the fur trade, taking Kaiana and three other natives as passengers on the latter vessel. Kaiana's friends at Canton put on board of each vessel several cattle, goats, and turkeys, besides lime and orange trees, and a large assortment of presents for him. Unfortunately the ships made a long trading voyage along the American coast, during which all of the live-stock perished before visiting the islands.

The "Iphigenia," Captain Douglass, arrived off the coast of Hana December 6th, 1788, and proceeded to Kealakekua Bay, where Kamehameha came off in state, with twelve large double canoes, beautifully adorned with feathers, and was honored with a salute of seven guns.

As Kaiana learned that Kaeo, king of Kauai, was very hostile to him, he decided to accept Kamehameha's offers and to enter his service. Accordingly he was landed December 29th, 1788, with his extensive collection of foreign goods, tools, and fire-arms, which made him immensely rich, in the estimation of the natives.

Captain Douglass afterward brought Kaiana's wife and child and his brother Namakeha from Kauai, and was persuaded to present Kamehameha with a swivel cannon, which was mounted upon a large double canoe, besides some muskets and ammunition. He touched again at Kealakekua in July, 1789, on his way to China, when he narrowly escaped a plot of the principal chiefs to massacre him and his crew. For about four years the islands remained at peace, the chiefs and people being all eagerly engaged in trade with their foreign visitors. The two harbors most frequented were those of Waimea, Kauai, and Kealakekua Bay, and it is probable that Kamehameha and his chiefs received the lion's share of this traffic.

The Olowalu Massacre.—About the end of the year 1789 Captain Metcalf, an American fur-trader, in command of the snow "Eleanor," visited the islands on his way to China. His son, only eighteen years of age, commanded a little schooner called the "Fair American," which had been detained by the Spaniards at Nootka Sound.*

* A plot was formed by Kaiana and other chiefs to capture the "Eleanor," but was prevented by Kamehameha, who went on board and ordered the treacherous chiefs ashore. After this Kameeiamoku, a high-chief of Kona, was insulted and beaten with a rope's-end by Metcalf for some trifling offense, on which he vowed to revenge himself on the next vessel that should come into his power.

Near the end of February, 1790, the "Eleanor" crossed the Hawaii Channel and anchored off Honuaula, Maui. There Kaopuiki, the chief of Olowalu, with his men, stole a boat one night from its moorings at the stern, and murdered the sailor who was sleeping in it. It was then broken up for the sake of the nails in it, after which the thieves returned to Olowalu. When Captain Metcalf found that the guilty persons had come from Olowalu, he proceeded thither in the "Eleanor," and after a certain tabu was over, resumed trade with the natives. A great number of canoes from far and near had crowded around his ship, when suddenly a broadside of cannon and musketry was fired upon them, and the waves were covered with the dead and dying. Over a hundred were killed and many more were wounded.

After this cruel and wanton massacre of innocent people Captain Metcalf returned to Hawaii, and lay off and on near Kealakekua Bay waiting for the tender, which arrived about this time off Kawaihae.

Capture of the "Fair American."—Kameeiamoku went off with a fleet of canoes as if to trade, and while the young captain was off his guard threw him overboard and killed all the crew except the mate, Isaac Davis. The vessel was hauled up on shore and stripped of its guns and ammunition. On the same or the next day (March 17th) John Young, the boatswain of the "Eleanor," who was on shore, found himself detained, and all canoes tabued by Kamehameha's orders lest Metcalf should hear of the loss of the schooner and the death of his son. The "Eleanor" lay off and on for two days longer, firing signal guns for Young's return in vain, and finally sailed for China. Young and Davis were treated with great kindness, presented with valuable lands, and raised to the rank of chiefs by the king; and in return they fully repaid him by their services both in war and in council. They were, however, for a long time closely watched whenever a foreign vessel was in sight. They mounted the small cannon obtained from the "Iphigenia" and the "Fair American" on carriages for land service, and trained a small body of troops in the use of muskets.

Invasion of Maui.—Kamehameha considering himself now strong enough to renew the invasion of Maui, sent a summons to Keoua of Kau and to Keawemauhili of Hilo to furnish him men and canoes for the war. Keoua flatly refused, but his uncle sent a large force commanded by his own sons.

In the summer of 1790 Kamehameha crossed the channel with his fleet, landing first in Hana and then in Hamakualoa, where he defeated the advance-guard of the Maui forces in a hard-fought battle. He then moved his fleet to Kahului, and marched to the Wailuku Valley, where he met the Maui army under Kahekili's sons, and drove them up the valley. The two field-pieces managed by Young and Davis, and the musketry, struck terror into the hearts of the Maui warriors, and decided the victory in his favor. No mercy was shown to the vanquished. They were driven over precipices and chased to the high peaks and crags of the mountains, where they were starved into surrender.*

Kalanikupule, with his brothers and the other chiefs, escaped through the Olowalu Pass, and sailed to Oahu.

War with Keoua.—Kamehameha did not, however, make any permanent conquest of Maui at this time; for in his absence Keoua had invaded Hilo, slain Keawe-mau-

* It is said that the brook Iao was choked with the corpses of the slain, whence the battle was called "Kapaniwai" (the damming of the waters).

hili in battle, overrun Hamakua, and cruelly ravaged

PEAK IN IAO VALLEY

Waipio and Waimea. On hearing this news, Kamehameha immediately sailed with all his forces from Molokai for Hawaii and landed at Kawaihae. Keoua retreated to Hamakua, where he awaited the attack, and fought two bloody but indecisive battles near Paauhau, in which Kamehameha's fire-arms gave him the advantage. Keoua fell back to Hilo, while Kamehameha returned to Waipio to recruit his losses.

The Eruption of Kilauea.—In November, 1790, Keoua, having divided the lands of Hilo between his chiefs, set out for Kau by the overland route that leads past the volcano of Kilauea. His followers encamped there two days, during which the crater was very active. On the third day, as they were on their way to Kau in three divisions, a terrific earthquake took place, after which an immense black cloud rose out of the crater and shut out the light of day. An enormous quantity of black sand and cinders was thrown to a great height, and came down in a destructive shower for many miles around. The rear body, which suffered the least, after the shower had passed over hastened forward, rejoicing at their escape, but they found the middle party all dead, some lying down, and others sitting up and clasping their wives and children in a farewell embrace. They did not dare to linger, but hurried on to overtake the advance company at their place of encampment. This disaster convinced Kamehameha that the goddess Pele was on his side, and must have discouraged Keoua.

During the following year (1791) the great heiau of Puukohola at Kawaihae was built in honor of the war-god Kukailimoku, by the advice of the priests, to secure to Kamehameha the kingdom of Hawaii. Kaiana was sent to Kau, where he carried on the war against Keoua without success.

The Sea-fight off Waimanu.—Meanwhile Kahekili and his brother Kaeo, king of Kauai, combined their forces for an attack on Hawaii. Kaeo took with him his nephew Peapea, his favorite gunner, Murray, and several large, fierce dogs. Stopping awhile at Maui on their way, the two fleets proceeded to Waipio, where they landed and committed many wanton outrages on the people.

Kamehameha sailed from Kona to meet them with his fleet of double canoes and the schooner "Fair American," carrying several small cannon, which were under the charge of Young and Davis. The two hostile fleets met off Waimanu, where a bloody battle was fought, in which Kamehameha's superiority in fire-arms gave him the victory. Kahekili and Kaeo returned crest-fallen to Maui with their shattered fleet.*

The Assassination of Keoua.—Toward the end of the year 1791 two of Kamehameha's chief counselors, Kamanawa and Keaweaheulu, were sent on an embassy to Keoua at Kahuku in Kau. Keoua's chief warrior urged him to put them to death, which he indignantly refused to do.

By smooth speeches and fair promises they persuaded him to go to Kawaihae, and have an interview with Kamehameha, in order to put an end to the war, which had lasted nine years. Accordingly he set out with his most intimate friends and twenty-four rowers in his own double canoe, accompanied by Keaweaheulu in another canoe, and followed by friends and retainers in other canoes.

As they approached the landing at Kawaihae, Keeaumoku surrounded Keoua's canoe with a number of armed men. As Kamakau relates: "Seeing Kamehameha on the beach, Keoua called out to him. 'Here I am,' to which

* This sea-fight was called *ka pu-waha-ula* (the red-mouthed gun).

he replied, 'Rise up and come here, that we may know each other.'"

As Keoua was in the act of leaping ashore, Keeaumoku killed him with a spear. All the men in Keoua's canoe and in the canoes of his immediate company were slaughtered but one. But when the second division approached, Kamehameha gave orders to stop the massacre. The bodies of the slain were then laid upon the altar of Puukohola as an offering to the blood-thirsty divinity Kukailimoku. That of Keoua had been previously baked in an oven at the foot of the hill as a last indignity. This treacherous murder made Kamehameha master of the whole island of Hawaii, and was the first step toward the consolidation of the group under one government. But, as Fornander says, "We may admire the edifice whose foundation he (Kamehameha) laid, but we must note that one of its cornerstones is laid in blood.'

CHAPTER XIX

1791–1795

VISITS OF VANCOUVER AND CONQUEST OF OAHU

Visitors in 1791.—Among others, a sloop called the "Princess Royal," which had been seized by the Spaniards at Nootka Sound, visited the islands in March, 1791, under Spanish colors. Kaiana, whose mind seems to have been constantly directed to the seizing of every small vessel that arrived, formed a plot for the capture of this sloop, but was again prevented by Kamehameha. In October of the same year, Captain Kendrick of Boston, in the sloop "Lady Washington," left three sailors at Kauai to collect sandal-wood and pearls against his return from New England. This was the beginning of the sandal-wood trade with China.

Vancouver's First Visit.—The three visits of Vancouver form an era in the history of these islands, and his name is justly cherished as that of a wise and generous benefactor to the Hawaiian people.

Captain George Vancouver was sent by the British Government to receive the cession of Nootka Sound and the adjoining country from a commissioner of Spain; and to make a complete survey of the northwest coast. He had under his orders the ship "Discovery" and the armed tender "Chatham," of one hundred and thirty-five tons, under Lieutenant Broughton. They first reached Hawaii March 2d, 1792, and sailed slowly along the

Kona coast. Kamehameha was on the other side of the island, probably engaged in dividing up Keoua's late dominions among his followers. Kaiana visited the ships, and was well received, but, strange to say, could not speak a word of English. Vancouver uniformly refused to sell any fire-arms or ammunition, but he gave Kaiana and Keeaumoku orange-trees, grape-vines, and other useful plants and seeds. He told the chiefs that the ship and all it contained belonged to King George, who had tabued all fire-arms and ammunition.

Kaiana falsely represented himself as the equal of Kamehameha, and as sovereign of the three southern districts of Hawaii. Captain Vancouver then touched at Waikiki, Oahu, where he learned that Kahekili and Kaeo, with most of their chiefs and warriors, were at Hana, Maui, to repel an expected invasion by Kamehameha. He next proceeded to Waimea, Kauai, where he remained a week. The ships were visited by Inamoo, the regent, and Kaumualii, son of Kaeo, a lad of twelve years of age, who greatly pleased Vancouver by his superior intelligence and amiability. The young prince was always accompanied by a guard of thirty men, armed with iron daggers, and carrying thirteen muskets made up into three bundles, with calabashes containing ammunition.*

Visit of the "Dædalus."—The store-ship "Dædalus," under Lieutenant Hergest, arrived off Waimea, Oahu, May 7th, 1792, and sent a small party ashore to procure fresh water. This party was attacked by a lawless band under one Koi, who killed Lieutenant Hergest and Mr. Gooch, the astronomer, who had gone farther inland than the rest.

*Vancouver was everywhere struck with the evidence of the decrease in population since Captain Cook's visit in 1778, and with the insatiable desire of the natives to obtain fire-arms.

The others escaped to their boat and fired on the natives, but did not succeed in recovering the bodies of the unfortunate officers. The "Dædalus" then sailed for Nootka Sound to join Vancouver.

Vancouver's Second Visit.—Vancouver returned from Monterey, California, and anchored off Kawaihae February 14th, 1793, where he landed a bull and a cow (the first of their kind on these islands), as a present to Kamehameha. On the 21st Kamehameha visited the ships, accompanied by John Young and by his favorite wife, Kaahumanu.*

The next day the ships anchored in Kealakekua Bay, where Kamehameha made them a grand state visit, wearing his feather cloak and helmet, with a fleet of eleven double canoes, and presented Vancouver with four feather helmets, ninety of the largest swine, and an immense quantity of fruit and vegetables. In return Vancouver landed his remaining live-stock, consisting of five cows and three sheep, which he gave to the king. The rival chieftains, Kaiana and Keeaumoku, could not repress their jealousy and avarice. On the 4th of March Kamehameha entertained his visitors with a sham battle between one hundred and fifty of his best warriors, in which he took an active part himself, and showed wonderful dexterity in the spear exercise. Vancouver, in his turn, gave a grand display of fire-works in the evening.

The object which he had most at heart was to bring about a lasting peace between Hawaii and the leeward islands. Having thoroughly discussed, and, as he thought, settled the conditions of peace, he sailed for Maui March 7th. The ships anchored off Lahaina on the evening

*Presents were liberally distributed among the party, and the king received a showy scarlet cloak, in which he displayed himself on deck to his admiring subjects.

of the 12th, and were visited first by Kamohomoho and then by Kahekili himself. Captain Vancouver discussed with him and the other principal chiefs the two objects for which he had made this visit.

The first was that of bringing to justice the persons guilty of the murder of Messrs. Hergest and Gooch, of the store-ship "Dædalus," committed at Waimea, Oahu. To this Kahekili replied that three of the murderers had already been executed by his orders, and that his brother Kamohomoho would accompany Captain Vancouver to Oahu and see that the rest of them should be duly punished.

The second object was to put a stop to the war which had so long continued between Kahekili and Kamehameha. The island of Maui had not yet recovered from the effects of the cruel ravages committed by Kamehameha's men during the last invasion. Besides, a large army had to be kept up in Hana, which was a heavy drain on the resources of both Maui and Oahu. This the chief admitted, and proposed to send Kaeo as ambassador to Hawaii on Vancouver's ship to negotiate a treaty in his presence.

As Vancouver could not spare the time for this, he proposed to write a letter to John Young, to inform Kamehameha that the Maui chiefs had consented to the terms of peace. This was done, but the chief bearing the letter was attacked and obliged to flee for his life without delivering it. Having presented Kahekili with some goats and a large assortment of useful articles, and given a display of fire-works, Vancouver sailed for Oahu with Kamohomoho on board, and anchored at Waikiki on the 20th.

Three men were then brought on board who were charged with the murder of Lieutenant Hergest, and several witnesses testified to their guilt. On the 22d they were placed in a double canoe alongside of the "Discovery," and shot by a chief, who is called "Tennavee" by Vancouver. This man afterwards confessed that they were innocent of the murder, although guilty of certain offenses against the tabu.

About this time a revolt had broken out in Kauai against the tyranny of Inamoo, which had been put down with the aid of the foreigners on the island. On his way thither in mid-channel Vancouver met a fleet of canoes carrying the news and prisoners to Kaeo, one of the canoes being sixty-one and a half feet long, made of a single pine log, and beautifully finished.

On the 28th of March he anchored off Waimea, where he landed two young women who had been carried off by Captain Baker in the "Jenny" the year before.*

Troubles on Kauai.—The "renegade white men," as Vancouver calls them, on Kauai were charged with inciting the natives to acts of piracy. They well-nigh succeeded in cutting off the brig "Hancock," of Boston, by scuttling her under water. They also urged Inamoo, the governor, to assert his independence, and fired on the messengers sent by Kahekili to investigate these matters.

Accordingly, in October, 1793, Kahekili, notwithstanding his advanced age, took passage for Kauai with Captain Brown on the ship "Butterworth," and summoned Inamoo to give an account of his conduct. Inamoo, however, seems to have convinced Kahekili of his loyalty, for he was allowed to retain his offices as governor and as guardian of the young prince.

Vancouver's Third Visit.—On the 9th of January, 1794, Vancouver, returning from the American coast,

* After taking great pains to secure land for them and to provide for their future protection, he sailed again for the Northwest Coast.

arrived off Hilo, Hawaii, where Kamehameha was residing. Although the *makahiki* or New Year's festival was in progress, he was persuaded to take passage with Vancouver to Kealakekua, where the ships remained six weeks.

Vancouver and his men were regarded as the guests of the nation, and treated with unbounded hospitality. He landed several more cattle as well as sheep for Kamehameha, and had a tabu laid upon them for ten years. On the first of February his carpenters laid the keel of the "Britannia," the first vessel ever built at the islands. Although only thirty-six feet in length, she formed an important addition to Kamehameha's navy. Vancouver gave the king much valuable advice in regard to his intercourse with foreigners, the management of his kingdom, the discipline of his troops, etc. He also told him of the one true God, Creator and Governor of all mankind, that their tabu system was wrong, and that he would ask the king of England to send him a teacher of the true religion. He also effected a reconciliation between Kamehameha and his favorite queen, Kaahumanu. He strongly recommended Young and Davis to his confidence, and would have removed seven runaway seamen of bad character, leaving only four white men on the islands, if the chiefs had consented to it.

On the 21st of February, 1794, a grand council of the chiefs was held on board of the "Discovery" for the purpose of placing Hawaii under the protection of Great Britain. They reserved, however, the right to regulate all their own internal affairs. On the 25th Lieutenant Puget hoisted the British flag on shore, and took possession of Hawaii in the name of his Britannic Majesty. A salute was then fired, and the natives shouted, "*Kanaka no Beritane*" ("We are men of Britain").

The next day Captain Vancouver sailed for Kauai, having promised the chiefs that he would return, accompanied by missionaries and artisans, to civilize and Christianize them, under the protection and support of the British Government.*

He anchored off Waimea, Kaui, March 9th, 1794, where he was visited by Inamoo and Kaumualii, with whom he left some sheep for breeding. He was entertained on shore by a dance performed by six hundred women, dressed in figured kapas, and finally sailed for England on the 13th.

War between Kaeo and Kalanikupule.—Kahekili died in July, 1794, at Waikiki, over eighty years of age. It is said that his bones were taken to Hawaii, and concealed in a cave at Kaloko, North Kona. After his death his kingdom speedily fell to pieces from the folly and treachery of his heirs, and became an easy prey to Kamehameha.

While his son remained the sovereign of Oahu, his brother Kaeo continued to rule over Maui and the adjacent islands. In November, 1794, Kaeo decided to visit Kauai and settle the affairs of that island, which were in great disorder.

Accordingly he embarked with a large force of chiefs and warriors, leaving Maui nearly defenseless. When he arrived at Waimanalo, Oahu, he found Kalanikupule's warriors drawn up to oppose his landing. A skirmishing fight was kept up until Kalanikupule arrived from Waikiki, and held a conference with his uncle, at which they came to a friendly understanding.

After a short stay in Koolau, Kaeo and his men em-

* The cession, however, was never ratified by the Home Government, and no steps were ever taken to carry out Vancouver's benevolent designs.

barked again in their canoes, landing first at Waialua, and then at Waianae, on their way to Kauai. But while resting at Waianae he was informed that a formidable conspiracy had sprung up among his troops, and that there was a plot to throw him overboard during the voyage to Kauai. "Better to die in battle," said he; "many will be the companions in death." He immediately ordered his men to haul up the canoes on shore and prepare to march overland against Kalanikupule. Upon this, the disaffection among his troops disappeared, and the people of Waianae and Waialua flocked to his banner. He would no doubt have carried all before him if his nephew had not been aided by foreigners.

Captain Brown in the schooner "Jackal," accompanied by Captain Gordon in the sloop "Prince Lee Boo," entered the harbor of Honolulu, (which he had discovered and named "Fair Haven"), November 21st, 1794. There Captain Kendrick joined him in the sloop "Lady Washington." Captain Brown sold Kalanikupule arms and ammunition for the war. As Kaeo was victorious in the first encounters, and was rapidly approaching, Mr. George Lamport, the mate of the "Jackal," with eight others, agreed to assist Kalanikupule to repulse the enemy. In the first battle at Punahawele, their native allies were routed, and one of the seamen was killed, the rest escaping to the canoes. After several skirmishes, during which Kaeo kept slowly advancing, a bloody battle was fought December 12th, in Kalauao, east of Pearl Lochs, in which Kalanikupule gained a complete victory. Kaeo himself was surrounded and slain, fighting desperately to the last.

Massacre of Captain Brown and his Men.—On the return of his men the next day, Captain Brown fired a salute in honor of their victory. A wad, as is supposed, from one of the guns entered the cabin of the "Lady Washington," and killed Captain Kendrick, who was at dinner at the time.

His funeral service was the first ceremony of the kind ever witnessed on Oahu, and the natives supposed it to be an act of sorcery to cause the death of Captain Brown. The "Lady Washington" then sailed for China, but Captain Brown remained in port, on the most intimate terms with the chiefs.

Kalanikupule kept his promise to pay him four hundred hogs for his services in the war, and most of the sailors were employed in butchering and salting them on shore. On the 1st of January, 1795, Captain Brown had sent Mr. Lamport with a boat and four men to procure more salt at the Kaihikapu pond in Moanalua, when Kamohomoho suddenly boarded the vessels with an armed force, killed the two captains and made the rest prisoners. At the same time, the unarmed seamen on shore were surrounded and overpowered by a multitude of natives. Mr. Lamport's party were also attacked and cruelly beaten, but their lives were spared, and they were brought to Honolulu.

Elated by the capture of these two vessels with all their guns and ammunition, Kalanikupule and his chiefs resolved to sail at once to Hawaii and attack Kamehameha. Mr. Lamport and several of the seamen were set to work under a guard to fit the vessels for sea. On the 11th the king had all his guns and ammunition put on board, and embarking with some of his chiefs, had the vessels warped out of the harbor, and anchored off Waikiki. Against Kamohomoho's advice he had ordered that the soldiers should accompany him in a fleet of canoes, reserving the vessels for himself and his train.

About midnight, at a preconcerted signal, the seamen in both vessels suddenly rose up and made a desperate attack on the natives. They soon cleared the decks of them, and confined the king, queen, and a few attendants in the cabin. They then set sail, and stood to the southward till day-break, when they put the king, queen, and a servant into a canoe which had been towing astern, and sent them ashore. They touched at Hawaii for provisions, where they landed the three remaining women, and informed Kamehameha of all that had occurred, after which they proceeded on their voyage to China, touching at Kauai for yams.

Conquest of Oahu by Kamehameha, 1795.—Kamehameha and his counselors saw that the time had now come to conquer the leeward islands. Without any delay, he ordered a levy of all the fighting men and war-canoes of Hawaii, and mustered the largest and best equipped army ever seen in the islands. He had sixteen foreigners in his service, of whom Young, Davis, and one Peter Anderson had charge of his cannons.*

In the month of February, 1795, he sailed to Lahaina, which he completely destroyed, and West Maui was laid waste. Koalaukane, who was in command, fled to Oahu without a battle. The great Armada next proceeded to Kaunakakai, Molokai, where the canoes are said to have lined the beach for four miles.

Of late years there had been a growing jealousy and suspicion between the old Kona chiefs and the turbulent Kaiana. As he was not invited to a council of war held at Kaunakakai, he concluded that his ruin or death had been determined upon. Accordingly, during the voyage to Oahu he and his brother, Nahiolea, separated from the

* A tradition reports the strength of his army at 16,000 men.—Broughton.

main fleet with their followers, and landed at Koolau whence they crossed over to Nuuanu and joined Kalani-

PALI OF NUUANU

kupule. In the mean time, Kamehameha landed his army in Waialae Bay, and after a few days spent in arranging and preparing his men, he marched up Nuuanu Valley, where Kalanikupule had posted his forces.

He encountered the enemy at Laimi and Puiwa, where the Oahu troops made a brave resistance until Kaiana, their leader, was killed by a cannon-ball, when they gave way. They were closely pursued up the valley, some escaping up the ridges on either side, while others were hemmed in and driven over the Nuuanu "Pali," or precipice, north of the road. Kalanikupule for several months wandered in the Koolau Mountains, until he was captured in a cave above Waipio, brought down and offered in sacrifice to the conqueror's war-god at Moanalua. His brother, Koalaukane, escaped to Kauai.

This battle, which was fought about the end of April, 1795, made Kamehameha master of all the islands except Kauai and Niihau, and was the beginning of a new era for the Hawaiian Islands.

Although no wholesale massacres were committed after the battle was over, the conquered people suffered the miseries of savage warfare. All the lands were confiscated and divided among Kamehameha's friends, while the immense horde that followed his banner plundered the people without mercy or restraint.

CHAPTER XX

1795—1810

FROM THE CONQUEST OF OAHU TO THE CESSION OF KAUAI

AFTER dividing the lands of Oahu among his followers, Kamehameha resolved to embark in an expedition against the two remaining islands of Kauai and Niihau, in order to complete the conquest of the entire group. Accordingly he set the foreign mechanics in his service to work in building a vessel of about forty tons, which he proposed to arm with his four-pound cannons.

Captain Broughton's First Visit.—About this time, in February, 1796, Captain Broughton, commanding the British discovery-ship "Providence," of sixteen guns, arrived at Waikiki, Oahu, on his way to Nootka Sound. Kamehameha visited the ship, clad in a European suit, over which he wore a splendid feather cloak. He made handsome presents to Captain Broughton, and begged for fire-arms and ammunition, but met with a firm refusal. Captain Broughton employed his men three days in making the first survey of the harbor of Honolulu. He was much impressed by the misery and destitution of the common people, and with the rapid depopulation that had been going on since his former visit with Vancouver. He labored in vain to dissuade Kamehameha from his proposed invasion of Kauai, and says that the conquerors

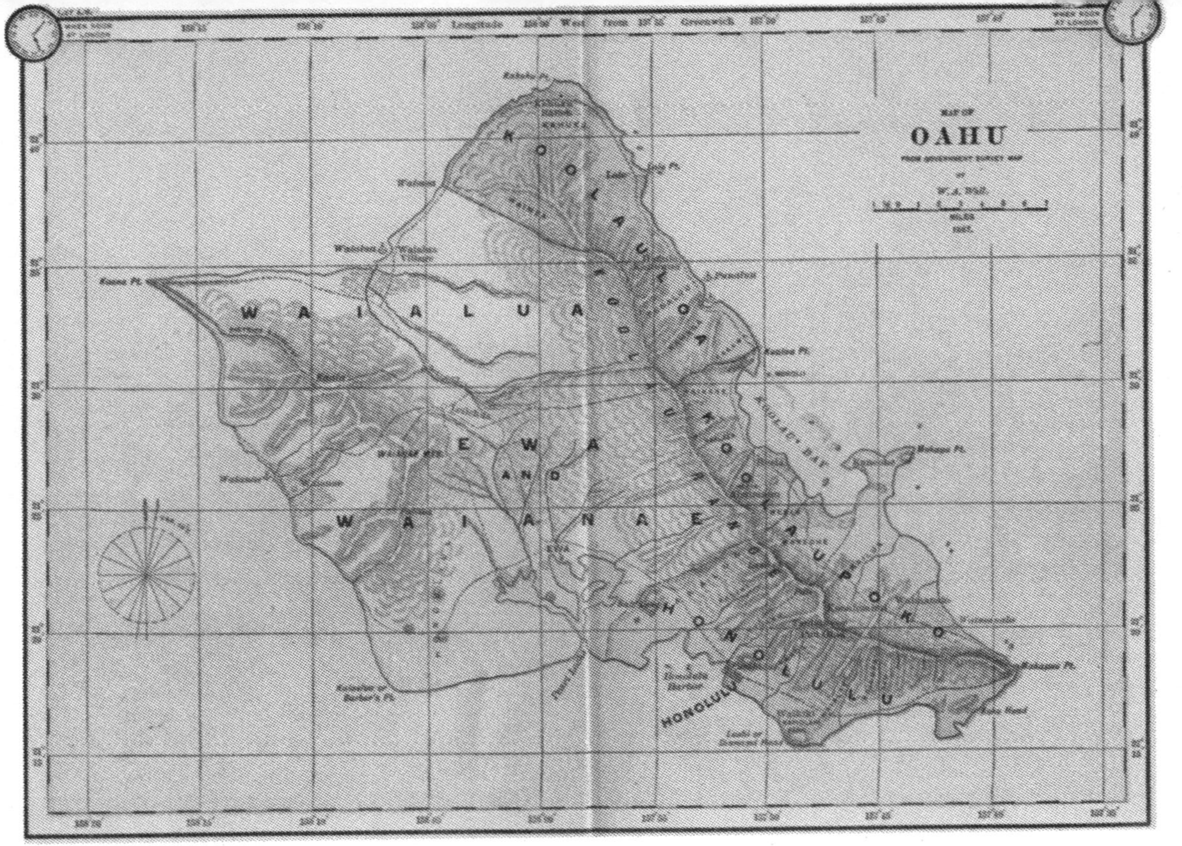
MAP OF
OAHU
Longitude West from Greenwich
W A I A L U A
E W A
A N D
W A I A N A E
HONOLULU
Kaena Pt.
Mokapu Pt.

"seemed intent upon nothing but seizing every thing that they could grasp."

He sailed on the 15th for the Northwest Coast, touching at the island of Kauai, which he found rent with civil war between the adherents of the young Prince Kaumualii and those of Keawe, a grandson of Peleioholani. Captain Broughton endeavored in vain to restore peace between the rival chiefs, and refused all requests for arms or ammunition.

The Attempted Invasion of Kauai.—Kamehameha did not wait to complete his schooner, but after dedicating a heiau in Ewa with human sacrifices, in April, 1796, he moved his army and fleet of war-canoes to Waianae. Thence they sailed for Kauai in the night (as they steered by the stars), expecting to land at Wailua. But before the fleet was more than one fourth of the way across the channel, it encountered a tempest that wrecked many of the canoes, and drove the rest back to Waianae. According to Captain Broughton, he had caused the whole stock of hogs on Oahu to be destroyed before sailing for Kauai. A severe famine ensued from the general destruction of live-stock and the neglect of cultivation.*

Rebellion on Hawaii.—Meanwhile Namakeha, Kaiana's brother, who had remained in Kau, raised a rebellion against Kamehameha, and the former partisans of Keoua flocked to his support. At first he carried every thing before him, and soon overran the districts of Kau, Puna, and Hilo. In one battle a European was killed.

Broughton's Second Visit.—The following July, 1796, Captain Broughton, returning from Nootka Sound, touched at Kealakekua Bay for water and supplies. He found

* Many of the people, to relieve their hunger, stole from the chiefs, and were cruelly punished, several being burned alive to terrify the rest.

that the cattle left by Vancouver had rapidly increased. On his arrival at Oahu, July 25th, Kamehameha boarded the ship and entreated Captain Broughton to take him and his principal chiefs to Hawaii, a request which he was obliged to refuse.*

At Kauai, Keawe, who seemed to be in power, had tabued the sale of supplies, except for arms and ammunition. He was afterward slain, leaving the sovereignty of the island to Kaumualii. Captain Broughton then crossed over to Niihau to buy yams, and at first all appeared friendly. On the 30th he sent the cutter ashore with two armed marines to bring off the remainder of the yams. While off their guard they were suddenly attacked, and the two marines were killed, the rest narrowly escaping to the boat. A strong armed party was sent to their assistance, which burned the village and destroyed sixteen canoes. Four natives were killed in this sad affair, the last of the kind that stains Hawaiian annals.

Wreck of Captain Barber's Ship.—The snow "Arthur," commanded by Captain Henry Barber, on his second voyage from Bengal to the Northwest Coast, visited the islands in October, 1796. After taking in supplies at Waikiki he sailed for Kauai in the evening of the 31st, and was wrecked off the point that bears his name. One of the boats was lost and six men were drowned, the rest escaping to the shore.

Fortunately Mr. John Young was on Oahu at the time, and by his orders the natives saved a large part of the ship's stores and of the cargo of furs, which were taken

*Queen Kaahumanu presented Captain Broughton with a canoe in which she had lately eloped, and had nearly reached Kauai before she was overtaken and brought back.—Bingham.

to Hawaii in the king's schooner. The king afterward succeeded in recovering the ship's cannon, which he kept for himself.

The Suppression of Namakeha's Revolt.—In August, 1796, Kamehameha embarked for Hawaii with the bulk of his army, to suppress the rebellion. He met the insurgents at Kaipalaoa, in the district of Hilo, and gained a complete victory over them. Namakeha was hunted down, and offered in sacrifice in the heiau at Piihonua, Hilo. This was the last of Kamehameha's wars. All opposition to his authority was now at an end.

KAMEHAMEHA I.

Consolidation of the Government.—The ancient system of government was radically changed by the conquest. Kamehameha's great object was to centralize all power in his own hands. All the lands in the kingdom he claimed as his by right of conquest, and apportioned them among his followers according to their rank and services, on condition of their rendering him military service and a part of the revenues of their lands. He broke up the old system of district chieftains by giving land in detached pieces, scattered through the group, and by keeping the more restless and ambitious chiefs about his person, obliging them to follow his court wherever he resided. He employed numerous informers and female spies, who were always on the watch for disaffection, and he appointed men whom he could trust as governors, *kiaaina*, over the principal islands. Thus John Young was governor of Hawaii, and Keeaumoku governor of Maui. In making appointments, he regarded ability and fidelity much more than rank. The governors, by his approval, appointed tax-collectors, heads of districts, and other petty officers. The four great Kona chiefs (see page 118) who had raised him to the throne and aided him in all his wars were his chief counselors, together with Kalanimoku, *alias* William Pitt, who acted as prime-minister and treasurer.

He now exerted himself to promote agriculture, to encourage industry, and thus to repair the ravages of his wars. He took energetic measures for suppressing brigandage, murder, and theft throughout his kingdom, until, as the old saying goes, "the old men and the children could sleep in the highways" unmolested.

As long as he lived he was a firm supporter of the ancient tabu system in all its rigor, and used it as a powerful engine of state. The tabus relating to the person of the king were strictly enforced, and the ceremonial etiquette of the court was increased in severity.

His policy toward foreigners showed his superiority in wisdom to other chiefs. He always protected them, and secured their trade and assistance by hospitality and fair dealing. He also showed his superior sagacity and insight into character by his selection of foreign advisers, and was never imposed upon by worthless adventurers.

His head queen was Keopuolani, who was admitted by all to be the highest chief living, uniting in herself the blood of the highest chiefs of Maui and Hawaii. Her children were heirs to the throne. But his favorite queen was Kaahumanu, though she, like the rest, had to suffer from occasional outbreaks of his ungovernable temper.

Kamehameha's Residence on Hawaii, 1796–1802.—Kamehameha remained six years on Hawaii, during which time the famous fleet of war-canoes called *peleleu* was built in the forests back of Hilo for the invasion of Kauai. These were wide and deep canoes, with a capacity for carrying men and stores on long voyages. Several small decked vessels were also built by native carpenters under the direction of Mr. James Boyd.* About this time two foreigners residing in Lahaina built for the king a two-story brick house, which stood for over seventy years, near the landing, on the site of the present market.

His heir, Liholiho, was born in 1797 at Hilo, Hawaii. When five years old he was proclaimed as heir-apparent, and was carried to the temples to take part in the sacred rites.

Eruption of Hualalai, 1801.—A great eruption of lava took place in 1801 from a crater in Kaupulehu on the western slope of Hualalai, which filled up the fish-pond of Paiea, and destroyed several villages and cocoanut groves. Many sacrifices were made to the goddess Pele, and hundreds of hogs were thrown into the fiery stream, but in vain.

At last Kamehameha cut off part of his own hair (which was considered sacred), and cast it into the flowing lava, which is said to have ceased to flow in a day or two after.

Kamehameha's Visit to Lahaina, 1802–3.—In 1802

*At this time certain fishermen of Puna, who had beaten Kamehameha's forehead with a paddle in a skirmish in the year 1783, were arrested and brought before him, together with their wives and children. The king's courtiers all advised that they should be stoned to death, but he forbade it, and protected them by a decree called *Mamalahoa*.

Kamehameha sailed to Lahaina with his fleet of *peleleu* canoes, touching at Kipahulu and Kaupo, where he consecrated several heiaus. He remained more than a year in Lahaina, making the "brick palace" his head-quarters, while he collected the taxes due from Maui and the three adjacent islands. He also consecrated numerous heiaus at Lahaina and other places with the usual cruel rites, in which the little heir to the throne officiated. At this time his old comrade, Kameeiamoku, died at Puuki in Lahaina, and was succeeded by his son Hoapili.

In May, 1803, Captain Cleveland touched at the islands on his way from California to China, bringing with him the first horses ever seen here. He landed a mare and foal at Kawaihae for John Young on the 24th, and two days later landed a horse and mare at Lahaina as a present to the king. Their beauty and mettle excited the wonder and admiration of the natives. In spite of his advanced age, Kamehameha afterwards became a good horseman.

Kamehameha's Return to Oahu, 1803.—Soon after this Kamehameha proceeded on his way to Oahu with his fleet and army. According to Cleveland's account, he possessed at that time twenty small vessels of from twenty to forty tons burden, some even copper-bottomed. In 1804 Mr. Shaler exchanged his brig, the "Lelia Byrd," of one hundred and seventy-five tons, which had been aground on the California coast and was leaking badly, with Kamehameha for his schooner and a sum of money to boot. Mr. George McClay, the king's carpenter, put in a new keel, and nearly replanked her in Honolulu Harbor. She afterwards made two or three voyages to China with sandal-wood, and finally sank near Canton.

The Pestilence, 1804.—After Kamehameha had made

vast preparations for the invasion of Kauai, and had collected an overwhelming force, a pestilence broke out among his troops, which spread through the island and carried off half the population. It was known among the natives by the name of "*mai okuu*," and is believed by many to have been the cholera. Kamehameha himself was attacked, but he recovered. All his chief counselors perished except Kalanimoku. Thus Kauai again escaped invasion.

A Human Sacrifice, 1807.—In 1807 Queen Keopuolani was dangerously ill at Waikiki. A priest declared that her illness was caused by the gods, who, he said, were angry because certain men had eaten tabu cocoanuts.

Upon this ten men were seized as victims by the king's orders, but as her alarming symptoms abated, only three of them were slain and offered up in the heiau at the foot of Diamond Head.

Honolulu in 1809.—Archibald Campbell, a Scotch sailor who arrived in Honolulu in 1809, and spent a year in Oahu, afterwards published an interesting account of his experience.*

During this year Kamehameha's younger brother, Keliimaikai, died, and Mr. Campbell was an eye-witness of the frightful scenes that took place, the knocking out of teeth, the deafening wailing, etc., and the general casting off of clothing and of all restraints of decency. When

*The village of Honolulu, which consisted of several hundred huts, was then well shaded with cocoanut-trees. The king's house, built close to the shore and surrounded by a palisade, was distinguished by the British colors and a battery of sixteen carriage guns belonging to his ship, the "Lily Bird" (Lelia Byrd), which lay unrigged in the harbor. "At a short distance were two large storehouses built of stone, which contained the European articles belonging to the king." The king's fleet of small vessels was hauled up on shore around Waikiki Bay, with sheds built over them. One small sloop was employed as a packet between Oahu and Hawaii. Captain Harbottle, an old resident, generally acted as pilot.

remonstrated with by the captain of a ship that lay in the harbor, Kamehameha replied that such was their law, and that he could not prevent it. Mr. Campbell also witnessed the *makahiki*, or New Year's ceremonies. Kamehameha sent a handsome feather cloak to England by Captain Spence of the "Duke of Portland," as a present to King George III., and dictated a letter to the captain, dated March 3d, 1810, reminding King George of Vancouver's promise that a vessel armed with brass guns should be sent to him.

Don Francisco de Paula Marin, from Jerez, Andalusia, Spain, who came to the islands in 1791, and died in 1837, deserves to be remembered for his services in introducing useful plants and setting an example of industry.*

* As early as 1809 he was raising oranges, figs, grapes, roses, pine-apples, and vegetables, making butter, salting beef for ships, and making wine. He acted as interpreter for Kamehameha I. until his death, and became wealthy by honest industry

CHAPTER XXI

1810—1819

CLOSING YEARS OF THE REIGN OF KAMEHAMEHA I.

Cession of Kauai, 1810.—Kaumualii, the king of Kauai and Niihau, had justified the high expectations formed of him by Vancouver and others who saw him in his youth. From his personal qualities, both of mind and body, he was the *beau ideal* of a Hawaiian chief, and was universally beloved by his subjects and by foreigners. He was the only Hawaiian who had learned to read and write the English language to any extent.

Although his warriors were well armed, he knew how inferior his forces were to those of Kamehameha, and therefore caused a schooner to be built by the white mechanics in his service, in which, as a last resort, he might escape from the island and seek refuge in some land to the west.

Several messages and presents had been interchanged between the two kings. At length Kaumualii sent his cousin Kamahalolani to Oahu with presents, offering to acknowledge Kamehameha as his feudal superior. In reply Kamehameha insisted on Kaumualii's making the cession in person, and pledged his honor for his safety. Remembering the fate of Keoua, Kaumualii hesitated, until Captain Jonathan Windship, a well-known sandal-wood trader, by leaving his mate as a hostage, persuaded him to visit Honolulu in his ship.

As soon as he arrived, Kamehameha went on board in state, and held a friendly interview with him. Kaumualii offered him his islands, upon which Kamehameha told him to continue to hold them in fief during his lifetime, on condition that Liholiho should be his heir.

Kaumualii then landed, and was hospitably entertained, although some of the chiefs urged Kamehameha to have him assassinated, to which he would not consent. A plot was then laid to poison him at a feast to be held at Waikahalulu, near the shore. Isaac Davis, however, warned him of it, so that instead of attending the feast he went on board of the ship and sailed for Kauai. For this good act Mr. Davis was soon afterward poisoned by the perfidious chiefs, and died in April, 1810.

The Sandal-wood Trade.—It was during the period from 1810 to 1825 that the sandal-wood trade was at its height. This wood was in great demand for the Canton market, where it was sold for incense and for the manufacture of fancy articles. It was purchased by the picul of 133⅓ pounds, the price varying from eight to ten dollars for the picul.

While it lasted, this wood was a mine of wealth to the king and chiefs, by means of which they were enabled to buy guns and ammunition, liquors, boats, and schooners, as well as silks and other Chinese goods, for which they paid exorbitant prices.* Great quantities of these costly goods, however, were never used, but being stored away in unsuitable storehouses were allowed to decay.

* This trade greatly increased the oppression of the common people multitudes of whom were obliged to remain for months at a time in the mountains searching for the trees, felling them, and bringing them down on their backs to the royal storehouses.

Distilling.—The art of distilling was introduced by some Botany Bay convicts before the year 1800. It is said to have been first practiced here by a William Stevenson, from New South Wales.

The root of the *ki* plant (Cordyline terminalis) was first baked for days in the ground, after which it became very sweet. It was then macerated in a canoe with water to ferment, and in five or six days was ready for distillation. The rude still was made of iron pots, procured from ships, with a gun-barrel used as a tube to conduct the vapor. The liquor obtained in this way, *okolehao*, was nearly pure alcohol. At one time almost every chief had his still. Large quantities of rum were also imported, and caused incalculable injury to the people. Kamehameha, although at first he indulged in it to excess, was soon convinced of the evil effects of the practice by John Young, and had the strength of mind to restrict himself to a very small fixed quantity, and finally to abstain entirely.*

On the 21st of February, 1811, John Jacob Astor's ship, the ill-fated "Tonquin," on its way to Astoria anchored off Waikiki, and remained a week, buying supplies from Kamehameha. Twenty-four natives entered the service of Astor's company.

Kamehameha's Return to Hawaii, 1811.—In 1811 Kamehameha returned to Hawaii for the purpose of receiving and disposing of the sandal-wood that had been collected for him on the Windward Islands. He first embarked in his own schooner, the "Keoua," accompanied by many canoes and other small vessels. The "Keoua"

*Near the end of his life he summoned all the leading men of Hawaii to a great assembly at Kailua, at which he ordered all the stills to be destroyed, and forbade the manufacture of any kind of liquor. His oldest son, Liholiho, however, and many of the other chiefs were in the habit of drinking to excess.

sprang a leak off Lanai, on which Waipa, a native ship-carpenter, leaped into the sea and nailed canvas over the leak, so that the vessel could be safely brought back to Honolulu. Kamehameha afterward sailed in Captain Windship's ship for Kealakekua, accompanied by some of his chiefs on board of another ship (commanded by Captain William Davis), Kalanimoku following on the "Keoua." From Kealakekua the king sailed to Lahaina and to Molokai to dispose of the taxes collected there.

In December, 1811, he sent a cargo of sandal-wood to China by Captain Windship, who brought him back a cargo of China goods in return the next year.

Soon after this there was a famine in Hawaii, caused by the neglect of agriculture while the people had been forced to spend their time in cutting sandal-wood. Kamehameha set his retinue to work in planting the ground, and also set an example of industry himself. The piece of ground which he tilled is still pointed out. As an illustration of his foresight, it is said that he forbade the cutting of young sandal-wood, and instructed his bird-catchers not to strangle the birds from which they plucked the choice yellow feathers for royal cloaks, but to set them free, that other feathers might grow in their place.

His second son by Keopuolani, Kauikeaouli, was born August 11th, 1813, at Keauhou.

About this time, Astor's ship, the "Lark," was cast away on the island of Kahoolawe. Kamehameha relieved the wants of the crew, but claimed the wreck for himself.

Russian Aggressions.—Mr. Baránoff, the Russian governor of Alaska, seems to have had some idea of forming a colony on the islands as early as 1809, when Archibald Campbell visited them in his ship "Neva." In 1812 he established a fortified trading-post on Bodega Bay, California, in defiance of the Spanish governor.

In the year 1814 Governor Baránoff sent the ship "Attawelpa" on a sealing voyage to the islands, in which she was wrecked at Waimea, Kauai. The ship's stores and cargo were left in the care of Kaumualii for the owners.

In 1815 Baránoff sent Dr. Scheffer to the islands on the American ship "Isabella," to look after the property.*

Shortly after, the "Discovery," a Russian ship in search of seals, arrived with thirty Kodiak Indians on board, who were left at Waimea with Dr. Scheffer. Next, a Russian brig, the "Elemenia," or "Ilmen," which had been trading on the coast of Mexico, ran down to the islands for repairs, and a Russian ship, the "Myrtle," sent by Governor Baránoff, arrived about the same time. The "Myrtle" anchored at Honolulu, where the Russians landed and built a block-house, mounting a few guns and hoisting the Russian flag. As soon as he was informed of it, Kamehameha sent Kalanimoku with a large force of chiefs and warriors, with orders to watch the Russians, and, if necessary, to resist them with arms.

On the night after their arrival at Honolulu, the "Myrtle" and the brig both sailed for Kauai, and remained some time at Hanalei, where a breast-work was thrown up and a few cannon mounted.

It is said that Kaumualii had been persuaded to give Dr. Scheffer the valley of Hanalei. Dr. Scheffer superintended the building of a fort at Waimea for Kaumualii,

* He landed with his goods at Kailua, Hawaii, where he was kindly treated by Kamehameha, until he obtained a passage to Kauai on the ship "Millwood.' After landing his merchandise at Waimea, he built a storehouse there, and engaged in trade.

over which the Russian colors were displayed, and even proposed to Kaumualii to lease the whole island of him for a term of years.

Building of the Honolulu Fort.—Meanwhile, by the advice and under the direction of John Young, Kalanimoku proceeded to erect a fort at Honolulu to command the harbor, which was commenced in January, 1816, and

OLD FORT AT HONOLULU

completed in a year. It was nearly square, measuring three hundred to four hundred feet on a side, with walls about twelve feet high and twenty feet thick, built of coral rock, with embrasures for cannons. It stood on the seaward side of Queen Street, and across the lower part of Fort Street. About forty guns, six, eight, and twelve-pounders, were afterward mounted, and it was placed under the command of Captain Beckley. Eight thirty-two-pounders were afterward placed on Punchbowl Hill.

Departure of the Russians.—By Kamehameha's orders, a messenger was sent to Kaumualii with orders to expel

Dr. Scheffer. The latter, on being informed of the order, sent his property on board of the brig, and sailed for Hanalei and thence to Honolulu. Here again they were soon requested to depart, which they did without resistance. The ship "Myrtle," however, being old and unseaworthy, was obliged to return, and sank in the harbor. Her crew were kindly treated on shore until they had an opportunity to leave. Soon after the Russian sloop of war "Diana" touched at Waimea for supplies. The captain made some inquiries about Dr. Scheffer's conduct and his treatment, and appeared to be satisfied.

In October, 1816, John Ebbets sold the ship "Albatross," of one hundred and sixty-five tons burden, to Kamehameha I. for four hundred piculs of sandalwood.

Kotzebue's First Visit, 1816.—Captain Kotzebue, in the Russian discovery-ship "Rurick," visited the islands near the close of the year 1816.

On his arrival at Kailua, November 24th, there was great excitement on shore, until he assured the king that Dr. Scheffer's proceedings were not authorized by the Russian Government.

After this he was treated with the utmost hospitality, in return for which he gave Kamehameha two eight-pounder mortars, together with a supply of shells, powder, etc. M. Choris, the artist of the expedition, painted the only authentic portrait of Kamehameha in existence. The king sent Manuia with Captain Kotzebue to carry messages to Kalanimoku and John Young.

On arriving at Honolulu the "Rurick" was towed into the harbor by eight double canoes, each manned by from sixteen to twenty rowers. The port charges were remitted, and she was supplied with provisions gratis. The next day a misunderstanding arose because the Russians in surveying the harbor had set up flags on shore. The people resented this and were taking up arms, when John Young explained matters, substituting brooms for flags, and tranquillity was restored.

Captain Kotzebue made an interesting trip to Pearl River, and a mock fight with spears was exhibited in his

PORT OF HONOLULU IN 1816

honor, in which over sixty chiefs took part. He sailed December 14th, 1816, exchanging salutes with the fort, the first time that this had ever been done.

Kotzebue had found in the harbor, besides the ship "Albatross" and other vessels, the brig "Forester," which had been purchased by the king from Captain Piggott in exchange for sandal-wood, and her name changed to "Kaahumanu." In March, 1817, Kamehameha sent her, under Captain Alexander Adams, with a cargo of sandal-wood to Canton, touching at Kauai to haul down the

Russian colors and hoist his own, and returning October 17th, 1817. The result was that the king lost about three thousand dollars by the speculation, partly because the Chinese authorities would not recognize the Hawaiian flag. The "Keoua" had previously been taken to Macao by Captain Davis, and never returned. The "Bordeaux Packet," a brig of one hundred and sixty tons, was purchased in 1817 with sandal-wood.

The Spanish Pirates.—In the early part of the year 1818 a suspicious-looking craft named the "Victory," *alias* "Santa Rosa," arrived at Kealakekua Bay under the command of an Englishman named Turner. The crew, who spoke Spanish, were a lawless set, and spent most of their time in carousing on shore. They had abundance of gold and silver, crucifixes, candelabras, cups, and other sacred vessels, taken from Roman Catholic churches. Kamehameha purchased the ship of her officers and crew, and renamed her the "Liholiho," intending to send her to Canton with a cargo of sandal-wood.

At last, in September, 1818, a Spanish man-of-war from Buenos Ayres, the "Argentina," commanded by Captain Bouchard, arrived, and seized the "Victory." The captain informed Kamehameha that its crew were pirates, who during the war of independence had run away with the "Santa Rosa," a sloop of war belonging to the province of La Plata, had pillaged a town on the Chilian coast, and stripped the churches of their sacred ornaments and furniture. Accordingly, the king immediately sent out his messengers, who captured most of the buccaneers and delivered them up to justice. The greater part of the church ornaments were also recovered by his orders and restored to Captain Bouchard, who appointed Don Marin consul of La Plata. Hearing that the first officer of the "Victory" had gone to Waimea, Kauai, Captain Bouchard sailed thither with an order from Kamehameha to the chiefs of Kauai. The pirate was given up, and summarily tried and executed on the beach at Waimea, after which both vessels laid in supplies at Honolulu, and finally sailed for California.

In 1817 the "Argentina" had cruised against the Spaniards, and captured a brigantine belonging to the governor of Guam. In November, 1818, Captain Bouchard made a descent on the California coast, and sacked the town of Monterey.

During this year three men were sacrificed at Kealakekua for petty violations of the tabu.

Death of Kamehameha I.—Kamehameha resided at Kailua seven years.* He died May 8th, 1819, at the age of eighty-two years, and in the faith of his ancestors. His work was done. He had consolidated the group under one government, put an end to feudal anarchy and petty wars, and prepared the way for civilization and Christianity. His faults were those of the age and society in which he lived, and both morally and mentally he stood far above the other chiefs of his time.

It is said that during his last illness, when the priests proposed that a number of human victims should be sacrificed to his patron deity in order to prolong his life, he replied, "The men are sacred to the king," meaning his son, Liholiho.

The funeral rites observed at that time have been described in Chapter XII. As the district of Kona was

* It is said that near the end of his life he heard of the changes that were taking place at the Society Islands, and asked some questions in regard to the nature of the Christian religion, but found no one who could answer his inquiries.

polluted for the time being, the heir to the throne had to leave at once for Kohala. The usual human sacrifice, *moepuu*, seems not to have been offered, but the *kuni* sorcerers performed their incantations to discover who had prayed the king to death. The conduct of the people in general was such as forbids description. "According to custom, all law was suspended and all restraints taken away." After the bones of the late king had been deified Hoapili took charge of them and had them concealed in some cave in North Kona. The place of their concealment has never been revealed.

PART III
LATER HISTORY

CHAPTER XXII

1819

ABOLITION OF IDOLATRY

INSTALLATION of Liholiho, or Kamehameha II.—By his will Kamehameha had left to his son, Liholiho, the sovereignty over all the islands, and the title of *Moi*, while the war-god Ku-kaili-moku was intrusted to the care of Kekuaokalani, the son of his late brother Keliimaikai.

From all accounts Liholiho appears to have been a heedless and dissolute young prince, entirely wanting in the great qualities of his father. Knowing his unfitness to govern, Kamehameha had appointed Kaahumanu, who was already the guardian, *kahu*, of the young princes, as premier or *kuhina nui*, to exercise equal authority with the king.

Undoubtedly the leading chiefs, as well as Hewahewa, the high-priest, had long since ceased to believe in the power of their ancient deities; and the highest female chiefs, especially the two queens, Keopuolani and Kaahumanu, had secretly resolved upon the abolition of the oppressive tabu system. Hence as soon as the iron hand of Kamehameha was withdrawn, the whole structure was ready to crumble into ruins. In fact, on the very morning of Kamehameha's death the six chiefs present proposed to Kaahumanu to renounce the tabu; but she thought the time for this step had not come.

About ten days after Kamehameha's death, Liholiho returned to Kailua, and on the second day after his arrival he was formally vested with the sovereign power. The ceremony took place at Kamakahonu, adjoining the old heiau, before a vast concourse of chiefs, soldiers, and common people.

Liholiho came forth from the heiau, arrayed in a feather cloak and a cocked hat, and attended by chiefs wearing feather helmets and mantles, and bearing magnificent kahilis or plumed staffs of state.

Kaahumanu, in similar costume, advanced to meet him, and publicly declared the will of his father, which constituted him king and herself premier with equal authority. She concluded by proposing that they should henceforth disregard the tabus. The king, however, remained silent, and withheld his consent.

Carefully trained as he had been in idolatry, and remembering the last injunctions of his father, on no account to forsake it, he was very slow to yield to the general sentiment of the chiefs. The same evening Keopuolani, the queen-mother, sent to the king for his younger brother, Kauikeaouli, a mere child, to come and eat with her in defiance of tabu. Liholiho permitted it, but was careful himself to refrain from any violation of tabu.

Soon after this he returned to Kawaihae, where he attempted to consecrate a heiau, and did the same at Honokohau in North Kona.*

*He failed in both cases to obtain a perfect *aha* or faultless ceremony, on account of the drunkenness and disorder that prevailed.

Freycinet's Visit.— While the king was still at Kawaihae, the French discovery-ship "Uranie," Captain Freycinet, arrived at Kailua August 8th, 1819. He was hospitably received by Kuakini, *alias* Governor Adams, and made a series of scientific observations on shore. On the 12th he proceeded to Kawaihae, where the king and most of the chiefs were assembled in council, and spent several days in friendly intercourse with them. A Frenchman from Bordeaux, named Jean Rives, who had been twelve years in the islands, acted as interpreter for the king.

In view of the disaffection of Kekuaokalani, and the impending danger of civil war, a grand council was convened on the 14th, at which Captain Freycinet, after referring to the cession to Vancouver, declared that France and England were allies, and were both ready to assist Liholiho in maintaining peace and order in his kingdom. Immediately after this council, Kalanimoku, at his own request, was baptized on board of the "Uranie" by the chaplain, the Abbé De Quelen.

The next day Captain Freycinet sailed for Lahaina, where he set up an observatory on shore, adjoining the "brick palace," and made a series of pendulum observations. Having laid in supplies of fresh provisions and water, he proceeded to Honolulu on the 26th, and exchanged salutes with the fort. Boki, a younger brother of Kalanimoku, was acting governor at Oahu.

Captain W. H. Davis, who was extensively engaged in the sandal-wood and fur trade, entertained Captain Freycinet at his residence on shore. The latter justly praises Don Marin for his industry and enterprise. Governor Boki, on learning from Captain Davis that Kalanimoku had been baptized, requested the same privilege for himself. He was accordingly baptized on board of the "Uranie" on the 27th.

There were then lying in the harbor the ship "Paragon," Captain Wildes, and the "Enterprise," both engaged in the sandal-wood trade, besides the new brig "Niu," which had been ordered by Kamehameha, and was sold to Liholiho for $51,750, paid for in sandal-wood at $10 per picul.

Captain Freycinet, after laying in supplies of fire-wood, etc., sailed for Port Jackson August 30th, 1819.

Abolition of Idolatry.—Meanwhile Kaahumanu sent for Liholiho again, requesting him to renounce idolatry on his return to Kailua. Accordingly, Liholiho with his retinue embarked in several canoes, and spent two days in a drunken debauch at sea, during which he committed several violations of tabu.

On his arrival at Kailua he found that a great feast had been prepared, at which he sat down with a large company of chiefs of both sexes, and openly feasted with them, while a multitude of common people looked on with mingled fear and curiosity to see what judgments would follow so impious an act. As they saw no harm ensue they raised a joyful shout, "The tabus are at an end, and the gods are a lie!"

The effect of it was like that of displacing the key-stone of an arch. The whole structure both of idol-worship and of the tabus fell at once into ruins. The high-priest himself set the example of setting fire to the idols and their sanctuaries, and messengers were sent even as far as Kauai to proclaim the abolition of the tabus, which was termed the *ai noa* or free eating, in opposition to the *ai kapu*. Kaumualii gladly consented, and a general jubilee pervaded the islands, attended with revelry and license; but the tabu system was too ancient and deeply rooted to be given up without a struggle.

Insurrection of Kekuaokalani.—Kekuaokalani, who was a brave and popular young chief, was highly indignant at the conduct of Liholiho, and retired to Kaawaloa. There the priests flocked around him and offered him the crown, repeating an ancient Hawaiian proverb: "A religious chief shall possess a kingdom, but irreligious chiefs shall always be poor." A large body of chiefs and common people rallied around the standard of this "defender of the faith," while his adherents took up arms in the district of Hamakua and killed a chief named Kainapau.

Kaahumanu and her friends, who had been reveling deeply at Kailua, suddenly awoke to a sense of their danger.

A few months before, the king had purchased over eleven thousand dollars' worth of muskets and ammunition from an American trader, which now stood them in good stead.

They decided, however, to try conciliatory measures first, and sent Naihe, the orator, and Hoapili, together with Keopuolani, to negotiate with Kekuaokalani; but all their entreaties were in vain, and they were glad to escape with their lives.

Battle of Kuamoo.—Kekuaokalani resolved to march immediately on Kailua, hoping to take the royal party by surprise. But Kaahumanu and her general, Kalanimoku, were equal to the crisis. That night the arms were given out, and in the morning the army advanced to meet the rebels. The two armies met near Kuamoo, about four miles north of Kaawaloa. As the royalist troops approached, they received a volley from a scouting party of rebels and several men fell, on which they fell back to the cover of a stone wall, but finding the party opposed to them to be small, they advanced again and pursued the rebels till they came up to the main body, and the battle became general. Kekuaokalani had fewer men and fewer muskets than Kalanimoku, and but little ammunition. His men were outflanked and driven down toward the sea-shore, where they were exposed to a flanking fire from a squadron of double canoes, one of which carried a mounted gun under the charge of a foreign gunner.

Kekuaokalani, although wounded early in the action, fought bravely, and repeatedly rallied his men, until, as Ellis relates, "unable to stand from loss of blood, he sat on a fragment of lava and twice loaded and fired his musket at the advancing foe. He now received a ball in the left breast, and covering his face with his feather cloak, expired in the midst of his men.

"His wife, Manono, during the whole of the battle had fought by his side with steady and dauntless courage. A few moments after her husband's death she called out for quarter, but the words had hardly left her lips before she received a bullet in her left temple, fell upon the lifeless body of her husband, and expired."

The rebels having lost their leader were soon scattered or taken prisoners.*

This battle was fought about December 20th, 1819.

Hoapili was then sent with a force to Hamakua, and made short work with the insurrection in Waipio. The people now turned with rage and contempt against their idols. They slew Kuawa, the priest who had been Kekuaokalani's chief adviser.

* An oblong pile of stones near the sea, covered with vines, long marked the resting-place of the brave but misguided Kekuaokalani and his heroic wife.

They now made more thorough work of destroying their images and sacred inclosures, with a few exceptions, such as the *Hale o Keawe* at Honaunau. All public worship and sacrifices ceased, and, in the words of Mr. Jarves, "Hawaii presented to the world the strange spectacle of a nation without a religion."

Still the ancient idolatry was cherished by many in secret; and many of their superstitions, especially those relating to sorcery and the cause of disease, were destined to survive for generations to come, and to blend with and color their conceptions of Christianity.

CHAPTER XXIII

1820–1823

COMMENCEMENT OF THE AMERICAN PROTESTANT MISSION

Obookiah.—A strong interest in the Hawaiian people was awakened in New England by several Hawaiian youths who had been taken to the United States as seamen, and especially by Opukahaia, commonly known as Obookiah. He was brought to New Haven by a Captain Brintnall in 1809, where he attracted the attention of Mr. E. W. Dwight and other kind friends, who gave him an education.*

Arrival of the Pioneer Missionaries.—The first company of American missionaries to these islands embarked at Boston, October 23d, 1819, in the brig "Thaddeus," Captain Blanchard. It consisted of two clergymen and five laymen, with their wives, besides three Hawaiian youths from the Cornwall school, who were to act as assistants, viz., Kanui, Hopu, and Honolii.

Humehume or George Tamoree, a son of King Kaumualii by a common woman, was also a passenger. He had been sent to America for an education in childhood,

* In 1817 the "Foreign Mission School" was instituted at Cornwall, Conn., for the instruction of young men from heathen lands, and five young Hawaiians were among its earliest pupils. Obookiah died while a member of the school in 1818.

and in later years had enlisted in the American navy, in which he served during the War of 1812 with Great Britain, and the war with Algiers. On his return to Boston he was sent to the Cornwall school for a time.

The "Thaddeus" approached the coast of Kohala March 31st, 1820, and a boat was sent ashore under Mr. J. Hunnewell, the first officer, to learn the state of the country. On his return he said: "Liholiho is king; the tabus are abolished; the idols are burned; the temples are destroyed. There has been war, but now there is peace."

The wonder and gratitude of the missionaries can not be described. Off Kawaihae they were boarded by Kalanimoku and two female chiefs, Kalakua and Namahana, who took passage with them to Kailua, where the king resided. They arrived at Kailua April 4th, where the captain, with Messrs. Bingham and Thurston, attended by Hopu as interpreter, called on the king to explain the objects for which they had come, and to ask permission to reside in the country. On the 6th the king and his family dined with them on board by invitation. Kalanimoku appeared quite civilized in his dress and manners, but Liholiho's royal costume consisted of a *malo*, a green silk mantle fastened over the right shoulder, a string of beads around his neck, and a wreath of yellow feathers on his head.

After a week's delay, permission was granted them on the 12th to reside in the islands one year, two of them at Kailua and the rest at Honolulu. John Young had used his influence in their favor, assuring the chiefs that they taught the same religion as the English missionaries whom Vancouver had proposed to send to them.

Establishment of the American Mission.—Mr. and Mrs.

Thurston and Dr. and Mrs. Holman were assigned a small thatched hut to occupy in common at Kailua, while the rest of the party proceeded in the brig to Honolulu. There Boki, who had been appointed governor of Oahu, gave Mr. Bingham and his associates a building-site on the arid, treeless plain half a mile east of the landing, and then some distance from the village.

Their firewood and water were brought a distance of several miles.

At Kaumualii's urgent request Messrs. Whitney and Ruggles went to reside at Waimea, Kauai. No chief gave Christianity so cordial a reception, or made such rapid improvement as Kaumualii. In August, 1820, one Jean Rives, a Frenchman in Liholiho's service, came from Kailua to Honolulu to expel all foreigners "who did not belong to the king or Kalanimoku." In consequence of this, several Americans removed to Fanning's Island.

The first whale-ship, the "Mary," Captain Joseph Allen, arrived at Honolulu in 1820, and was soon followed by many others.

In November, as the king and court removed to Honolulu, Mr. and Mrs. Thurston were obliged to accompany them, and sailed as far as Lahaina in a small brig with four hundred and seventy-five passengers besides a numerous live-stock. This crowding was not an unusual occurrence.

The first pupils of the missionaries were the chiefs and their favorite attendants, and the wives and children of foreigners. At first their teaching was entirely in English, but by degrees they devoted their time and energies more and more to the task of mastering the Hawaiian language, and of reducing it to writing, until they made it their chief medium of instruction.

The foreigners in Honolulu at this time subscribed upwards of six hundred dollars for the education of orphan children.

Commander Vassilieff, of the Russian Exploring Expedition, who visited the islands in April and again in December, 1821, strongly recommended the mission to the favor of the chiefs, and treated both parties with the utmost kindness and courtesy.

In 1821 the frame of a dwelling-house was sent out from Boston for the mission, and with much difficulty permission was obtained from the king to build it. At first he said, "My father never allowed a foreigner to build a house in this country except for the king." When the cellar was dug, a report was spread that it was intended to be a magazine for arms and ammunition to be used against the king. The first church, a thatched building, was built in August, 1821.

During the summer of 1821, Kaumualii proposed to send his brig, the "Becket," to open intercourse with the Society Islands, and offered two of the American missionaries a free passage thither to confer with the English missionaries and to obtain copies of their publications. In consequence, however, of the opposition of Mr. Jones, the American consul, and of the traders, this expedition was given up.

Character of Liholiho, Kamehameha II.—The conduct of Liholiho formed a striking contrast to that of his father. Discarding the old counselors of his father, he chose his favorites out of the lowest class of whites, and spent most of his time in revelry and debauchery. He spent much time in roving from place to place with a numerous train of worthless retainers, who ravaged the land like a swarm of locusts. The treasures accumulated by his father were squandered, and he was soon involved in ruinous debts.*

Many other chiefs followed his example of extravagance and dissipation, to support which the common people were taxed and plundered, until, as they expressed it, "debt was more oppressive than war." Vast quantities of sandal-wood were collected and sold, but the debts increased still more rapidly, and new methods of extortion were devised. All trade with foreigners was subject to the monopoly of the chiefs, and the common people had nothing that they could call their own.

Liholiho's Visit to Kauai.—On the 21st of July, 1821, without disclosing his intention, Liholiho left Honolulu for Ewa in an open sail-boat with Boki, Naihe, and about thirty attendants, including two women.

But on arriving at Puuloa he refused to enter the lagoon and passed around Barber's Point. Then, to their surprise and consternation, he ordered the helmsman to steer for Kauai, nearly one hundred miles distant. They were without water, provisions, chart, or compass, the channel was rough and the wind strong; but the king, half intoxicated, would not listen to advice, and spreading out the fingers of one hand, said, "Here is your compass; steer by this." Twice the boat was nearly capsized, the seas broke over them, and his companions begged him to put back. "No," said the king, "bail out the water, and go on. If you return with the boat, I will swim to Kauai."

After a night of peril and fatigue they arrived off

* For example, in 1820 he purchased from Captain Suter a beautiful yacht called "Cleopatra's Barge," built in Salem, Mass., for $90,000, to be paid in sandal-wood. Her name was then changed to "Haaheo o Hawaii," "Pride of Hawaii." The brig "Thaddeus" was also bought for $40,000.

Waimea at the dawn of day, where they threw themselves entirely into the power of Kaumualii.

That noble chieftain, as soon as he heard of their arrival, instead of taking advantage of their helpless condition, went off in a canoe to meet Liholiho, gave him a hospitable reception, and took every pains to entertain him with honor. He then sent his brig to Oahu to inform Liholiho's people of his safety, and to bring his wives to Kauai. The following day, in an assembly of chiefs, Kaumualii addressed his guest, Liholiho, offering to surrender to him his kingdom, his fort, guns, and vessels. After this a deep silence prevailed for a short time, all awaiting with anxiety the reply of Liholiho. At length he answered: "I did not come here to take away your island. Keep your country and take care of it as before, and do what you please with your vessels."

The two kings then spent several weeks in a tour around the island of Kauai.

On their return, September 16th, Kaumualii was invited on board of the "Cleopatra's Barge" in the evening. While the unsuspicious prince was seated in the cabin, orders were secretly given to make sail, and he was torn from his kingdom, to remain henceforth a virtual prisoner of state. Soon after his arrival at Honolulu, October 9th, he was induced to marry the haughty Kaahumanu, who also took to husband his son, Kealiiahonui.

The First Printing.—The first printing in Hawaii was done January 7th, 1822. Keeaumoku II. (also called Governor Cox) was present and assisted in taking a few impressions of eight pages of a Hawaiian spelling-book. The king and other chiefs came in to see the wonderful machine, and a new impulse was given to the desire for knowledge among them. Much pains had been taken in settling upon the best method of expressing the sounds of the language. An alphabet of twelve letters was finally decided upon, the vowels having the same powers as in the Italian language. All the leading chiefs, including the king, now eagerly applied themselves to learn the arts of reading and writing, and soon began to use them in business and correspondence.

Visit of the English Deputation.—The arrival of Mr. Ellis and his associates at Honolulu, April 16th, 1822, was of great service to the cause of Christianity.

To fulfill a promise made by Vancouver to Kamehameha I., a schooner of seventy tons, called the "Prince Regent," with an armament of six guns, had been built and fitted out at Port Jackson, New South Wales. Captain Kent, of the brig "Mermaid," was commissioned to present this vessel to Liholiho in the name of the British Government. Having touched at the Society Islands on his way, and finding that Messrs. Tyerman and Bennett, who were there as a deputation from the London Missionary Society, and the Rev. W. Ellis, with two converted chiefs of Huahine, were desirous of proceeding to the Marquesas Islands, he offered them a free passage thither by way of the Hawaiian Islands, which they accepted.

They were most cordially received both by the native chiefs and by the American Mission, and were detained at Honolulu four months, while Captain Kent made a trip to Fanning's Island for *bêche de mer*. Their original plan of a mission to the Marquesas Islands was finally given up. The Tahitian teachers, Auna and Matatore, were immediately taken into the confidence of the chiefs, to whom they described the character and influence of the English missionaries among their own people. The English members of the party were able to refute many false reports that had been circulated, and to dissipate any lingering jealousies by joining harmoniously in the work of the American missionaries. Such is the similarity between the Tahitian and Hawaiian dialects, that in two months Mr. Ellis was able to preach fluently to the natives, and composed several hymns in their language.

The "Prince Regent" was formally presented to the king May 1st, but a few months after was wrecked on the east side of Oahu.

Other Events in the Year 1822.—Kaahumanu and Kaumualii, with a large retinue, including Auna, made a tour through the windward islands in May and June, 1822. Immense quantities of provisions, kapas, etc., were laid at their feet in different places (*hookupu*). Feasting, dancing, and revelry went on together with the burning of idols. Kamehameha's poison-god, Kalaipahoa, was burned at Hilo June 4th, and at Kailua on the 26th one hundred and two idols collected from various hiding places were consumed in one bonfire.

The first Christian marriage in the islands was solemnized August 11th, 1822, between Thomas Hopu and Delia, before a large assembly. On the 13th of August, Kaahumanu and the nominal king of Kauai, with their immense retinue of chiefs and servants, numbering nearly twelve hundred persons, sailed for Kauai on board of two brigs and two schooners, the decks of which were so crowded that the people could scarcely find room to sit or stand. They took Auna and others with them as teachers. The object of this expedition was to receive homage and presents from their subjects and to collect sandal-wood.

As the king and chiefs and American missionaries united in inviting Mr. Ellis to take up his residence at the islands with his family as well as Auna, the deputation gave its consent. The whole party sailed for the Society Islands in August by the brig "Mermaid." Mr. and Mrs. Ellis, with Taua and Tute, Tahitian teachers, returned from Tahiti in the "Active," Captain Richard Charlton, arriving in Honolulu February 4th, 1823.

Arrival of the First "Reinforcement."—The first reinforcement to the mission, consisting of six missionaries and their wives, arrived at Honolulu April 27th, 1823, on the "Thames," Captain Clasby, and were well received by the chiefs. During the last three years much progress had been made in civilization. The English deputation had found twenty-four vessels at anchor at Honolulu, mostly whalers from the United States. The village contained from two thousand to three thousand inhabitants, and boasted four mercantile establishments, well supplied with goods, which carried on trade with the northwest coast of America, the Spanish Main, and China. The chiefs appeared on state occasions dressed in civilized style, and their houses began to be supplied with costly furniture. Many of them had learned how to read and write, and several had embraced Christianity. The poverty and misery of the common people, however, had increased.

A Grand Pageant.—The annual feast in commemoration of Liholiho's accession to the throne was celebrated this year (1823) with barbaric magnificence. In the grand procession of the last day (May 8th), each of Liholiho's wives and his younger brother and sister were borne in state with all the pomp and splendor that the country could furnish.

The head queen, Kamamalu, was seated in a whaleboat, fastened to a platform of spars, and borne on the shoulders of seventy men. The boat and platform were covered with fine broadcloth, relieved by richly colored native cloth. The bearers marched in a solid phalanx, the outer ranks of which wore scarlet and yellow feather cloaks and helmets. The queen wore a scarlet silk *pau* and a coronet of feathers, and was screened from the sun by a huge umbrella of scarlet damask, supported by a chief wearing a scarlet malo and a feather helmet. On one quarter of the boat stood Naihe, and on the other Kalanimoku, similarly clad, and each holding a scarlet *kahili* or plumed staff of state, thirty feet in height.*

Meanwhile the king and his suite, nearly naked, and intoxicated, rode from place to place on horses without saddles, followed on the run by a shabby escort of fifty or sixty men.†

* One of the queen-dowagers wore seventy-two yards of orange and scarlet kerseymere, which was wrapped around her waist until her arms were sustained by it in a horizontal position, and the remainder was formed into a train supported by her attendants.

† Companies of dancing and singing girls, to the number of several hundreds, met the procession in different places, encircling the highest chiefs, and chanting their praises.

CHAPTER XXIV

1823–1824

LIHOLIHO'S VOYAGE TO ENGLAND AND DEATH

Death of Keopuolani, 1823.—About the end of May, 1823, Keopuolani, the queen-mother, who was the highest chief in the nation by blood, moved her residence to Lahaina, Maui. At her request, Messrs. Stewart and Richards, with Taua, her Tahitian chaplain, accompanied her, and founded a mission-station there under her patronage.*

On the 21st of August, Kaahumanu, Kaumualii, Kalanimoku, and other chiefs arrived at Lahaina in a fleet of three brigs and two schooners, of which not only the decks, but also the chains, bowsprits, and tops, were crowded with people. Soon after, Keopuolani was taken with her last illness, and expired September 16th, after receiving baptism from Mr. Ellis. She had previously given strict orders forbidding all heathen practices at her death. Many of the natives, however, fled to the mountains from fear that anarchy would be let loose, as in former times, but their fears were groundless. Her funeral was conducted in a quiet and orderly manner, with solemn religious rites, which was considered a signal triumph of Christianity over pagan superstition.

* Of a remarkably interesting and amiable character, she had already embraced Christianity in spite of bitter opposition, and had set her face against the debauchery and revelry of the court.

Mr. Wm. Ellis, accompanied by Messrs. Thurston, Bishop, and Goodrich, was engaged from the beginning of July to the end of September in making a thorough exploration of the island of Hawaii, of which he published a very interesting and valuable report.

Liholiho's Voyage to England and His Death.—About this time Liholiho decided to visit England and the United States. In this he was actuated partly by curiosity to see foreign lands, and partly by a desire to secure protection for his country, especially against Russia. A council of the high-chiefs was held at Lahaina to consider the subject, at which Kaahumanu was acknowledged as regent with Kalanimoku as her prime-minister, and Kauikeaouli confirmed as heir-apparent.

KAMEHAMEHA II.

The king embarked in an English whale-ship, "L'Aigle," commanded by Captain Starbuck, an American. He was accompanied by Kamamalu, the queen, by Boki and his wife, Liliha, by Kekuanaoa, Kapihe, Manuia, and James Young.

The king and chiefs were very anxious that Mr. Ellis should accompany the party, and offered a large sum for his passage, but Captain Starbuck positively refused to receive him. Jean B. Rives, the Frenchman, secretly took passage with them, and was employed as interpreter. They sailed from Honolulu November 27th, 1823, amid the sad forebodings of the people.

The king had placed on board twenty-five thousand dollars in coin, which Captain Starbuck took charge of. The "L'Aigle" touched at Rio Janeiro, where they received distinguished attentions from the British consul-general and the emperor, Dom Pedro. During the voyage, "no pains were spared to induce the chiefs to drink and gamble."

On arriving at Portsmouth, May 22d, 1824, Captain Starbuck landed them without providing for their comfort or giving notice to the government. On being informed of their arrival by the owners, the government appointed the Hon. F. Byng as their guardian, and paid all their expenses while in England.

When their cash-chests were opened at the Bank of England, only ten thousand dollars were found, and no account was ever rendered of the balance by Captain Starbuck, who alleged that three thousand dollars had been spent at Rio Janeiro, and some more on the way from Portsmouth to London. Rives was dismissed from his office as interpreter on account of gross misconduct, and James Young was appointed in his place.

The royal company received great attention from the English nobility, were feasted and flattered, and taken to see all the sights and shows of London.

About the 10th of June, Manuia, the steward, was attacked by the measles, and soon the whole party were taken ill. The inferior chiefs soon recovered, but the queen grew rapidly worse, her lungs were affected, and in spite of the best medical attendance she died on the 8th of July.

This sad event so affected the spirits of the king that he sank rapidly and expired on the morning of the 14th. The survivors were treated with great kindness, and were received by the king, George IV., at Windsor Castle, September 11th, where he advised them to attend to the instructions of the missionaries, and promised to protect them from foreign aggression.

The Rebellion on Kauai, 1824.—Meanwhile the nation had suffered a great loss in the death of Kaumualii, king of Kauai, May 26th, 1824. His remains were deposited in Lahaina by the side of Keopuolani.*

By his will he bequeathed his dominion to Kaahumanu and Kalanimoku in trust for Liholiho.

When the news of his death reached Kauai, there was an outbreak of the heathen party, and many outrages were committed in different parts of the island. Kahalaia, a nephew of Kalanimoku, a young man unfit for the place, was appointed governor, upon which a conspiracy was formed to throw off the yoke. But Kapule, the widow of Kaumualii, remained loyal.

Soon after this Kalanimoku went to Kauai to settle the affairs of the island, and to look after the wreck of the "Cleopatra's Barge" at Hanalei. In a council which he called at Waimea, he declared the will of Kaumualii, and refused to make the new division of lands demanded by the disaffected chiefs.

On this Kiaimakani and other heathen chiefs invited George Humehume, who was living at Wahiawá, to put himself at their head, and offered to make him king of Kauai and Niihau. He accepted the offer, and before light on the morning of the 8th of August they made a desperate attack on the fort at Waimea. After half an hour's hard fighting the rebels were repulsed with a loss

* Of him Mr. Stewart testifies that "he never knew of a word or action of his that was unbecoming a prince or even inconsistent with the character of a pious man."

of ten men, while six of the garrison were killed, including two young Englishmen.

The next day Kalanimoku sent a schooner to Oahu and Maui with the news of the rebellion, and by his advice Messrs. Bingham and Whitney took passage in it for Honolulu.*

The news of the war caused great excitement both at Honolulu and Lahaina. A thousand warriors from Oahu and two companies from Maui soon sailed for Kauai under the command of Hoapili, and landed at Waimea. After organizing and arranging his forces, Hoapili marched to meet the rebels August 18th.

As he was versed in ancient astrology, he spent night after night in studying the positions of the planets and principal stars in order to learn the result of the impending conflict. He gave orders to spare the vanquished, and to abstain from cruelty to prisoners and non-combatants.

The two armies met east of Hanapepe, two miles inland, where the insurgents were posted, with two field-pieces. These, however, in the hands of ignorant gunners, did little or no execution, and Hoapili's men, steadily advancing, captured them with the loss of only one man. Disheartened at this, the rebels gave way, and were pursued without mercy. In the action and pursuit forty or fifty of them were killed. Kiaimoku was shot, but George Humehume escaped to the mountains, where he was concealed for several weeks. At length he was captured and brought before Kalanimoku, who treated him kindly, and soon after sent him to Oahu, where he remained until his death in 1826.

* During the voyage Kamakakini, a young chief who had been taken prisoner, was stabbed in the night and thrown overboard.

Kaahumanu and the other high-chiefs held a grand council at Waimea, for the final settlement of the island of Kauai, which was now treated as a conquered province. The disaffected chiefs were distributed on the other islands, and their lands were divided among the loyal chiefs and their favorites. Kaikioewa, a famous warrior chief, was appointed governor.

At this time Mr. Ellis was obliged by the ill-health of his wife to return to England.

Progress of Education.—After the war was over, the leading chiefs exerted themselves more than ever to suppress drunkenness and vice, and to promote education.

Before the end of 1824, two thousand people had learned to read, and a peculiar system of schools was spreading rapidly over the islands. Each chief sent the most proficient scholars in his retinue to his different lands to act as teachers, with orders to his tenants to attend school. The eagerness of the people to acquire the new and wonderful arts of reading and writing was intense, and at length almost the whole population went to school. The time of school was from one to two hours in the afternoon, and the pupils were called together by the blowing of a conch-shell.

Kapiolani's Defiance of Pele.—Kapiolani, daughter of the great chief, Keawe-mauhili, of Hilo, was one of the noblest characters of her time. Her husband, Naihe, called the national orator, was the son of Keawe-a-heulu of Kaawaloa, where they generally resided.

Though at one time intemperate and dissolute, Kapiolani became an example to her countrywomen of virtue and refinement, and excelled them all in the readiness with which she adopted civilized habits and sentiments.

In December, 1824, she determined to break the spell of the belief in Pele, the dread goddess of the volcano. In spite of the strenuous opposition of her friends, and even of her husband, she made a journey of about one hundred and fifty miles, mostly on foot, from Kealakekua to Hilo, visiting the great crater of Kilauea on her way, in order to defy the wrath of Pele, and to prove that no such being existed.

On approaching the volcano, she met the priestess of Pele, who warned her not to go near the crater, and predicted her death if she violated the tabus of the goddess. "Who are you?" demanded Kapiolani. "One in whom the goddess dwells," she replied. In answer to a pretended letter of Pele, Kapiolani quoted passages from the Scriptures, setting forth the character and power of the true God, until the priestess was silenced, and confessed that *ke akua*, the deity, had left her. Kapiolani then went forward to the crater, where she was much surprised to find Mr. Goodrich, who had come from Hilo to meet her. "Mr. Ruggles, having been for six months without shoes, was unable to come." On the eastern brink of the crater a hut was built for her, in which she spent the night.

The next morning she and her company of about eighty persons descended over five hundred feet to the "Black Ledge." There, in full view of the grand and terrific action of the inner crater, she ate the berries consecrated to Pele, and threw stones into the burning lake, saying: "Jehovah is my God. He kindled these fires. I fear not Pele. If I perish by her anger, then you may fear Pele; but if I trust in Jehovah, and he preserve me when breaking her tabus, then you must fear and serve him alone. . . ." They then united in singing a hymn of praise to the true God, and knelt in adoration to the Creator and Governor of the universe.*

The "New Kaahumanu."—Scarcely less remarkable was the change in the character of Kaahumanu, the regent. Superior in intellect and in decision of character to most of the chiefs, she was haughty, overbearing, and cruel before her conversion. At first she treated the missionaries with disdain, but her mind became interested, first in the novel arts of reading and writing, and then in the new doctrines which they taught, and finally her heart and conscience were completely won over.

As she did nothing by halves, the change in her conduct and in her treatment of her people was so striking that they called her "the new Kaahumanu." From the beginning of the year 1825 she devoted herself with her wonted energy to the improvement of her countrymen, and made frequent tours among the islands, to promote education, and to urge the people to the practice of industry and virtue.

* This has justly been called "one of the greatest acts of moral courage ever performed."

CHAPTER XXV

1825–1827

VISIT OF LORD BYRON AND OUTRAGES BY FOREIGNERS

HILO VILLAGE

Visit of Lord Byron in the "Blonde."—In January, 1825, Captain Kotzebue made a second visit to the islands in the Russian sloop-of-war "Pretpriatie," in the course of his voyage around the world.

Captain Richard Charlton, who had been appointed by the British Government consul-general for the Society and Hawaiian Islands, arrived at Honolulu in the "Active" April 16th, 1825.

The 46-gun frigate "Blonde," commanded by Lord Byron, a cousin of the poet, was commissioned to convey the remains of the late king and queen and their attendants back to their native land. The "Blonde" arrived off Lahaina May 4th, 1825, and sent a boat ashore with Boki, Liliha, and their suite, who were received by Hoapili and a multitude of people with old-fashioned wailings, a few old veterans burying their faces in the sand. The little princess, Nahienaena, and other chiefs took passage in her to Honolulu, where the whole party landed on the 6th, and were received by the queen regent and other chiefs on the beach. The meeting between the survivors of the royal party and their old friends was an affecting scene. The next day a formal state reception of Lord Byron and his officers took place at the house of Kalanimoku. After the ceremonies of introduction Lord Byron made a courteous speech, and distributed the presents from the British Government, a gold watch to Kalanimoku, a silver teapot for Kaahumanu, and a rich suit of Windsor uniform, with hat and sword, for the little prince Kauikeaouli. "He instantly put it on, and strutted about the whole morning in an ecstasy."

On the 21st of May the remains of Kamehameha II. and his queen, Kamamalu, enclosed in triple coffins covered with crimson velvet, were landed and conveyed to a temporary mausoleum, with impressive funeral ceremonies, in which European and Hawaiian customs were combined.

On the 6th of June a national council of chiefs was held at Honolulu, for the purpose of settling the succession to the throne and other important affairs of government, at which Lord Byron was present. The young prince Kauikeaouli was proclaimed king with the title of Kamehameha III., and Kaahumanu was continued in the regency during the minority of the king, with Kalanimoku as her minister. Lord Byron expressed his approval of the objects and labors of the American mission, and gave the chiefs some useful suggestions. In particular, a set of port regulations were drawn up by his advice and published.

The next day the "Blonde" sailed for Hilo, taking Kaahumanu and her suite as passengers. Lord Byron, with his corps of scientific men, visited the volcano of Kilauea, where they occupied Kapiolani's hut, and surveyed the crater. He also caused an accurate survey to be made of the bay, which has since been called "Byron's Bay." He returned to Honolulu, where he remained four days, when he sailed for England, touching at Kealakekua Bay, where he erected a monument to the memory of Captain Cook.

Lord Byron was a worthy successor of Vancouver, and won the gratitude and respect of both the natives and the better class of foreigners. If he had left here a suitable representative of his government, imbued with his own humane and enlightened views, the subsequent history of the islands would have been very different.

Collisions with Foreigners.—Encouraged by Lord Byron's advice, the chiefs now proceeded to take more active measures for suppressing the vices which were destroying their race, and for promoting education. In the seaports of Honolulu and Lahaina this policy immediately brought them into collision with a lawless and depraved class of foreigners. It is said to have been the motto of the buccaneers that "there was no God this side of Cape Horn." Here, where there were no laws, no press, and no public opinion to restrain men, the vices of civilized lands were added to those of the heathen, and crime was open and shameless.

Accordingly, in no part of the world has there been a more bitter hostility to reform. As soon as laws began to be enacted to restrict drunkenness and prostitution, a series of disgraceful outrages were perpetrated to compel their repeal. Mr. Charlton, the British consul, put himself at the head of this faction, and from that time on persistently labored to embarrass the native government, and finally to overthrow its independence. He even denied the right of the native chiefs to make laws or treaties without the approval of the British Government.

Outrage at Lahaina, 1825.—The ship "Daniel," of London, commanded by Captain Buckle, arrived at Lahaina October 3d, 1825, and the crew soon found that a change had taken place on shore since their last visit. Two days later several of them entered Mr. Richards's house and threatened him and his wife with death if he did not procure the repeal of the obnoxious law.

Their calm and heroic demeanor seems to have saved their lives for a time. On the 7th a larger company, armed with knives and pistols, landed under a black flag and forced an entrance into the yard, when the natives interfered, barely in time to rescue the lives of their teachers. A strong armed guard was then kept on the place by Hoȧpili's order until the departure of the "Daniel."

A shower of meteoric stones fell at Honolulu September 27th, 1825.

Outrage of the "Dolphin," Lieutenant Percival.—On the 23d of January, 1826, the United States armed schooner "Dolphin," Lieutenant John Percival, arrived

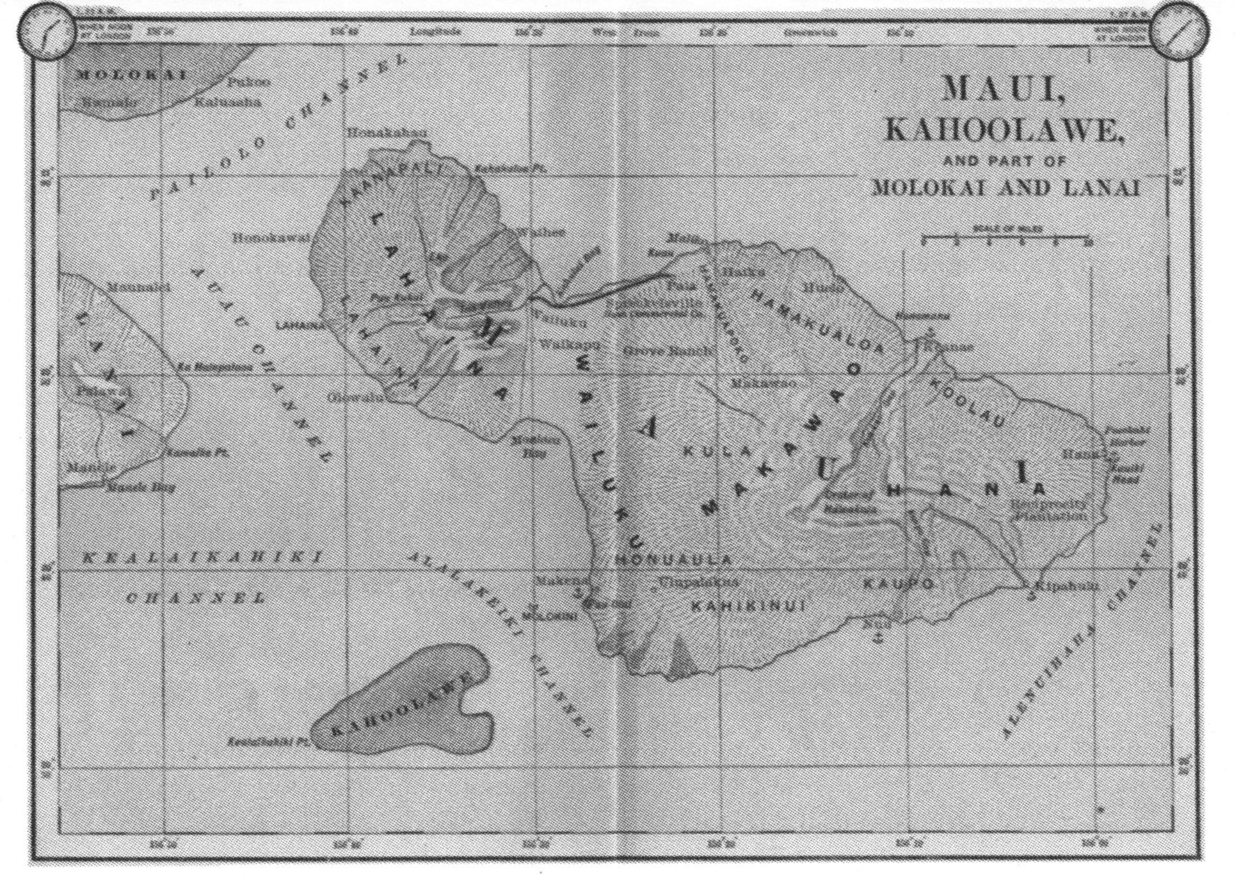
MAUI,
KAHOOLAWE,
AND PART OF
MOLOKAI AND LANAI
SCALE OF MILES
Longitude
West
Greenwich
MOLOKAI
Pukoo
Kaluaaha
PAILOLO CHANNEL
Honakahau
KAANAPALI
LAHAINA
Honokawai
Wailuku
Waikapu
Grove Ranch
Paia
Haiku
Huelo
HAMAKUALOA
Makawao
KOOLAU
HANA
KULA
MAKAWAO
WAILUKU
HONUAULA
Makena
Ulupalakua
KAHIKINUI
KAUPO
Kipahulu
ALENUIHAHA CHANNEL
AUAU CHANNEL
LAHAINA
Olowalu
LANAI
Palawai
Manele
KEALAIKAHIKI
CHANNEL
ALALAKEIKI CHANNEL
MOLOKINI
KAHOOLAWE

at Honolulu from the Marshall Islands, where he had taken off the surviving mutineers of the whale-ship "Globe." About this time the American ship "London" was wrecked at Lanai, and the "Dolphin" went there to save the cargo. On his return, February 22d, Lieutenant Percival called on the queen regent, and demanded the repeal of the law against vice, threatening violence if it were not done.

"My vessel is small," said he, "but she is just like fire."

On the 26th his men attacked the houses of Kalanimoku, who was ill, and the mission premises, and did considerable damage before they were driven off. Mr. Bingham was rescued from their hands by the natives, narrowly escaping with his life.

In the evening Lieutenant Percival waited on the chiefs, and again insisted on the repeal of the law. At length Governor Boki and Manuia, the captain of the fort, intimidated by his threats, permitted its violation, at which it is said that "a shout of triumph rang through the shipping." The "Dolphin" remained in port two months longer, and the pernicious influence exerted by its crew during that time cannot be described.*

Captain Beechey, in command of the British exploring ship "Blossom," visited the islands in May, 1826.

During this year mosquitoes, hitherto unknown in the islands, were introduced at Lahaina by the ship "Wellington," from San Blas, Mexico.

Second Outrage at Lahaina.—In October, 1826, the

* After Lieutenant Percival's return to the United States, a court of inquiry was convened at Charlestown, Mass., in May, 1828, to inquire into his conduct at Honolulu. The session lasted thirty-six days, and brought out a mass of evidence, sustaining most of the charges against him.

crews of several whale-ships landed at Lahaina, threatening to massacre Mr. Richards and his family, who happened to be absent at Kailua, Hawaii. They went in a body to demolish his house, but found it strongly guarded. They continued rioting several days, breaking open and plundering the houses of the natives. The native women had all fled to the mountains with Kekauonohi, who was acting as governess in Hoapili's absence, and remained there until the ships sailed for Oahu.

Visit of the "Peacock," Captain Jones.—Several memorials had been presented to the President of the United States by the ship-owners of Nantucket, complaining of the frequent mutinies and desertions of their crews, and representing that there was danger that the "Sandwich Islands would become a nest of pirates and murderers." They stated that nearly one hundred whale-ships visited the islands every year, and sometimes thirty were lying at the port of Honolulu at once.

Accordingly, Captain Thomas Ap Catesby Jones, commanding the United States sloop-of-war "Peacock," was sent to the islands to attend to these complaints, and "to secure certain debts due to American citizens by the native government." He arrived at Honolulu in October, 1826, and remained at the islands nearly three months.

He first turned his attention to the American runaway sailors, and rid the islands of thirty or more of them. He then took up the claims of American traders against the king and chiefs. Unfortunately, no list or schedule of these claims has ever been published. Captain Jones is said to have reduced them considerably, and yet he estimated them at the enormous sum of five hundred thousand dollars. There is reason to believe that many of them were exorbitant and unjust.

To provide for the payment of these claims an edict was issued, December 27th, that every able-bodied male subject should deliver half a picul of sandal-wood or pay four Spanish dollars before the 1st of September, 1827, and that every woman of age should deliver a mat twelve feet by six, or pay one dollar; the whole to be applied exclusively to the payment of these claims. The population of the islands at that time was estimated at one hundred and forty thousand.

On the 22d of December, 1826, a great council of chiefs was convoked by the queen regent, at which Captain Jones and the British consul were present. At this council Mr. Charlton declared that the islanders were subjects of Great Britain, and denied their right to make treaties, to which Captain Jones replied that Charlton's own commission as consul recognized the independence of the islands. The council then proceeded to business, and soon agreed to the terms of a commercial treaty with the United States, the first between the Hawaiian Government and any foreign power.

At a general meeting of the missionaries held at Kailua in October, a circular letter was drawn up and published, stating briefly the course which they had pursued, and challenging investigation. The challenge was accepted by their opponents, and they assembled in Honolulu early in December. A public meeting was held on the 8th at Governor Boki's house, which was presided over by Captain Jones, the opposition being headed, as usual, by Mr. Charlton.*

* Of this famous trial Commander Jones afterward wrote that "not one jot or tittle, not one iota, derogatory to their characters as men, or as ministers of the Gospel of the strictest order, could be made to appear against the missionaries by the united efforts of all who conspired against them."

After some desultory talk, the circular was read, and the opposition was invited to present charges in writing, and to support them by credible evidence. This they refused to do, and the meeting broke up *sine die.*

Boki's Relapse.—Boki, younger brother of Kalanimoku, on his return from England, had been reappointed governor of Oahu, and given the personal charge of the young king by Kaahumanu, an appointment which she soon had reason to regret. After a year or two, he and his wife, Liliha, relapsed into intemperance, ran into debt, and squandered much of the sandal-wood which had been collected for extinguishing the debts of the late king. He was led by designing foreigners to intrigue against the queen regent, and to lead the young king into habits of dissipation.

Death of Kalanimoku.—Kalanimoku, the prime minister, who was called by his countrymen "the iron cable of Hawaii," died at Kailua on February 8th, 1827, of the dropsy, from which he had suffered for several years. Originally of low rank, he had gained this high position by his ability and integrity. His death was a great loss to the cause of reform.

Third Outrage at Lahaina.—In October, 1827, another assault was made at Lahaina by the crew of the "John Palmer," an English whaler, commanded by Captain Clarke, an American. Governor Hoapili, having learned that several native women were on board, contrary to law, demanded that they should be landed. The Captain evaded and ridiculed the demand from day to day. At last one evening the governor detained him on shore, and seized his boat to enforce his demand. Upon Captain Clarke's promise to return the women in the morning, he was released. Meanwhile the crew had opened fire on the village with a nine-pound gun, aiming five shots at Mr. Richards's house, which, however, did little damage. The next morning Captain Clarke sailed for Honolulu, without keeping his promise.

Trial of Mr. Richards.—About the same time Captain Buckle arrived at Honolulu, and learned that a full report of his conduct in Lahaina in 1825 had been published in the United States. It was now seen that crimes committed at the islands were liable to be published on the other side of the globe, and the rage of Captain Buckle and his party knew no bounds. Even some of the chiefs, as Boki and Manuia, joined in condemning Mr. Richards.

Such threats were made against his life that the regent sent to Lahaina for him and the chiefs to attend a council in Honolulu. On their arrival two meetings were held, at which the chiefs decided that, as there was no question about the truth of Mr. Richards's statements, they would protect him at all hazards.

This ended the matter. Heavy guns were mounted on the fort at Lahaina, and the guard strengthened.

A few days after this affair, December 8th, 1827, the first written laws were published against murder, theft, adultery, rum-selling, and gambling. We read of no more outrages at Lahaina.

CHAPTER XXVI

1828–1832

CLOSING YEARS OF KAAHUMANU'S REGENCY

Arrival of Roman Catholic Missionaries.—Jean Rives, after being dismissed from the suite of Liholiho in England, went to France, where he represented himself as having great wealth and influence at the Hawaiian Islands. He purchased a cargo of goods on credit, chartered a ship to carry them to the islands, and advertised for laborers to cultivate his estates, and for priests and artisans to instruct his people.

A religious order had recently been founded by the Abbé Coudrin, which is often called the "Picpusian order," from the name of the street, Picpus, in Paris on which its headquarters are situated. It is more properly named the "Congregation of the Sacred Hearts of Jesus and Mary." In September, 1825, Pope Leo XII. gave to this Society the task of introducing the Catholic faith into the Hawaiian Islands. Accordingly, three priests of this order, Alexis Bachelot, prefect apostolic, Patrick Short, and M. Armand, were set apart for this mission.

They embarked at Bordeaux in the ship "Comet," Captain Plassard, in November, 1826, together with three lay brothers, who were mechanics. Church ornaments were shipped to the amount of several thousand dollars, which, together with the cargo, were to be paid for by Jean Rives at Honolulu. He himself took passage on the ship "Le Heros," Captain Duhaut-Cilly, to the western coast of America, and never appeared at the islands. He died in Mexico August 18th, 1833. Mr. Armand died during the voyage. After touching at Valparaiso, Callao, and Mazatlan, the "Comet" arrived at Honolulu July 7th, 1827, and anchored outside.

Captain Plassard, unable to sell his cargo, landed his passengers without a permit. Being ordered to take them away, he refused to do so, and sailed without them. The priests celebrated their first mass July 14th, and opened a small chapel about January 1, 1828, in which a small congregation was soon gathered. Boki and Mr. Charlton favored them, in the hope of enlisting them in their political party.

Boki's Conspiracy.—Meanwhile Governor Boki continued his course of extravagance, intemperance, and disloyalty. He set up a tavern on the harbor front, the "Blonde Hotel," and leased for a distillery a building which Kalanimoku had built for a sugar-house. To supply sugar-cane for this distillery he leased land in Manoa Valley, but Kaahumanu cancelled the lease, and had potatoes planted instead of cane.

Instigated by the two foreign consuls, he plotted to destroy Kaahumanu and supplant her as regent. In pursuance of this design, he sounded nearly every high-chief in the country without success, and labored in vain to shake the young king's attachment to the queen regent. About the beginning of 1829, he collected armed men at Waikiki, and civil war seemed imminent, when Kekuanaoa, his fellow-voyager to England, boldly went alone to his camp, and dissuaded him from his mad designs.

The First Laws, etc.—Soon after this an immense thatched house of worship was erected at Honolulu, which measured one hundred and ninety-six feet by sixty-three, and could seat four thousand people. It was opened for divine worship July 3d, 1829, the king taking a prominent part in the ceremonies of dedication.

In September, 1829, laws were published against murder, theft, gambling, and drunkenness, and also on the subject of marriage and the observance of Sunday. These laws were violently opposed by many of the foreign residents, who denied that they were amenable to the laws or courts of the kingdom. In reply to a memorial by Charlton and others, a proclamation was issued October 7th, addressed to the foreign residents, in which they were notified that these laws would be equally enforced on natives and foreigners.

The Visit of the "Vincennes."—At this juncture the United States sloop-of-war "Vincennes," Captain Finch, arrived at Honolulu, October 14th, bringing presents to the king and the principal chiefs, and a letter from the Secretary of the Navy, in which he congratulated them on their "rapid progress in acquiring a knowledge of letters and of the true religion." *

In a conference held to consider the claims of American merchants, the chiefs acknowledged about $50,000 as due to different merchants and ship-masters, and promised to pay the whole in nine months in sandal-wood, giving their note for four thousand seven hundred piculs. These claims, however, were not fully settled until 1843.

* The letter also contained the following important passage:

"Our citizens who violate your laws or interfere with your regulations violate at the same time their duty to their own government and country, and merit censure and punishment. We have heard with pain that this has sometimes been the case, and we have sought to know and to punish those who are guilty." In addition to this well-timed assurance from the American Government, Captain Finch gave the chiefs much valuable advice in regard to their rights and duties as an independent nation.

Mr. Stewart, chaplain of the "Vincennes," was greatly surprised at the progress made by the chiefs since 1824, not only in education, but also in luxury and refinement.

A new thatched palace had been built south of the fort, and elegantly furnished, and several two-story houses had been erected in the town. The ship-yard and wharf of Robinson & Co. had been established in 1827. The "Vincennes" sailed November 23d, having done much to repair the injury done by the visit of the "Dolphin."

Boki's Fatal Expedition.—Boki had been lavish in his presents to his partisans; his debts began to press hard upon him, and sandal-wood had become scarce. In November, 1829, an adventurer from Port Jackson reported that an island had been discovered in the South Pacific, which abounded in sandal-wood, and offered to guide an expedition to it. Boki immediately took the bait, and, against the advice of his best friends, hastily fitted out the king's brig "Kamehameha" and the "Becket." Kaahumanu was absent at the time on Kauai. Boki took command of the "Kamehameha," with about three hundred men, while Manuia, his confidential agent, had charge of the "Becket," with one hundred and seventy-nine men. Almost the whole company of opposers that he had collected went on this wild expedition. They sailed December 2d, 1829, touching at the island of Rotumá, where Boki remained four days, and took on board a large number of natives to assist in cutting sandal-wood. The "Becket" lay there ten days longer, and then followed on her way to their destination, which was the island of Eromango, in the New Hebrides.

Nothing more was ever seen or heard of Boki's vessel, the "Kamehameha," and her fate is still a mystery.

The "Becket" remained at Eromango five weeks, but the hostility of the inhabitants, and sickness among the people on board, defeated the object of the expedition. Many of them fell victims to the deadly climate, among whom was Manuia.

The survivors set sail for home, touching again at Rotumá, where they left twenty of their sick. They suffered dreadfully during the voyage from disease and privation, and when they arrived at Honolulu on the 3d of August, 1830, out of the whole company only twenty remained, eight of whom were foreigners.

The mournful sound of wailing was heard for weeks by night and by day throughout the district.

Kaahumanu's Tour of Hawaii and Maui.—In May, 1830, Kaahumanu, accompanied by the young king and Hoapili, made the circuit of the windward islands, leaving Liliha and Kinau in joint charge of affairs on Oahu for nine months. Their object was not to plunder the people, but to lighten their burdens, and to promote education and good morals.

It seems to have been on a previous trip in 1829 that she visited the *Hale o Keawe*, or mausoleum at Honaunau, Kona. On account of the heathen superstitions attached to the place, she caused the bones of twenty-four chiefs to be placed in coffins and entombed in a secret cave at Kaawaloa, and the house to be demolished.

The sacred *kauwila* rafters in it were used in building a government house in Honolulu, south of the fort, which was called the *Hale Kauwila.*

Liliha's Sedition.—During the absence of all the leading chiefs, and after the return of the "Becket," Liliha, fearing that she would lose her position as governess of Oahu, made warlike preparations. Encouraged by foreign sympathizers, she purchased arms and ammunition, and filled the fort with armed men from Waianae.

While the leading chiefs were assembled at Lahaina, Kinau managed* to send them information of Liliha's plot to detach the king from the regent and to overthrow the government.

As it was thought best to try peaceable measures first, Hoapili was sent to use his influence with his daughter, Liliha. The old warrior landed without troops or arms, called on Liliha, and required her to give up the fort to him, and to repair to Lahaina with her captain, Pakí. She obeyed, on which Hoapili took command of the fort, established a new garrison, and calmly awaited the arrival of the regent and the other chiefs, who arrived at Honolulu about the end of March, 1831.

At a national council held April 1st, 1831, Kuakini (Governor Adams), brother of Kaahumanu, was appointed governor of Oahu, and Naihe governor of Hawaii. Kuakini proceeded to vigorously enforce the laws of 1829, which had been allowed to become a dead letter under Boki and Liliha.*

Persecution of Catholics.—Governor Boki, by Kaahumanu's order, on the 8th of August, 1829, had published an order forbidding the natives to attend Catholic worship.

On Kaahumanu's return from Kauai, about the beginning of 1830, she undertook to reform some evils that had grown up under Boki's protection. At this time her attention was called to the progress of the Catholic faith, and she ordered the priests to desist from propagating it

* "Armed bands," says Jarves, "paraded the streets; grog-shops, gaming-houses, and other haunts of dissipation were suppressed; even riding was forbidden on Sunday."

among the natives. She commanded certain natives to give up their crucifixes, and threatened them with punishment if they continued to use them in their devotions.

Louisa, a native woman who had been baptized in California, was taken into her train, and, remaining firm in her belief, was treated with severity. Kaahumanu even intended to send her to Kahoolawe (which was then used as a place of banishment), but was dissuaded from doing so by Mr. Richards, and sent her back to Honolulu. During her absence at the windward, Kinau caused several persons to be punished for the same offense by hard labor in building stone walls or in braiding mats.

On her return from the windward, Kaahumanu continued the same policy, and in some cases had the offenders put in irons for what she considered insolent language.

Banishment of the Priests.—At the council of the high-chiefs, April 2d, 1831, a formal order was passed for the departure of the priests within three months, which was twice repeated afterwards. Meanwhile they continued their labors, chiefly among the adherents of Liliha.

In July, 1831, a Prussian ship, the "Princess Louisa," Captain Wendt, touched at the islands, bringing presents from the king of Prussia to Kamehameha III., among which were portraits of the king and of Marshal Blücher. Captain Wendt, being requested to take the priests away, refused to receive them on board unless he was paid five thousand dollars.

Letters had been received from the prefect of the Franciscan Missions in California inviting the priests to come to their assistance.

At length the chiefs fitted out a vessel of their own, the brig "Waverly," Captain Sumner, at an expense of about $4,000, and issued a proclamation December 7th, 1831, stating their reasons for taking this course. Accordingly, Messrs. Bachelot and Short sailed December 24th, and landed at San Pedro, California, on the 28th of January, 1832, where they were cordially received by the Franciscan fathers. The lay brothers remained behind to keep alive the embers of the faith.

With the lapse of two generations, the bitter animosities of those days have nearly died out, and all parties now regret that any religious persecution should ever have taken place in this kingdom.

Justice to the native government, however, requires some further explanation. It would have been strange, indeed, if the chiefs of that generation, brought up under the old *régime*, had been able to understand the principle of religious toleration or the distinction between church and state.

In ancient times each reigning family had its own tutelar deities, and the worship of those of a rival chief by a subject would have been considered an act of sedition. The civil war of 1819 was purely a religious war, and so was that of 1824 in a great measure. From that time any act that to their minds suggested image worship was regarded as a grave political offense.

This was the ground taken by Kaahumanu when Mr. Bingham remonstrated with her for compelling certain Catholic converts to work on the stone wall at Kulaokahua. In the minds of the chiefs they were also identified with the faction of Boki and Liliha, who were plotting the overthrow of the government. It was therefore not strange that the older chiefs regarded them not merely as an element of discord, but as a political party, dangerous to the state.

This persecution being confined to Honolulu, few of the American missionaries knew of it at the time.*

While many believed that the Hawaiian Government had a legal right under the law of nations to exclude foreigners whom it considered dangerous to the state, there is no evidence that as a body or as individuals they advised the exercise of that right.

From this time on the native government greatly needed a wise and able civilian in its service as a political adviser.

Lahainaluna Seminary.—In September, 1831, the Lahainaluna Seminary was founded, under the care of Rev. Lorrin Andrews. The scholars supported themselves in part by cultivating a tract of land granted by the chiefs to the school, and had to erect their own school-house and lodgings under the greatest disadvantages. A printing-press and book-bindery were afterwards attached to the school, at which many text-books were printed.

Death of Kaahumanu.—On the 29th of December, 1831, Governor Naihe died at Kaawaloa, and Kuakini (Governor Adams) returned to Hawaii to resume his former place as governor of that island. Kaahumanu paid a last visit to Kapiolani, and returned to Honolulu in very feeble health. She lived to receive the fourth reinforcement of American missionaries, which arrived in the "Averick," May 19th, 1832. She then retired to a cottage in Manoa Valley, where she had the pleasure of receiving the first complete copy of the New Testa-

* There is abundant evidence, however, that several of them remonstrated with the chiefs against persecution for religious opinions. A published letter, addressed by Kamehameha III. to the American consul, relates several instances of this.

ment in Hawaiian, and where, on the 5th of June, 1832, she passed away. Her place could not be filled, and the events of the next few years showed the greatness of the loss which the nation had sustained. The "days of Kaahumanu" were long remembered as days of progress and prosperity.

CHAPTER XXVII

1832-1836

THE BEGINNING OF KAMEHAMEHA III.'S REIGN

Kinau Premier.—The death of Kaahumanu marks an era in the history of the nation. Although the four succeeding years were years of peace and quiet as far as the foreign relations of the country were concerned, they were years of reaction, uncertainty, and disorder in its internal affairs.

Kinau had been appointed by Kaahumanu, by and with the advice of the council of chiefs, as her successor, with the title of Kaahumanu II. A joint declaration by her and the king was published July 5th, 1832. She was the daughter of Kamehameha I. and Kalakua, and a half-sister of the king. She had married Kekuanaoa, a chief of secondary rank, but of commanding ability, in October, 1827, and two of her sons afterwards succeeded to the throne. In a public address she declared her intention to carry out the policy of Kaahumanu. She was a princess of more than ordinary discretion and firmness, but could not fill the pre-eminent position of Kaahumanu.

Visit of the "Potomac."—The United States frigate "Potomac," Commodore Downes, from the East Indies, arrived July 23d, 1832, and anchored outside of the harbor. Commodore Downes and his officers had much friendly intercourse with all parties on shore. Having been informed that a company of Roman Catholics were forced to labor on the stone wall of Kulaokahua, he strongly represented to the chiefs the injustice and folly of punishing men for their religious opinions. They were liberated, and the persecution seems to have been discontinued for several years.

The claims of the traders were also discussed before the Commodore.

Arrival of a Japanese Junk.—A Japanese fishing-junk with four men on board, after drifting many months, arrived at Waialua, Oahu, December 23d, 1832. In an attempt to take the junk around to Honolulu it was wrecked on Barber's Point, January 1st, 1833, but no lives were lost.

KAMEHAMEHA III.

Accession of Kamehameha III.—After the death of Kaahumanu, the king came more under the influence of Liliha and Charlton, who did their best to lead him into dissipation, and to prejudice him against his old friends.*

He had surrounded himself with a company of dissipated young men of Liliha's faction, called "Hulumanu" (bird feathers), among whom one Kaomi, a renegade teacher of Tahitian descent, for a time had unbounded

* He had set his heart on buying a brig, which was offered to him for $12,000, but Kinau and the council refused to sanction the purchase, thinking it unwise to increase the public debt, which already pressed hard upon the poor people. The king yielded the point, but felt deeply the disappointment.

influence over him. This Kaomi was nicknamed "ke lii kui" (the engrafted king). Kinau was treated with insult, and forbidden to enter the king's presence, while Kaomi usurped her authority.

It was given out that all laws were abrogated except those against murder, theft, and rioting. Distilleries were set up in many places, grog-shops were multiplied, and heathen dances and drunken revels were encouraged as in Liholiho's time. Hoapili, the king's foster-father, hastened to Honolulu, to reclaim him if possible, but in vain.

About the middle of March, 1833, the king announced to his chiefs his intention "to take into his possession the lands for which his father had toiled, the power of life and death, and the undivided sovereignty." He summoned a public meeting, at which it was expected that he would set aside Kinau, and appoint either Liliha or the low-born Kaomi in her place. A great assembly was convened in the open air. Kinau came in, and saluting her brother, said: "We cannot war with the word of God between us." Civil war had indeed been apprehended by some.

The king made a speech, declaring his minority to be at an end, and asserting his claim to the sovereignty. Then, lifting his hand to appoint the second person in the kingdom, to the disappointment of Liliha's partisans, he solemnly confirmed Kinau as premier. When afterwards asked why he had done so, he replied, "Very strong is the Kingdom of God." "The effect was electrical. All felt that the days of misrule were numbered." (Jarves.)

For a time, however, there was a great reaction, as it was generally understood that the king was no longer on the side of morality. On Oahu, especially, the effect was disastrous. Schools were deserted, congregations thinned, and in a few places there was a partial revival of heathen practices. This year of disorder is known as "ka wa o Kaomi" (the time of Kaomi). But on the whole, the effect of the king's course was to sever whatever connection may have existed between church and state, and to settle Christianity on a more solid basis.

Most of the high-chiefs, including the governors of the other islands, stood firm, and used their authority to repress crime and disorder. After the shock of 1833 had passed over, a change for the better took place. The king's adoption of Kinau's third son, Alexander Liholiho, born February 9th, 1834, as his heir, helped to complete the reconciliation of the families.

In March, 1834, Hoapili and the other chiefs made the circuit of Oahu, and destroyed every distillery. Kaomi soon afterwards fell into neglect and ill-health. He lingered awhile in a hovel at Lahaina, and died on board of a schooner on his way to Honolulu.

Visit of the "Challenger."—The British ship-of-war "Challenger," Captain Seymour, arrived in 1834, to demand the execution of two Hawaiian sailors, who had murdered their commander, Captain Carter, an Englishman, on the voyage from California, on the "William Little," after which they had run the little vessel to Fanning's Island, and scuttled her there. Accordingly, they were arrested and hanged at the yard-arm of the king's brig, the "Niu." Captain Seymour thanked Kinau for her assistance in bringing them to justice.

Progress in Education and Religion.—The Rev. John Diell, seaman's chaplain, arrived in Honolulu May 1st, 1833, bringing with him from New London the frame of a chapel. This was erected on a lot given by the king and Kinau in the heart of the town, "in the very midst of grog-shops." It was opened for worship November 28th, 1833, under the name of the "Bethel Church," and henceforth formed a central rallying point for the better elements among the foreign residents and seamen. Its flag was "a welcome signal of peace and hope to many a mariner."

It was in 1832 that schools began to be opened for native children, which gradually took the place of those for adults.*

At the same time a subscription was opened among the foreign residents of Honolulu for the erection of a school-house for the instruction of English-speaking children, which was liberally aided by the ship-masters in port, and by the officers and men of the frigate "Potomac." A neat building of brick was erected, and opened on the 10th of January, 1833, under the name of the "Oahu Charity School," near the site of the present government building.

The first girls' boarding-school was opened in Wailuku in 1837, and a manual-labor school for boys was established the same year in Hilo, which still exists.

The first census of the kingdom was taken in 1832, and gave 130,313 as the total population of the islands at that time.

Another census was taken in 1836, which gave only 108,579 as the total. By all accounts the decrease of the native population at that period was alarming.

The first newspapers published in the Pacific Ocean were the *Lama Hawaii*, issued at Lahainaluna in February, 1834, and the *Kumu Hawaii*, printed at Honolulu in October of the same year.

The first English newspaper in Honolulu was published

* The number of readers that year amounted to 23,127.

during the year beginning July 30th, 1836, under the name of *The Sandwich Island Gazette.*

Trade and Agriculture.—The export of sandal-wood had fallen off from $400,000 worth in a year to only $30,000 worth in 1835, and the chiefs were burdened with debts in consequence of their former extravagance. Their principal resources were the sale of fire-wood and hides, and of supplies to the whale-ships, of which from fifty to one hundred a year called at Honolulu.

A tract of land at Koloa, Kauai, was leased to Ladd & Co. for a sugar plantation July 26th, 1835, and at the same time a silk plantation was started by Peck & Titcomb. Cotton now began to be raised and manufactured, and in 1837 Governor Kuakini built a stone cotton factory at Kailua, Hawaii.*

Second Visit of the "Peacock."—The United States frigate "Peacock," Commodore Kennedy, and the United States brig "Enterprise," Captain Hollins, arrived at Honolulu September 7th, 1836, and remained a month. During this time the commodore held conferences with the chiefs, at which the subjects of land titles and of the claims of traders were discussed without any decided result.

An old claim for $60,000 was acknowledged, besides another much smaller one.

The First Government House.—Until the death of Kinau nearly all of the actual administration of the government was left to her, as premier, and to her hus-

* The old system of land tenure was a great hindrance to progress. The idea of absolute ownership in land was unknown to the Hawaiians. No one could possess more than a life interest in it. It could not be bought and sold like movable property. Foreigners could not obtain more than a permission to occupy land at the pleasure of the chiefs, and it reverted to the king at their departure or death.

band, Kekuanaoa, the governor of Oahu, who also acted as judge. The "Hale Kauila," already mentioned, was the Government House, where the court records, the accounts of taxes, leases, etc., and the correspondence with foreign consuls were kept by a staff of native clerks, under the superintendence of Kekuanaoa. It was there that the consuls came to enter their complaints, and the commanders of ships of war to make their demands, and many scenes of thrilling interest took place within those walls.

KEKUANAOA

The idea, however, of a government as distinct from the person of the king, and of a treasury apart from his private income, had not yet taken shape in the native mind.

CHAPTER XXVIII

1836-1839

TROUBLES WITH FOREIGN POWERS

Causes of Dispute.—The chiefs were particularly tenacious of their rights on two points, which involved them in many disputes with foreigners.

The first was the ownership of land, which, according to their theory, belonged to the king as head of the nation, and could not be transferred without his consent, so that all foreign residents were but tenants at will. The second point was the right of the king to refuse permission to enter the kingdom to any foreigner who might be obnoxious to him.

While they denied that they had any intention to hinder foreigners from worshiping God in their own way, they forbade them to propagate the Roman Catholic religion among the natives, fearing that it would foment discord and sedition; and under this apprehension they persisted in harsh and impolitic measures, which imperiled the independence of the kingdom.

Arrival of the Rev. R. Walsh.—In 1835 the two exiled priests in California received a brief from the Pope exhorting them to persevere in their attempt to establish a mission in the Hawaiian Islands. On the 30th of September, 1836, the Rev. Robert Walsh, an Irish priest educated in Paris, arrived in Honolulu by the brig "Garafilia," from Valparaiso. He was ordered to leave the country, but by the intervention of the British consul obtained permission to remain until the arrival of the British sloop-of-war "Acteon," Lord Edward Russell.

Meanwhile, on the 8th of October the French corvette "Bonite," Captain Le Vaillant, arrived from Guayaquil.

Having been appealed to by Mr. Walsh, Captain Le Vaillant obtained permission for him to reside in the islands on condition that he should make no attempt to propagate his religion among the natives. Lord Russell arrived on the 23d, and after long and warm discussions, and not without threats, negotiated a convention, which was signed November 16th, defining the right of British subjects to land, reside, and build houses on the islands "with the king's consent." Damages were paid to a Mr. Geo. Chapman, whose house had been pulled down by Paki, the owner of the land. Lord Russell then sailed for Tahiti.

Death of Nahienaena.—The princess Harieta Nahienaena, once the pride of the nation, at last gave way to the temptations surrounding her, and after a brief career of dissipation died at Honolulu December 30th, 1836. She was born in 1815, and was married to Leleiohoku, son of Kalanimoku, in 1835. Her funeral took place with more than usual pomp February 4th, 1837.

The king was married February 2d to his favorite Kalama, the daughter of Kapihe (*alias* Naihekukui), a chief of low rank.

At this time the bark "Don Quixote" was purchased for the Hawaiian navy, and armed with fourteen guns, her name being changed to "Kai." On the 12th of April, 1837, the king took the remains of his sister to Lahaina in the "Kai," accompanied by a fleet of eight schooners. Her body was interred by the side of her mother, Keopuolani.

On the 9th of the same month the bark "Mary Frazier" arrived from Boston with the largest company of missionaries ever sent to the islands.

Return of Messrs. Bachelot and Short. — We now come to the second stage of this unhappy contest. The Rev. Fathers Bachelot and Short embarked from Santa Barbara in the "Clementine," a brigantine under English colors, the property of Mr. Jules Dudoit of Honolulu, and arrived at Honolulu April 17th, 1837. In the absence of the king and Kinau, Governor Kekuanaoa ordered the captain and the owner of the "Clementine" to receive the priests on board again, which they both refused to do. On the 19th he delivered an order to the priests to return to California in the vessel in which they had come, and his course was approved by the king and Kinau.

After many long and fruitless discussions, when the vessel was ready to sail, the order was reluctantly carried into effect on the 20th of May. After some remonstrance on the part of the mate, the priests were put on board of the "Clementine" without violence, on which Mr. Dudoit ordered the crew ashore, hauled down the flag, and carried it to Mr. Charlton, who burnt it in the street. Mr. Dudoit then made his protest before the British consul, affirming that the "Clementine" had been seized by the Hawaiian Government, and claiming $50,000 damages. The American consul also claimed heavy damages for Mr. W. French, who had chartered her on the 10th of May for another voyage.*

Arrival of the "Sulphur" and "Venus."—On the 7th

* Meanwhile Kinau kept the priests supplied with provisions.

of July, 1837, the British sloop-of-war "Sulphur," Captain Edward Belcher, arrived at Honolulu from San Blas, and on the 10th the French frigate "Venus," Captain Du Petit Thouars, from Callao. They were immediately applied to for the liberation of the priests imprisoned on board of the "Clementine." The two commanders, with the two consuls and other gentlemen, called upon Kinau at the Kauila House the same afternoon, and had a stormy interview. Captain Belcher so far forgot himself as to shake his fists in her face.

After he had left, Mr. Charlton returned and informed Kinau that the harbor was under blockade, and that all vessels except the "Clementine" were forbidden to leave. After inquiring about the meaning of this proceeding, she said: "My vessel shall sail." He replied: "No; she will be fired upon. If you wish to write to the king, your messenger can go upon our vessel with the letter." This Kinau refused. "No," she said, "my vessel shall sail."

In fact, it did sail without molestation. A body of marines from the "Sulphur" was sent to the "Clementine," and landed the priests, after which both commanders escorted them to their former residence. The British flag was now hoisted on the "Clementine," and she was sent to Lahaina for the king, who arrived on the 20th on his own man-of-war bark, the "Kai," accompanied by several schooners. The next day he gave audience to the two commanders, and had a long discussion with them, of which there is a full report.

Both commanders, while condemning the king's course, admitted his rights under the law of nations. During this conference Rev. H. Bingham was insulted and threatened by a foreign officer, so that the chiefs were obliged to interpose for his protection.

As a compromise, Captain Du Petit Thouars signed a pledge that M. Bachelot "would seize the first favorable opportunity to go to Lima, Valparaiso, or some other part of the civilized world," and that "in the mean time he should not preach." Captain Belcher signed a similar obligation for Mr. Short, and the king signed an agreement that the two priests might reside unmolested at Honolulu until such opportunity should occur. At another conference, he signed a brief convention with Captain Du Petit Thouars, guaranteeing to the French "equal advantages with the subjects of the most favored nation."

Both men-of-war sailed on the 24th, without exchanging salutes with the fort.

Visit of the "Imogene."—On the 24th of September, 1837, the British frigate "Imogene," Captain Bruce, arrived from Valparaiso, and remained until October 12th. Captain Bruce held four friendly conferences with the chiefs, in which he recommended a liberal system of toleration, but fully recognized the king's rights as an independent sovereign. He received a letter from the chiefs thanking him for his courtesy and valuable advice, and took charge of a petition to the British Government for the removal of Mr. Charlton.

He also offered Messrs. Bachelot and Short a free passage. Mr. Short sailed for Valparaiso October 30th, 1837, in the ship "Peru."

Arrival of Messrs. Maigret and Murphy.—The contest now entered on its third stage.

On the 2d of November, 1837, the ship "Europa," Captain Shaw, arrived from Valparaiso, bringing as passengers the Rev. L. D. Maigret, pro-vicar, and Mr. J. C. Murphy, or Brother Colomban, a catechist. Mr. H. Skinner, the owner of the vessel, had required his passengers, when in Valparaiso, to give bonds that they would not land in the islands without permission.

On their arrival, Kinau had the captain bound in the sum of ten thousand dollars not to allow the landing of the priests without a permit. Three Chilean political refugees who were on board were allowed to land. A long correspondence followed, in which Mr. Maigret stated that his object was to "remain here until he could get a passage to the Marquesas, or Dangerous Archipelago." The government, however, refused to permit him to land unless Mr. Dudoit would give pecuniary security for his departure within some definite time. Mr. Murphy was allowed to land on the certificate of the British consul that he was not a priest. He afterward returned to Tahiti, where he took an important part in affairs.

At length Mr. Maigret purchased a schooner, the "Missionary Packet," or "Honolulu," for $3,000, and sailed for Micronesia on the 23d. Mr. Bachelot, who was in feeble health, embarked with him; but unfortunately, instead of improving in health, he grew worse, and died at sea on the 4th of December. He was buried on the Island of Bonabe, where Mr. Maigret remained a short time, and then proceeded to the Gambier Islands, or Mangareva.

Volcanic Wave.—On the 7th of November, 1837, an extraordinary commotion of the sea was observed at all the islands. At Hilo the sea first receded, and then suddenly rose twelve feet above high-water mark, carrying away houses and doing great damage. Twelve lives were lost at Hilo, where many were saved by the boats of the "General Cockburn," an English whaler. A great earthquake took place in Chile on the same day. At Kahului,

Maui, two persons lost their lives. A similar phenomenon took place in May, 1819.

Persecution of Catholics.—On the 18th of December, 1837, the king and chiefs issued a severe "ordinance rejecting the Catholic religion," which forbade the teaching of that religion, or the landing of any teacher of it except in cases of necessity. During these years of angry controversy, it is to be deplored that the persecution of native Catholics was renewed. Toward the end of 1835, and at different times during the next three years, nearly thirty persons were set at forced labor, and a few were even required to work as scavengers in the fort, which then served as a prison.*

Edict of Toleration.—At last better counsels prevailed, and mainly through the influence of Mr. Richards, the king was induced to issue an edict of toleration, June 17th, 1839, which ordered that all who were then in confinement should be released, and that no more punishment should be inflicted on account of religion. The following week two women were found to be confined in the fort in irons, but were promptly released by order of Kekuanaoa, as soon as he was informed of it. This seems to have been the last case of religious persecution in the islands.

Temperance Legislation.—After being petitioned by many shipmasters, and by their own people, to restrict the sale of ardent spirits at Honolulu, the king and his council enacted the first license law, March 20th, 1838, under which the number of licenses was reduced from

* Foreign visitors remonstrated with as little effect as the missionaries. As late as September, 1838, Kinau, in reply to a letter from Captain Eliot of the British sloop-of-war "Fly," asked him: "What shall we do? Shall we return to idolatry and the shedding of blood?"

twelve to two. In August of the same year a law was passed prohibiting the importation of ardent spirits after January 1st, 1839, and imposing a duty on wines of fifty cents per gallon.

At the request of the Hawaiian Government, the President of the United States removed Mr. Jones in 1838, and appointed Mr. P. A. Brinsmade as American consul in his place.

Political Instruction.—The king and chiefs were well aware that their whole system of government needed to be remodeled, and had written to the United States in 1836 for a legal adviser and instructor in the science of government. Failing to procure such a person, in 1838 they chose Mr. Richards to be their adviser and interpreter. He was accordingly released from his connection with the American mission, and entered upon his duties in 1839 by delivering lectures on the science of government and assisting in drawing up the first constitution and code of laws.

The Great Revival.—The years 1838–1839 were memorable for the great religious revival, which extended to all the islands and affected nearly all the people. Over five thousand were admitted to the Protestant churches in 1839, and ten thousand the next year. During the years 1837 to 1839 seven thousand three hundred and eighty-two converts were admitted to the church in Hilo, under the charge of the Rev. Titus Coan. The effects of this revival were felt for many years after.

Death of Kinau.—Kinau died April 4th, 1839, after a short illness. The king appointed Kekauluohi or Auhea, daughter of Kalaimamahú and Kalakua (*alias* Kaheiheimalie) and niece of Kamehameha I., as her successor, thus keeping up the tradition of a female *kuhina nui.*

She was far inferior to Kinau in fitness to rule, but had been carefully trained in her youth, and made a repository of traditional lore.

Hostile Visit of the "Artémise."—The French sixty-gun frigate "Artémise," Captain Laplace, arrived at Honolulu July 9th, 1839. In the course of his voyage around the world the commander had received instructions at Sydney which obliged him to proceed to Tahiti and then to Honolulu. The French ministry of that day had adopted a vigorous colonial policy, of which the Marquesas, Tahiti, and New Zealand, as well as the Hawaiian Islands, felt the effects.

Captain Laplace, without waiting for any further information, or making any investigation, immediately issued a manifesto, the principal points of which are as follows:

"His Majesty, the king of the French, having commanded me to come to Honolulu, in order to put an end, either by force or persuasion, to the ill-treatment to which the French have been victims at the Sandwich Islands, I hasten to employ the latter means as more conformable to the noble and liberal political system pursued by France toward the powerless. Misled by perfidious counselors, the principal chiefs of the Sandwich Islands are ignorant that there is not in the whole world a power capable of preventing France from punishing her enemies, or they would have endeavored to merit her favor instead of incurring her displeasure, as they have done in ill-treating the French. . . . They must now comprehend that to tarnish the Catholic religion with the name of idolatry, and to expel the French under that absurd pretext from this archipelago, was to offer an insult to France and to her sovereign. . . . Among all civilized nations there is not one that does not permit in its territory the free exercise of all religions. I consequently demand—

"1. That the Catholic worship be declared free throughout all the islands subject to the king.

"2. That a site at Honolulu for a Catholic church be given by the government.

"3. That all Catholics imprisoned on account of their religion be immediately set at liberty.

"4. That the king place in the hands of the captain of the 'Artemise' the sum of twenty thousand dollars as a guarantee of his future conduct toward France; to be restored when it shall be considered that the accompanying treaty will be faithfully complied with.

"5. That the treaty, signed by the king, as well as the money, be brought on board of the frigate 'Artemise' by a principal chief; and that the French flag be saluted with twenty-one guns.

"These are the equitable conditions at the price of which the king of the Sandwich Islands shall preserve friendship with France. . . . If, contrary to expectation, and misled by bad advisers, the king and chiefs refuse to sign the treaty I present, *war* will immediately commence, and all the devastations and calamities which may result shall be imputed to them alone, and they must also pay the damages which foreigners injured under these circumstances will have a right to reclaim."

The king being absent at Lahaina, dispatches were sent to request his presence, while his secretary, Haalilio, was kept on board of the frigate as a hostage. The harbor was also declared to be in a state of blockade.

Notes were sent to the British and American consuls announcing Captain Laplace's intention to commence hostilities on the 12th at noon, and offering protection on board of his frigate to such of their countrymen as should desire it. In his note to the American consul he added: "I do not, however, include in this class the individuals who, although born, it is said, in the United States, form a part of the Protestant clergy of the chief of this group, direct his counsels, influence his conduct, and are the true authors of the insults offered to France. For me, they compose part of the native population, and must undergo the unhappy consequences of war which they will have brought on this country."

The American missionaries therefore inquired of their consul whether the government of the United States would protect their lives and property, to which he replied that within the inclosure of his consulate, under the flag of his country, he could guarantee them an asylum.

At the request of the premier, Kekauluohi, the date for commencing hostilities was postponed until Monday, the 15th, in order to give time for the king to arrive. But on Saturday afternoon, as the king had not arrived, Kekuanaoa went on board of the frigate, and delivered to Captain Laplace the treaty signed by Kekauluohi and himself on behalf of the king, together with the twenty thousand dollars, part of which had been loaned by some of the foreign merchants to the government.*

The next morning, at nine o'clock A.M., the 14th, the king arrived, and soon after Captain Laplace, accompanied by one hundred and fifty men with fixed bayonets and a band of music, proceeded to a thatched building belonging to the king, where a grand military mass was celebrated by Rev. R. Walsh, the service concluding with the Te Deum.

As the Hawaiian Government, contrary to Captain

*The money was carefully counted and packed in four boxes, which were sealed with red wax with the seal of the Hawaiian Government.

Laplace's expectation, had been able to satisfy the demands made upon it, a further "convention" was drawn up and presented to the king at 5 P.M. on the 16th, which he was required to sign by breakfast time the next morning. No amendment of its objectionable clauses was allowed; it must be signed as received, or not at all. The king requested time to consult with his chiefs, but Captain Laplace refused to grant it, and the "convention" was signed. Its most important articles were the fourth and the sixth; the former stipulating that no Frenchman should be tried for any crime, except by a jury of foreign residents nominated by the French consul, and the latter providing that "French merchandise, especially wine or brandy, shall not be prohibited, nor pay a higher duty than five per cent. ad valorem." Having accomplished its errand, the "Artemise" sailed on the 20th.

Visit of Commodore Read.—On the 19th of October, 1839, the United States frigate "Columbia," Commodore Read, and the "John Adams," Captain Wyman, arrived at Honolulu, and remained until November 4th. The claims of Mr. Dudoit and of Mr. French for damages on account of the delay of the "Clementine" in 1837 were referred to Captain Read as umpire, and settled, on the 25th of October, by the payment of three thousand dollars to each of them. The commodore having been petitioned to hold a court of inquiry to ascertain whether the American missionaries had "lost their citizenship," or had been the cause of any persecution, declined to do so from want of time, but assured them of the protection of the United States.*

* Sixteen of the officers of the squadron signed a testimonial in their favor, and ordered one thousand copies of a pamphlet containing an account of the affair of the "Artemise" and a vindication of the American missionaries to be printed.

CHAPTER XXIX

1839–1842

FIRST CONSTITUTION—DISPUTES WITH CONSULS

The First Constitution.—During the year 1839 the first draft of the constitution was drawn up in the Hawaiian language at Lahaina by the council, aided by certain graduates of Lahainaluna.

A Declaration of Rights was signed by the king and promulgated June 7th, 1839, which may be considered as the Magna Charta of Hawaiian freedom.*

This act produced a feeling of security unknown before, and formed the first step in establishing individual property in land. Religious liberty was also guaranteed by the declaration: "All men of every religion shall be protected in worshiping Jehovah and serving Him according to their own understanding."

The first constitution was proclaimed October 8th, 1840. It perpetuated the offices of *kuhina nui* and of the four governors instituted by Kamehameha I., and defined their powers and duties. It constituted a legislative body, consisting of fifteen hereditary nobles and seven representatives, who sat together in one chamber and met annually. The representatives were elected by the people

* It contained the following important passage: "Protection is hereby assured to the persons of all the people, together with their lands, their building lots, and all their property, while they conform to the laws of the kingdom, and nothing whatever shall be taken from any individual except by express provision of the laws."

in a rather informal manner. The legislative body was to appoint four judges, who, together with the king and premier, should form the Supreme Court of final appeal.

New Laws.—The old laws were revised and new ones added, and the collection was published in 1842. They established a uniform system of government taxation, and abolished all the oppressive local and arbitrary taxes. They also abolished all arbitrary forced labor, and most of the oppressive tabus that formerly rested on fishing. The first school laws were enacted in 1841.*

On the 15th of May, 1842, all government property was set apart, and a treasury board created, consisting of four persons, of which Dr. G. P. Judd was chairman. By instituting a regular system of keeping the accounts, of paying government officers, and of collecting taxes, he soon established the credit of the government, and paid off the most pressing debts.

Deaths of High Chiefs.—About this time five of that noble band of chiefs who first welcomed Christianity passed from the stage of life, none of whom except Kinau left any children to fill their places. These were Kinau, the late premier, Kaikioewa, the veteran governor of Kauai, Hoapili, the brave and upright governor of Maui, his wife, Kalakua Kaheiheimalie, and the heroic Kapiolani. The loss was irreparable. The places of these natural leaders of their race could not be filled by foreigners or by natives of plebeian birth.

An Heroic Deed.—At noon on Sunday, the 10th of May, 1840, the schooner "Keola" foundered and sank a considerable distance west of Kohala Point. As there was

* That the laws were impartially carried out was proved by the public execution of the high chief Kamanawa, October 20th, 1840, for poisoning his wife, Kamokuiki.

a strong current running to the northward, the passengers and crew, seizing on oars, boards, etc., swam for Kahoolawe, then about thirty miles distant.

A Mr. Thomson of Lahaina was drowned, but his wife and two young men reached Kahoolawe the next day. Mauae of Lahaina and his noble wife, Kaluahinenui, swam together, each with an empty bucket for a support, until Monday afternoon, when his strength failed. His wife then took his arms around her neck, holding them with one hand and swimming with the other, until she found that he was dead, and was obliged to let him go in order to save her own life. After sunset she reached the shore, where she was found and taken care of by some fishermen, having been thirty hours in the sea.

Eruption and Volcanic Wave.—A great eruption from Kilauea commenced May 30th, 1840. The lava stream forced its way under-ground to the eastward, showing itself above ground at intervals, until it finally broke out twelve miles from the coast, and flowed into the sea at Nanawale in Puna. The flow continued for three weeks. A few small hamlets were overwhelmed, but no lives were lost.*

A volcanic wave took place May 17th, 1841, similar to that of 1837, but no lives were lost.

The United States Exploring Expedition.—The United States Exploring Expedition, commanded by Commodore Wilkes, was at the islands from September, 1840, until April, 1841. The squadron consisted of the flag-ship "Vincennes," the sloop-of-war "Peacock," under Captain Hudson, the brig "Porpoise," and the schooner "Flying Fish," with an accomplished corps of scientific observers.

* During this eruption the finest print could be read by its light at midnight at places forty miles distant.

Their intercourse with the king and people was of the most friendly nature, while their researches have proved to be of great value to science. An observatory was built on the summit of Mauna Loa, and occupied for three weeks in the middle of winter, and surveys were made of the principal craters on Hawaii as well as of all the important harbors of the group.

Educational Matters, etc.—A family school for the education of the young chiefs was founded in May, 1840. Fifteen young chiefs of high rank were educated in it through the medium of the English language for about ten years.

A school was founded at Punahou in 1842 by the American mission, which has since been chartered as Oahu College.

The translation of the Bible into the Hawaiian language was completed and published May 10th, 1839.

As far back as 1836 the project of building a large stone church at Kawaiahao in Honolulu had been discussed, and the sum of six thousand dollars was raised at that time by subscription, half of which was given by the king. The corner-stone was laid June 8th, 1839, and the edifice completed in 1841.

Progress of the Catholic Mission.—In May, 1840, the "Clementine" arrived from Valparaiso, bringing as passengers M. Etienne Rouchouse, bishop of Nilopolis, and vicar-apostolic, Rev. L. D. Maigret, and two other priests.

The erection of a cathedral was begun at Honolulu in July, 1840, and a considerable number of natives were soon enrolled as converts to their faith. In 1841 the Bishop of Nilopolis returned to France to procure a reinforcement, and in 1842 he sailed for the islands in the ship "Joseph and Mary," accompanied by seven priests, seven catechists, nine lay brothers, and ten nuns, with a large supply of silver crosses, chalices, and other church ornaments, and a cargo of goods for their mission. The ship foundered off Cape Horn, and was never heard from again.*

Difficulties with France.—In the mean time a number of petty disputes arose between Catholics and Protestants (especially in regard to the working of the new school and marriage laws), which seem to have been fomented by the French consul. He also objected to any restraint on the internal traffic in ardent spirits as an infraction of the Laplace convention; and such was the fear of France that for some years the license law of March 20th, 1838, was not enforced, to the great injury of the morals and health of the people.

On the 24th of August, 1842, the French corvette "Embuscade," Captain Mallet, arrived at Honolulu, but did not exchange the usual salutes. The captain called on Governor Kekuanaoa, and informed him that the French Government had taken the Marquesas Islands in July, and that there were complaints of violations of the Laplace convention, which he had been sent to investigate. On the 1st of September Captain Mallet sent a letter to the king, complaining that "French citizens and ministers of the Catholic religion have been insulted and subjected to divers unjust measures, concerning which Your Majesty probably has not been informed." He then made eight demands, chiefly relating to school matters, such as that "Catholic schools should be placed under the exclusive supervision of Catholic school agents, nominated by priests of the same faith and approved by the

* After this deplorable event, M. Maigret was appointed bishop of Arathia *in partibus*, and vicar-apostolic of Eastern Polynesia.

king," that land should be given for a Catholic high-school, etc., and expressed the opinion that the license law violated the Laplace convention by restricting the sale of French liquors.

To this the king made a courteous and dignified reply, assuring Captain Mallet that the convention had been faithfully observed, and that complete religious toleration was secured by the constitution and laws of his kingdom; that "the school laws were framed to promote education in these islands and not sectarianism, and ought not to be altered in the interest of any particular sect"; that "if there had been any instances of abuse, they were not authorized by the government," and that the courts of justice were open to all, and would afford redress, if appealed to. He added that the object of the license law was to regulate the *retail* sale of liquor, and prevent abuses, and that licenses could be obtained from the proper officers. In conclusion, he informed Captain Mallet that an embassy had been sent to France to ask for a new treaty. Captain Mallet replied that he would deliver the king's letter to Admiral Du Petit Thouars, who might be expected the next spring. The admiral was fully occupied in the mean time with the affairs of the Society Islands, which came under the French Protectorate September 10th, 1842.

Controversies with the British Consul.—The difficulties with France seem to have stimulated Mr. Charlton in the manufacture of grievances, which he hoped would eventually lead to the annexation of the islands to the British Empire. Happily, since the time of Boki no Hawaiian chief has ever been induced to act a disloyal part, or to join a foreign party, as was done at Tahiti.

At this time a number of complicated lawsuits arose

out of business transactions in Honolulu, which were tried before the governor with foreign juries, and led to bitter feeling between British and American residents. The report of one famous case, the "Estate of French and Greenway," fills two stout volumes.

In 1826 the chiefs had given two pieces of land to the British Government, one near the landing for a consulate, and another farther inland for an official residence. In April, 1840, Mr. Charlton put forward for the first time a claim for a tract of land adjoining the former, called Pulaholaho, and comprising nearly all of the block lying between Kaahumanu and Nuuanu Streets, on the strength of a pretended lease from Kalaimoku for two hundred and ninety-nine years, dated in 1826. The king replied that the land in question belonged by the most undoubted testimony and by virtue of continuous possession to Kaahumanu and her heirs, and that Kalaimoku had no authority to transfer any land without the consent of Kaahumanu, the regent. The alleged deed had been kept in abeyance until thirteen years after the death of Kalaimoku, and many houses had been built on the land without any objection having ever been made by Mr. Charlton.*

Ladd & Co.'s Contract, etc.—The Hawaiian Government, fully aware of the designs of its enemies, and that a crisis was approaching, had already taken steps to obtain the formal recognition of its rights as an independent state from the Great Powers, and to negotiate equitable treaties with them. As early as March 17th, 1840, Mr. T. J. Farnham, an American lawyer from Oregon, was commissioned as minister to the govern-

* It is believed by the best judges that the document either was a forgery, or was signed in ignorance of its real contents.

ments of Great Britain, France, and the United States, but nothing came of it. By an ill-advised measure the foreign relations of the government became involved with the schemes of a private firm. The firm of Ladd & Co. had taken the lead in developing the agricultural resources of the islands by their sugar plantation at Koloa and in other ways, and had gained the entire confidence of the king and chiefs. On the 24th of November, 1841, a contract was secretly drawn up at Lahaina by Mr. Brinsmade, a member of the firm, and Mr. Richards, and duly signed by the king and premier, which had serious after-consequences. It granted to Ladd & Co. the privilege of "leasing any now unoccupied and unimproved localities" in the islands, for one hundred years, at a low rental, each mill-site to include fifteen acres, and the adjoining land for cultivation in each locality not to exceed two hundred acres, with privileges of wood, pasturage, etc. These sites were to be selected within one year, which term was afterwards extended to four years from date, and cultivation was to be actually commenced within five years, which was also extended to ten years from date. The rights of native land-holders were to be strictly respected. It was further agreed that the said contract was to be null and void unless the governments of Great Britain, France, and the United States should acknowledge the Hawaiian Kingdom as an independent state. Mr. Brinsmade immediately left with the lease, in order to effect a sale of it to some joint-stock company, leaving one of his partners, Mr. Hooper, as acting consul. He was also intrusted with letters from the king to the three powers, proposing a triple guarantee of the independence of the Hawaiian Kingdom. In pursuance of these objects, he proceeded first to Washington, and afterwards to Europe.

The First Embassy to Foreign Powers.—In February, 1842, Sir George Simpson and Dr. McLaughlin, governors in the service of the Hudson Bay Company, arrived at Honolulu on business, and became interested in the native people and their government. After a candid examination of the controversies existing between their own countrymen and the Hawaiian Government, they became convinced that the latter had been unjustly accused. Sir George offered to loan the government ten thousand pounds in cash, and advised the king to send commissioners to the United States and Europe with full power to negotiate new treaties, and to obtain a guarantee of the independence of the kingdom.

Accordingly Sir George Simpson, Haalilio, the king's secretary, and Mr. Richards were appointed joint ministers-plenipotentiary to the three powers on the 8th of April, 1842.

Mr. Richards also received full power of attorney for the king. Sir George left for Alaska, whence he traveled through Siberia, arriving in England in November. Messrs. Richards and Haalilio sailed July 8th, 1842, in a chartered schooner for Mazatlan, on their way to the United States.*

Proceedings of the British Consul.—As soon as these facts became known, Mr. Charlton followed the embassy in order to defeat its object. He left suddenly on September 26th, 1842, for London *via* Mexico, sending back a threatening letter to the king, in which he informed him that he had appointed Mr. Alexander Simpson as acting-

* Their business was kept a profound secret at the time.

consul of Great Britain. As this individual, who was a relative of Sir George, was an avowed advocate of the annexation of the islands to Great Britain, and had insulted and threatened the governor of Oahu, the king declined to recognize him as British consul. Meanwhile Mr. Charlton laid his grievances before Lord George Paulet, commanding the British frigate "Carysfort," at Mazatlan, Mexico. Mr. Simpson also sent dispatches to the coast in November, representing that the property and persons of his countrymen were in danger, which induced Rear-Admiral Thomas to order the "Carysfort" to Honolulu to inquire into the matter.

Recognition by the United States.—Messrs. Richards and Haalilio arrived in Washington early in December, and had several interviews with Daniel Webster, the Secretary of State, from whom they received an official letter December 19th, 1842, which recognized the independence of the Hawaiian Kingdom, and declared, "as the sense of the government of the United States, that the government of the Sandwich Islands ought to be respected; that no power ought to take possession of the islands, either as a conquest or for the purpose of colonization; and that no power ought to seek for any undue control over the existing government, or any exclusive privileges or preferences in matters of commerce." *

* The same sentiments were expressed in President Tyler's message to Congress of December 30th, and in the Report of the Committee on Foreign Relations, written by John Quincy Adams.

CHAPTER XXX

1843

SUCCESS OF THE EMBASSY IN EUROPE, AND CESSION TO LORD PAULET

THE king's envoys proceeded to London, where they had been preceded by Sir George Simpson, and had an interview with the Earl of Aberdeen, Secretary of State for Foreign Affairs, on the 22d of February, 1843.

Lord Aberdeen at first declined to receive them as ministers from an independent state, or to negotiate a treaty, alleging that the king did not govern, but that he was "exclusively under the influence of Americans to the detriment of British interests," and would not admit that the government of the United States had yet fully recognized the independence of the islands.

Sir George and Mr. Richards did not, however, lose heart, but went on to Brussels March 8th, by a previous arrangement made with Mr. Brinsmade. While there, they had an interview with Leopold I., king of the Belgians, who received them with great courtesy, and promised to use his influence to obtain the recognition of Hawaiian independence. This influence was great, both from his eminent personal qualities and from his close relationship to the royal families of England and France.

Encouraged by this pledge, the envoys proceeded to Paris, where, on the 17th, M. Guizot, the Minister of Foreign Affairs, received them in the kindest manner, and at once engaged, in behalf of France, to recognize the independence of the islands. He made the same statement to Lord Cowley, the British ambassador, on the 19th, and thus cleared the way for the embassy in England.

They immediately returned to London, where Sir George had a long interview with Lord Aberdeen on the 25th, in which he explained the actual state of affairs at the islands, and received an assurance that Mr. Charlton would be removed. On the 1st of April, 1843, the Earl of Aberdeen formally replied to the king's commissioners, declaring that "Her Majesty's Government are willing and have determined to recognize the independence of the Sandwich Islands under their present sovereign," but insisting on the perfect equality of all foreigners in the islands before the law, and adding that grave complaints had been received from British subjects of undue rigor exercised toward them, and improper partiality toward others in the administration of justice. Sir George Simpson left for Canada April 3d, 1843.

The Belgian Contract.—Messrs. Richards and Haalilio then returned to the Continent in order to obtain the official recognition by France, in procuring which they met with unexpected delays.

Unfortunately they were induced by Mr. Brinsmade to join him at Brussels in negotiating a contract with the "Belgian Company of Colonization," a wealthy corporation, in which the king of the Belgians was a stockholder. The contract was signed May 17th, 1843, by the three parties interested. The firm of Ladd & Co., through Mr. Brinsmade, was to cede to the Belgian Company the lease of November 24th, 1841, and its other property in the islands, while the king of the Hawaiian Islands, represented by Mr. Richards, was to guarantee four per cent. interest on the capital for six years, secured by a mortgage on the revenues of the country, besides making other concessions, and the Belgian Company was to organize a branch society under its own control (to be called "The Royal Community of the Sandwich Islands"), and to transfer to it all the property and privileges which it had received under the contract. The king was to be a partner and Mr. Richards a director in the new company, which, however, never went into operation, although its "statutes" were drawn up in fifty-three articles, and signed April 13th, 1844.

The interest of Ladd & Co. was fixed at one million and sixty-seven thousand francs, or about two hundred thousand dollars. The capital of the branch society was to consist of four thousand shares of one thousand francs each. Each of the emigrants sent to the islands was to receive twenty hectares or nearly fifty acres of land in fee simple.

It was agreed, however, that the contract was not to be carried out until the independence of the Hawaiian Islands should be officially acknowledged by France, and that if it was not ratified by the council-general of the Belgian Company within one month after the said acknowledgment, it should be null and void. This ratification does not appear to have ever been given. Whether the ratification of the king of the Hawaiian Islands was necessary, has been a disputed question. It was certainly required and given for the acts of Mr. Richards as ambassador. The Belgian contract was signed by Haalilio with great reluctance, and received by the king and chiefs with strong disapprobation, which was justified by its pernicious consequences.

The Demands of Lord George Paulet.—Meanwhile,

events of thrilling interest had been taking place at the islands. On the 10th of February, 1843, the British frigate "Carysfort," commanded by Lord George Paulet, arrived at Honolulu, and showed displeasure by withholding the usual salutes. The commander seems to have placed himself completely under the direction of Mr. Alexander Simpson. The United States sloop-of-war "Boston," Captain Long, arrived on the 13th.

The king, who had been sent for at Lord Paulet's request, arrived from Lahaina on the 16th. Lord Paulet refused to treat with him through Dr. Judd, his agent, and late in the evening of the 17th sent him a peremptory letter, inclosing six demands, with the threat that if they were not complied with by four o'clock P.M. the next day, "immediate coercive steps would be taken." The substance of these demands was as follows:

1st. That an attachment laid on Charlton's property, at the suit of an English firm for an old debt, be removed, that the land claimed by him be "restored," and reparation be made to his representatives for the losses which they had suffered through the alleged injustice of the government.

2d. The immediate recognition of Mr. Simpson as British consul, and a salute of twenty-one guns to the British flag.

3d. A guarantee that no British subject should be put in irons, unless for a felony.

4th. That a new trial should be held in the case of Skinner *vs.* Dominis.

5th. That all disputes between British subjects and others be referred to mixed juries, one half of whom should be British subjects approved by the consul.

6th. A direct communication between the king and

the acting British consul for the immediate settlement of all complaints on the part of British subjects.

The next morning, February 18th, the frigate was cleared for action, and her battery brought to bear on the town. Some English families went on board of the brig "Julia," lying outside of the harbor, while Americans and other foreigners placed their funds and valuable papers on board of the "Boston."

The first impulse of the king and chiefs was to resist, but wiser counsels finally prevailed, and before the hour set for hostilities had arrived, a letter was sent on board of the "Carysfort," informing Lord Paulet that ambassadors had been sent to England with full power to settle these very difficulties; that some of these demands were "calculated to seriously embarrass this feeble government by contravening the laws established for the benefit of all," but that nevertheless the king would comply with them under protest, and appeal for justice to the British Government.

At 2 P.M. salutes were interchanged between the fort and the frigate, and Monday, the 20th, was appointed for the reception of Mr. Simpson as vice-consul. The attachment on Charlton's property was removed by public advertisement.*

The Provisional Cession.—On the 20th the king visited the "Carysfort," where he was received with royal honors, and the next day was fixed for a private interview with Lord Paulet and Mr. Simpson. At this and another interview on the 23d, the most extravagant and unjust demands were pressed upon the king, who was treated

* At the same time the king and premier published their solemn protest against the proceedings of Lord Paulet, and their appeal to the justice and magnanimity of the queen of England for redress.

with insolence, and not allowed any opportunity of consulting with his advisers.

Under the first demand, the king was intimidated into signing the pretended deed from Kalaimoku to Mr. Charlton. He was also forced to sign a note for $3,000, to Henry Skinner, a nephew of Charlton, for "indirect damages" caused by the attachment. Under the fourth demand, it was shown that the case had been settled a year before by the arbitration of Sir George Simpson, and a receipt given in full of all demands, but this was of no avail. Under the sixth head, Simpson demanded the arbitrary reversal of several decisions of the courts, and brought in a new list of claims for damages, so that a "mushroom debt" of $80,000 had grown up in a few hours.

Under these circumstances, the king resolved to bear it no longer. "I will not die piecemeal," said he; "they may cut off my head at once. Let them take what they please; I will give no more."

Dr. Judd advised him to forestall the intended seizure of the islands by a temporary cession to Lord Paulet, pending an appeal to the British Government. The event proved the wisdom of this advice.

At the same time, the king was strongly urged by the leading foreign residents to cede his kingdom to France and the United States jointly, until his difficulties could be settled by the mediation of these two powers, and such an act of cession was offered him to sign, which he declined to do.

On the next day the subject was discussed by the king and his council, and preliminaries were arranged with Lord Paulet for the cession. On the morning of the 25th the king and premier signed a provisional cession of the islands to Lord George Paulet, "subject to the decision of the British Government after the receipt of full information from both parties."

At three o'clock P.M. February 25th, the king, standing on the ramparts of the fort, read a brief and eloquent address to his people.*

The act of cession was then publicly read, and a proclamation by Lord Paulet, after which the Hawaiian flag was lowered by natives. The British colors were then hoisted over the fort by a lieutenant from the "Carysfort," and saluted by the ship and the fort. At the same time the flag over the British consulate was struck. It chanced that the day was the forty-ninth anniversary of Kamehameha's cession to Vancouver.

The British Commission.—The proclamation issued by Lord Paulet declared that the government should be carried on, as far as natives were concerned, by the native king and chiefs and their officers; and in all that concerned foreigners by a commission, consisting of a deputy appointed by the king, Lord George Paulet, D. F. Mackay, Esq., and Lieutenant Frere of the "Carysfort." All laws enacted by the legislature and all *bona fide* engagements of the late government were to remain in force. The king and premier appointed Dr. Judd as their deputy in the commission, and left for Maui on the 27th.

Nothing more was heard of the claims brought

* The following is a translation of the address: "Where are you, chiefs, people, and commons from my ancestors, and people from foreign lands! Hear ye! I make known to you that I am in perplexity by reason of difficulties into which I have been brought without cause; therefore I have given away the life of our land, hear ye! But my rule over you, my people, and your privileges will continue, for I have hope that the life of the land will be restored when my conduct shall be justified."

against the late government. The commission now proceeded as if it had been settled that the islands should permanently remain a British colony. Every Hawaiian flag that could be found was destroyed. All foreigners holding land in any way were notified to send in their claims to the commission before June 1st, 1843, and new registers were given to vessels owned at the islands, putting them under the British flag. The government vessels were taken as "tenders for H. B. M.'s ship 'Carysfort,'" the name of the "Hooikaika" being changed to "Albert," and that of the "Paalua" to "Adelaide." An additional duty of one per cent. was added to the three per cent. required by law, to pay the expenses of the commission. The principal business of the commission was of the nature of a police court. No jury trials were held during its existence.

Without investigation or trial by any court, Lord Paulet had already seized the land claimed by Mr. Charlton, and had it cleared of its occupants, twenty-three houses being demolished, and one hundred and fifty-six persons expelled from their homes.

On the 11th of March the "Albert" was dispatched to San Blas, Mexico, to carry Mr. Alexander Simpson with letters for the British Foreign Office. As the firm of Ladd & Co. had previously chartered this vessel, they reserved the right to send a commercial agent by her.

It was of vital importance to the king that he should be represented in London at this critical juncture. Accordingly, Mr. J. F. B. Marshall (who acted as Ladd & Co.'s messenger) was secretly commissioned as His Majesty's envoy, and took passage in the same vessel with Mr. Simpson without exciting any suspicion on his part.

A canoe had been sent beforehand with a picked crew from a distant part of Oahu, to notify the king and premier, who came down in a schooner, landed at Waikiki by night, read and signed the prepared documents, and immediately returned to Wailuku. The "Victoria" sailed March 17th for Valparaiso with letters for Admiral Thomas.

During the month of April the legislative body held a session at Lahaina. At this session a complete register was made for the first time of all the lands in the kingdom, with the names of their respective holders. This work occupied about ten weeks. It proved that no large tract of land was unoccupied.*

The commissioners, having been informed that there was gross corruption in the management of the prison in the fort, made it a pretext for abrogating certain laws against licentiousness. Orders to this effect were issued April 27th, and sent to the governors of the other islands, and all prisoners under arrest were set free. The effect on public morals was disastrous. Vice became open and shameless, as in the days of Liholiho.

In consequence of this action, Dr. Judd presented his resignation May 10th, withdrawing the king from any further responsibility for the acts of the commission. Mr. Mackay had previously resigned on account of ill-health, so that the commission was now reduced to two persons, viz., Lord Paulet and Lieutenant Frere.

Meanwhile a secret correspondence was kept up between the king at Lahaina and his officers at Honolulu by means of canoes manned by trusty retainers.

* During this session, April 26th, the first anniversary of the Lahaina Temperance Society was celebrated, and a large quantity of liquor, which had lain for a year untouched in the king's cellar, was emptied into the sea.

A small standing army of natives had been enlisted by the commission under the name of the "Queen's Regiment," who were made to swear allegiance to the queen of England, and were commanded and drilled by British officers.

Heavy drafts were made on the government treasury for their support. On the 12th of June Dr. Judd received directions from the king not to pay any more money for the support of the army. On the 20th the commissioners demanded $713 for the "Queen's Guard" and the police, and threatened to put another person in the treasury office if he refused. Accordingly, on the 24th the king and premier published a manifesto, charging the commission with having broken the terms agreed upon at the cession, by abrogating some of the laws, and by draining the treasury for the support of a useless standing army.

Fearing imprisonment and the seizure of the national archives, Dr. Judd removed these from the government house and concealed them in the royal tomb.*

On the 1st of July the "Carysfort" sailed for Lahaina and Hilo, returning on the 16th. The next day the British sloop-of-war "Hazard," Captain Bell, arrived from Tahiti. On the 6th the U. S. frigate "Constellation," Commodore Kearney, arrived from China. On the 11th the commodore issued a protest against the cession and the proceedings of the British Commission. The young chiefs and Governor Kekuanaoa, on visiting the "Constellation," were saluted under the Hawaiian flag, at which Lord Paulet took great umbrage. The king returned from Lahaina

* "In this abode of death," says Jarves, "surrounded by the former sovereigns of Hawaii, and using the coffin of Kaahumanu for a table, for many weeks he nightly found an unsuspected asylum for his labors in behalf of the kingdom."

on the 25th, and on the next day the British flag-ship "Dublin" arrived from Valparaiso, bearing the pennant of Rear-Admiral Thomas, commander-in-chief of H. B. M.'s naval forces in the Pacific Ocean.

The Restoration.—Hardly had the "Dublin" come to anchor before the admiral in the most courteous terms solicited a personal interview with the king, and in a few hours it became known that he had come to restore the independence of the islands. On the following day the terms of the restoration were agreed upon, and arrangements were made for the ceremonies to take place on Monday, the 31st.

A proclamation was issued by Admiral Thomas, in which he declared in the name of his sovereign that he did not accept of the Provisional Cession of the Hawaiian Islands, and that "Her Majesty sincerely desires King Kamehameha III. to be treated as an independent sovereign, leaving the administration of justice in his own hands." A convention of ten articles was signed by the king and Admiral Thomas, which stringently guarded British interests, although it fully recognized the king's rights.*

The 31st of July, a day memorable in Hawaiian history, was clear and cloudless. An open space on the plain east of the town, since called "Thomas Square," had been selected for the ceremonies of the day, two pavilions having been erected and a flag-staff planted. Thither poured the entire population of Honolulu, to witness the restoration of the flag. At ten o'clock A.M., the marines of the "Dublin," "Carysfort," and "Hazard" being drawn

* The king also published an "Act of Grace," pardoning all offenses committed during the interregnum, and granting ten days of rejoicing, during which all government work was to be suspended.

up in line, with a battery of field-pieces on their right, the king, escorted by his own troops, arrived on the ground. As the Hawaiian royal standard was hoisted, a salute of twenty-one guns was fired by the field battery, after which the national colors were raised over the fort and on Punchbowl Hill, and saluted by both forts and by the four men-of-war in port, followed by loud and long cheering from the assembled multitude. After the saluting, various evolutions were performed by the marines, after which the king was escorted to his residence, where the natives belonging to the late "Queen's Regiment" came before him to sue for pardon, and to swear allegiance to their rightful sovereign.

At one o'clock P.M. the king attended a thanksgiving service in the Kawaiahao church, where he addressed the people, informing them that, as he had hoped, "the life of the land" had been restored, using the words which have since been adopted as the national motto, "*Ua mau ke ea o ka aina i ka pono*"—the life of the land is perpetuated by righteousness.*

Before the festival was over, the American frigate "United States," Commodore Jones, arrived (August 3d), and soon afterwards the "Cyane," Captain Stribling, bringing news of the success of the king's envoys in Europe.

Admiral Thomas took up his residence on shore while awaiting the approval of his own government. In the mean time, he gave his assistance in establishing order and morality, and in harmonizing the conflicting parties. His noble act of justice was fully approved by the home

* The admiral's declaration was then interpreted, after which John Ii addressed the assembly, announcing the general amnesty and a festival of ten days.

government, as, in the words of Lord Canning, "marked by great propriety and admirable judgment throughout, and as calculated to raise the character of the British authorities for justice, moderation, and courtesy of demeanor, in the estimation of the natives of those remote countries, and of the world."

CHAPTER XXXI

1843-1847

RECOGNITION OF THE INDEPENDENCE OF THE ISLANDS

As was stated on page 246, Messrs. Simpson and Marshall sailed together on the "Albert" for San Blas, the former having no suspicion of Mr. Marshall's real errand. They have well been compared to the acid and alkaline powders lying quietly side by side in a box of seidlitz powders. They landed at San Blas on the 10th of April, 1843, and traveled in company across Mexico to Vera Cruz, where they parted, Mr. Simpson proceeding directly to England, while Mr. Marshall hastened to Washington, where the news of the cession of the islands created great excitement.

He arrived in Liverpool June 28th, a week later than his rival, Mr. Simpson. Lord Aberdeen had already, on the 13th of June, assured the Hawaiian envoys that "Her Majesty's government had no intention to retain possession of the Sandwich Islands," and a similar declaration was made to the governments of France and the United States.

Mr. Marshall was soon joined by Messrs. Richards and Haalilio from Paris, after which the three commissioners opened a correspondence with the Foreign Office in reply to the charges brought by Messrs. Simpson and Charlton against the Hawaiian Government. In this they were aided by the ready pen of Mr. Brinsmade, as well as by the influence and advice of the Hudson Bay Company. At their urgent request the whole controversy was referred to the law advisers of the crown, who decided in favor of the Hawaiian Government on every point except the Charlton land claim. In regard to this last, they required "that Mr. Charlton, having first produced the original deed and shown it to be genuine, should be put in possession of the land by the government." Lord Aberdeen, however, declined to consider any claim for damages caused by the illegal acts of Lord Paulet, for the alleged reason that the cession was "a voluntary act" on the part of the king.

At length, on the 28th of November, 1843, the two governments of France and England united in a joint declaration to the effect that "Her Majesty, the queen of the United Kingdom of Great Britain and Ireland, and His Majesty, the king of the French, taking into consideration the existence in the Sandwich Islands of a government capable of providing for the regularity of its relations with foreign nations, have thought it right to engage reciprocally to consider the Sandwich Islands as an independent state, and never to take possession, either directly or under the title of a protectorate, or under any other form, of any part of the territory of which they are composed. . . ."

This was the final act by which the Hawaiian Kingdom was admitted within the pale of civilized nations. Finding that nothing more could be accomplished for the present in Paris, Messrs. Richards and Haalilio returned to the United States in the spring of 1844. On the 6th of July they received a dispatch from Mr. J. C. Calhoun, the Secretary of State, informing them that the President regarded the statement of Mr. Webster and the appointment of a commissioner "as a full recognition on the part of the United States of the independence of the Hawaiian Government."

A Mr. George Brown had previously been sent out as United States commissioner, arriving at Honolulu October 16th, 1843.

General William Miller had been appointed consul-general for Great Britain August 25th, 1843. He had greatly distinguished himself in the Chilean war of independence, and had risen to the rank of lieutenant-general in the Chilean army. He had visited the islands in 1831, in the Prussian ship "Princess Louisa." It may be said, however, that he was a better soldier than diplomatist.

General Miller arrived at the islands in February, 1844, bringing with him a convention with England, which was nearly a copy of that exacted by Captain Laplace, and which was signed by the king with the express understanding that it was to be only temporary. Admiral Thomas then took leave of the islands, where his name will long be held in grateful remembrance.

Organization of the Government.—The Hawaiian ship of state might then be regarded as safely launched. Much, however, remained to be done in order to organize a civilized government, "capable of providing for the regularity of its relations with foreign nations."

It was early seen by the king's advisers that in order to constitute a permanent government it would be necessary to combine the foreign and native elements together as subjects and officers of one common government, to make the king the sovereign not merely of one race or class, but of all, and to extend equal and impartial laws over all residents.

The office of Secretary of State was instituted, and held

by Dr. Judd from November 2d, 1843, until March 26th, 1845, when, at his instance, it was given to Robert Crichton Wyllie, Esq.*

The want of a competent legal adviser of the crown had long been felt. Accordingly, on the 9th of March, 1844, Mr. John Ricord, who had then just arrived from Oregon, and who was versed in the civil as well as the common law, was appointed attorney-general. Mr. Richards arrived at Honolulu March 23d, 1845, after a long voyage around Cape Horn. His colleague, Haalilio, who had long been in feeble health, died at sea, December 3d, 1844. His remains were brought to Honolulu, and deposited in the royal tomb with much ceremony and sincere mourning.

In the spring of 1845 a severe epidemic of influenza passed over the islands, and among others Kekauluohi, the premier, died June 7th, 1845, and was succeeded in office by John Young, Jr.

About this time Mr. Richards was appointed Minister of Public Instruction, and proceeded to organize and improve the public schools. At his death, on the 7th of November, 1847, Mr. Armstrong was appointed as his successor, and held the office until his death, in 1860.

On the 20th of May, 1845, the legislature was formally opened for the first time, by the king in person, with fitting ceremonies. At this session Mr. Ricord was ordered by a joint resolution to draft a series of acts organizing the five executive departments of the government. The duties on imports were raised to five per cent.

Meanwhile there was considerable agitation among the

* He was a Scotchman by birth, who had spent many years in South America. For twenty years he employed his multifarious learning, indefatigable energy, and sagacity in the service of his adopted country.

natives, especially on Maui, headed by David Malo, the historian, who petitioned the king to dismiss all foreigners from his service except Mr. Richards, not to allow any more to be naturalized, and not to sell any land to foreigners.* The king and John Young made a tour around the island of Maui, and addressed the people at several places, explaining and defending the policy of the government.

At the legislative sessions of 1846 and 1847, the first two volumes of statute laws drafted by Mr. Ricord were finally passed, and the complicated machinery of the government was set in operation, very nearly as it has been run ever since.†

Land Commission.—The king and chiefs were now fully convinced that their ancient system of land tenure (described on pages 27 and 215,) was the great hindrance to their further progress in civilization, and saw that it was continually involving them in disputes with foreigners.

By Dr. Judd's advice the legislature passed an act on the 10th of December, 1845, constituting a "Board of Commissioners to quiet Land Titles," before which all persons were required to file their claims to land within two years, or be forever barred. This board continued in office until March 31st, 1855.

After a long investigation it was finally settled that there were but three classes of persons having vested rights in land, viz.: 1st, the king, 2d, the chiefs, and 3d, the tenants or common people. The Land Commission decided that if the king should allow to the landlords one

* About three hundred and fifty foreign residents had been naturalized up to 1846.

† At this session the Minister of Finance was able to report that the national debt (which had amounted to $160,000 in 1842) was then entirely extinguished. The government remained out of debt during the rest of this reign.

third, to the tenants one third, and keep one third himself, "he would injure no one but himself."

The king and chiefs for years endeavored in vain to make some division among themselves which would enable each of them to hold land independently in fee simple. At last the subject was brought before the Privy Council in December, 1847, when the principles of the division among the king, the chiefs, and the government were finally settled. A committee was appointed, of which Dr. Judd was the chairman, to bring about this division.

The work was commenced January 27th, 1848, and completed in forty days.*

The day after the first partition with the chiefs was closed, the king again divided the lands which had been surrendered to him, setting apart half of them for the government, and reserving the remainder for himself as his own private estate. The former were known as government lands, and the latter as crown lands. By this grand act Kamehameha III. set an illustrious example of liberality and public spirit. Most of the chiefs afterwards (in 1850) gave up a third of their lands to the government, in order to obtain an absolute title to the remainder.

The common people were offered fee-simple titles for their house lots and the lands which they actually cultivated for themselves, commonly called *kuleanas*. The number of claims finally confirmed amounted to eleven thousand three hundred and nine. The awards for these were recorded in ten huge folios, which were deposited in the Land Office. Aliens were not allowed to own land in fee simple until July 10th, 1850.

* The book in which it is recorded is called the "Mahele Book," or book of division.

Thus a solid foundation was laid for individual property in land, and the poor serfs became owners of their homesteads.

The Judiciary.—The weakest point in the government, of which its enemies took every possible advantage, was the administration of justice in foreign cases. Hitherto, all such cases had been tried by juries composed of foreigners, with Governor Kekuanaoa as judge. The fact that the judge had to depend on the attorney-general for advice on points of law gave occasion for numerous complaints. Party spirit ran very high, while the course of the attorney-general was not conciliatory or calculated to inspire confidence in his impartiality.

At this juncture the brig "Henry" arrived from Newburyport, October 12th, 1846, with fifteen passengers on board, bound for Oregon. Among these was Mr. William L. Lee, a talented young lawyer, highly recommended by Professor Greenleaf and Judge Story. Fortunately he was persuaded to remain and accept the position of chief-justice, which he held until his death. To say that he was "the right man in the right place" gives but a faint idea of his eminent services to the country. He organized the courts of justice, and so conducted the highest tribunal that it soon acquired universal confidence and respect, and instead of being a source of weakness, became the strongest pillar of the government.

As president of the Board of Land Commissioners he performed a most arduous and responsible task. Although he was not the originator of that great reform, his was the guiding mind in carrying it on.*

Material Progress in the '40's.—The progress of the

*Mr. Ricord's departure in July, 1847, threw additional labors upon Judge Lee, to be mentioned hereafter.

country during these years in wealth and resources was steady but slow, from the want of convenient markets. The revenue of the government rose from forty-one thousand dollars in 1843 to one hundred and fifty-five thousand dollars in 1848, and the national debt was paid off. Among the public improvements made at this time may be mentioned the first horse-road over the Nuuanu Pali, opened June 7th, 1845, the old custom-house built in 1848, and a palace of coral stone, built on the site of the present one in 1844.

The exports were still small, averaging about seven hundred thousand dollars per annum, of which only one third was domestic produce. The furnishing of supplies to the whaling fleet was a great resource in those days. Over fifty whalers were sometimes at anchor off Lahaina at once, and about five hundred touched at the islands during the year 1845. Their influence on the morals and health of the people was pernicious.

Agriculture.—As has been stated, the first sugar plantation was started at Koloa, Kauai. Another was started in Kohala in 1841, and one in Wailuku soon afterwards. The wages then paid to laborers only averaged twenty-five cents a day. The amount exported rose to five hundred tons in 1843, but then fell off, and did not reach that figure again for ten years. The methods in use were rude and wasteful, the mills being mostly worked by oxen or mules, and the molasses drained in the old-fashioned way.

The first coffee plantation was started at Hanalei, Kauai, in 1842, and promised well at first, but the growers became discouraged by the blight, and gave it up. The export rose to two hundred and eight thousand pounds in 1850, but then fell off.

The first silk was exported in 1844, having been raised at Hanalei by Mr. Charles Titcomb. Although the quality was excellent, the enterprise was not a financial success.

The first experiments in wheat-raising were made in Makawao in 1845, and a few years later it became a flourishing branch of industry.

The Discovery of Gold in California.—The discovery of gold in California in 1848 formed an era in the history of the islands. In August of that year the first party left Honolulu for the gold diggings, and the rush continued for several months. It opened a new market for the productions of the islands, which has been increasing in importance ever since.

Decrease in Population.—No census of the kingdom was taken between 1836 and 1850, but it is certain that the decrease in population was rapid. Of the high chiefs, besides the premier, Governor Adams or Kuakini died December 9th, 1844, Kekauonohi June 2d, 1847, and Leleiohoku, son of Kalanimoku, October 21st, 1848. During the year 1848 the measles was introduced from California, and spread through the group for the first time. The mortality was dreadful.*

Relations with France.—For five years the relations between the islands and France continued to be of the most friendly nature. From 1843 until 1848 scarcely a complaint was made, and the bishop of Arathia, speaking for his countrymen, said: "We esteem ourselves happy in living under a government that so well understands the liberty of conscience." This was largely owing to the ability, tact, and courtesy shown by the French consul, M. Dudoit.

*It is supposed that it carried off one tenth of the people.

On the 22d of March, 1846, the French frigate "Virginie," Rear-Admiral Hamelin, arrived at Honolulu. On the following day the admiral restored the twenty thousand dollars which had been delivered to Captain Laplace July 13th, 1839. The money was brought on shore in the original cases and with the seals unbroken.*

The New Treaties.—The same ship brought Mr. Em. Perrin, special commissioner from the king of the French, who brought with him new treaties with the Hawaiian Government, concerted between England and France in identical terms, which did away with all former conventions. Although a decided improvement on the Laplace convention, they contained two objectionable clauses, which proved to be a fruitful source of trouble in subsequent years. The third article provided that no French or British subject should be tried except by a jury nominated by the consul of his country. The sixth article provided that import duties should not exceed five per cent., except for "wines, brandies, and spirituous liquors," which should "be liable to any reasonable duty which did not amount to a prohibition."

No modification being allowed, the two treaties were signed by the king, March 26th, 1846. At this same time he sent to both governments a strong remonstrance against the third and sixth articles.

Consular Grievances.—For several years the small foreign community of Honolulu was kept in a state of turmoil, and rent by party animosity.

On the one hand, the king's ministers claimed for him all the rights of an independent sovereign, while on the other, the representatives of England and the United

* Nothing could exceed the courtesy shown by the admiral during his short stay in port.

States claimed the rights of "ready access" to the king and of "diplomatic interference" with the internal affairs of the kingdom. In 1845 extraordinary efforts were made to discredit the government abroad and to break it down at home. The dispute over the "Belgian Contract" added to the excitement. In 1846, by order of the legislature, Mr. Wyllie prepared a table of "consular grievances," which formed a roll one hundred and twenty feet long. At length the course of Mr. Brown, the American commissioner, became so hostile and insulting that all official intercourse with him was suspended July 29th, 1845.

On the 1st of June, 1846, the United States ship "Congress," Commodore Stockton, arrived at Honolulu, bringing A. Ten Eyck, Esq., the new commissioner, and Joel Turrill, Esq., the new consul. All the outstanding petty disputes were immediately settled, and for nearly ten years not a single complaint was made by an American consul.

Captain Steen Bille, of the Danish corvette "Galathea," in the course of a scientific voyage around the world, arrived at Honolulu October 5th, 1846. On the 19th he negotiated the first fair and honorable treaty with this country, and one which has served as a model for other treaties.

End of the Belgian Contract, 1846.—While Mr. Brinsmade was in Europe, vainly endeavoring to persuade the Belgian Company to carry out their contract (page 240), the firm of Ladd & Co. had failed in business, and in November, 1844, the government, which had aided them with loans, levied on their property, and sold it for the benefit of their creditors.

In May, 1845, the firm claimed the right of selecting lands under the original contract of November, 1841 (page 236), which the government denied, on the ground that they had transferred it to the Belgian Company. On Mr. Brinsmade's return in March, 1846, he brought a claim against the government for damages to the amount of $378,000, chiefly for having, as he alleged, prevented the Belgian contract from being carried out.*

On the part of the government it was held that the Belgian contract of May 17th, 1843, was contrary to the constitution and laws of the islands, and inconsistent with existing treaties, and that its execution would have been fatal to the native race, and would have ruined all foreign trade except through the Belgian Company.

Difficulties with the British Consul.—For several years the government was involved in unfortunate disputes with General Miller, which were finally referred to the British Government, and settled in 1847. The Charlton land claim gave rise to a misunderstanding as to the meaning of Lord Aberdeen's decision (page 253). The Hawaiian Government held the view that Mr. Charlton was to produce his title before a court, and there prove its genuineness and validity. General Miller limited the question to the genuineness of the handwritings, and evidently considered it a mere matter of form. After a long correspondence he presented a peremptory demand from the British Government, and on the 23d of August, 1845, took possession of the land in question, without having even shown the alleged deed. An investigation was held at the palace during the month of October, 1845,

* The government agreed to refer this claim to the arbitration of Messrs. J. F. B. Marshall and S. H. Williams, and offered its archives for their inspection. Mr. Ten Eyck acted as counsel for Ladd & Co., and Mr. Ricord for the government. After the trial had lasted four months, and filled six hundred and thirteen printed pages, Ladd & Co. withdrew from it, before the government had brought in its evidence. Other attempts to effect a compromise failed, and the question long remained unsettled, to divide and embroil the foreign community.

when a mass of evidence was taken on the subject, which was sent to England, and also published here, and which to most minds was entirely conclusive against Mr. Charlton's claim.

While this appeal was pending, H. B. M.'s eighty-gun ship "Collingwood," Admiral Seymour, having been sent for by General Miller to enforce his demands, arrived August 6th, 1846. The admiral, however, consented to act as umpire in the matter, his decision being subject to revision by his own government. Accordingly, a second investigation was held at the palace, from August 25th until September 1st, a full account of which was sent to England.

The final award of the British Government, which confirmed that of Admiral Seymour, was not received until August 13th, 1847. It decided that Mr. Charlton was not to be disturbed in the possession of the land called Pulaholaho, but sustained the Hawaiian Government on the other points in dispute, viz.: that the government might erect wharves in front of the land of Pulaholaho, and that a certain James Ruddack should submit his petty boundary quarrels to the local courts.

CHAPTER XXXII

1848–1851

FOREIGN RELATIONS

The Grievances of Consul Dillon.—On the 1st of February, 1848, the French corvette "Sarcelle" arrived at Honolulu, bringing Mr. Patrick Dillon, the new French consul, commissioned to exchange the ratifications of the treaty of March 26th, 1846.

On the 15th a full-length portrait of Louis Philippe, the king of the French, was presented to Kamehameha III. with much ceremony and with the most friendly assurances.

But these pleasant relations did not continue long. Mr. Dillon was soon involved in personal quarrels with his predecessor and with Mr. Wyllie, and reversed the policy of the past five years, endeavoring to reopen all the old disputes which had been closed, and to manufacture new grievances in every possible way. He carried to the last extreme the policy of "diplomatic interference" with the internal affairs of the kingdom.*

His principal grounds of complaint were the high duty on brandy and the alleged partiality shown to the English language.

The Ten Demands.—In April, 1849, the questions at issue between the Hawaiian Government and Mr. Dillon were referred directly to the French Government, and his recall was requested.

* In six months his correspondence with Mr Wyllie filled nearly four hundred printed pages.

At the same time Mr. Dillon wrote to the French admiral for a naval force to support his demands.

On the 12th of August, 1849, the French frigate "Poursuivante," Admiral De Tromelin, arrived at Honolulu, and was joined the next day by the steam corvette "Gassendi," from Tahiti. On the 22d Admiral De Tromelin sent the king a peremptory dispatch containing ten demands which had been drawn up by Mr. Dillon, as follows:

1. The complete and loyal adoption of the treaty of March 26th, 1846.
2. The reduction of the duty on French brandy to fifty per cent. *ad valorem*.
3. The subjection of Catholic schools to the direction of the chief of the French Mission, and to special inspectors not Protestants, and a treatment rigorously equal granted to the two worships and to their schools.
4. The use of the French language in all business intercourse between French citizens and the Hawaiian Government.
5. The withdrawal of the (alleged) exception, by which French whalers, which imported wine and spirits, were affected, and the abrogation of a regulation which obliged vessels laden with liquors to pay the custom-house officers placed on board to superintend their loading and unloading.
6. The return of all duties collected by virtue of the regulation the withdrawal of which was demanded by the fifth article.
7. The return of a fine of twenty-five dollars paid by the whale ship "General Teste," besides an indemnity of sixty dollars for the time that she was detained in port.
8. The punishment of certain school-boys, whose impious conduct (in church) had occasioned complaint.
9. The removal of the governor of Hawaii for allowing the domicile of a priest to be violated (by police officers, who entered it to make an arrest), or the order that the governor make reparation to that missionary.
10. The payment to a French hotel keeper of the damages committed in his house by sailors from H. B. M.'s ship "Amphitrite."

The Hawaiian Government was allowed three days in which to make a satisfactory reply to these demands. If they were not acceded to, the admiral threatened to cancel the existing treaty, and to "employ the means at his disposal to obtain a complete reparation."

About noon of the 25th, a firm but courteous reply was sent to the admiral, declaring that the government had faithfully observed the treaty of 1846; that the existing duty on brandy was so far from being "an absolute prohibition" that the importation of French brandy had greatly increased under it; that rigorous equality in the treatment of different forms of worship was already provided for, but that public schools supported by government funds should not be placed under the direction of any mission, whether Catholic or Protestant; and that the adoption of the French language in business was not required by the treaty or by international law, and was impracticable in the state of the islands.

In reply to the fifth and sixth demands, it was stated that the laws in question applied equally to all vessels of whatever nation, that the ship "General Teste" had violated the harbor laws, and that the penalty in her case had already been reduced from five hundred dollars to twenty-five dollars. In regard to the last three demands, the admiral was informed that the courts of the kingdom were open for the redress of all such grievances, and that until justice had been denied by them there could be no occasion for diplomatic interference.

The government offered to refer any dispute to the mediation of a neutral power, and informed the admiral that no resistance would be made to the force at his disposal, and that in any event the persons and property of French residents would be scrupulously guarded.

The "Reprisals" made by Admiral Tromelin.—The same afternoon an armed force was landed with two field-pieces, scaling-ladders, etc., which met with no opposition, and took possession of an empty fort. The Hawaiian flag, which was flying over it at the time, was never hauled down. The invaders also took possession of the custom-house and other government buildings, and seized the king's yacht, together with seven merchant vessels in port. Perfect order prevailed during the whole time of the occupation, and no French citizen was molested in any way.

The occupation continued for ten days, during which nearly all business was interrupted. All communication with the other islands was stopped. No coasting vessels were allowed to leave, and all arriving from the other islands were at once taken and anchored under the guns of the "Gassendi." On the 28th, at the suggestion of the admiral, a conference was held on board of the "Gassendi," between himself and Mr. Dillon on the one side, and the king's commissioners, Messrs. Judd and Lee, on the other side.*

During this conference the work of dismantling the fort was going on, and was continued until noon of the 30th. The guns were spiked and broken; the magazine was opened, and the powder poured into the sea. The furniture, calabashes, and ornaments in the governor's house were destroyed.

On the 30th the admiral issued a proclamation, declaring that by way of "reprisal" the fort had been dismantled, and the king's yacht, "Kamehameha III.," confiscated, but that private property would be restored. He also declared

*At this conference the duty on brandy was discussed for several hours, but no agreement was arrived at, and the admiral refused to refer any point to arbitration.

the treaty of 1846 to be annulled, and replaced by the Laplace Convention of 1839. This last act, however, was promptly disavowed by the French Government. The British and American consuls had both protested against his proceedings, the former declaring them to be a violation of the convention of November 28th, 1843.

The yacht "Kamehameha" sailed for Tahiti, September 4th, and on the following day both men-of-war left, the "Gassendi" for Valparaiso and Europe, and the "Poursuivante," with Mr. Dillon and family on board, for San Francisco, where Mr. Dillon afterwards held the office of French consul-general.

The Second Embassy to Europe.—It was immediately resolved by the king and council to send Dr. Judd as special commissioner to France, together with the two young princes, Alexander Liholiho, the heir-apparent, and his brother, Lot Kamehameha. They sailed for San Francisco September 11th, 1849, in the schooner "Honolulu," amid hearty cheering from the shore, while all the ships in port manned their yards in their honor.

In San Francisco they met Charles Eames, Esq., United States commissioner, with whom Dr. Judd negotiated the draft of a new treaty. On their arrival in New York, they received flattering attentions from the city authorities, but deemed it necessary to take the first steamer for Liverpool. In England they were shown much kindness by Admiral Thomas and Lord Palmerston.

On arriving in Paris, they found that Mr. Dillon had preceded them, and still possessed the confidence of the Minister of Foreign Affairs. Dr. Judd was referred to Mr. Perrin, who seemed to be fully imbued with the views of Mr. Dillon. After remaining in Paris ten weeks, vainly endeavoring to negotiate a new treaty, they returned to

England, where the young princes were treated with the utmost hospitality and courtesy, and enjoyed glimpses of the aristocratic society of London.

Having agreed with Lord Palmerston upon the basis of a new treaty with England, the embassy returned to the United States in May, 1850. After visiting Washington, they came home by way of Panama, arriving in Honolulu September 9th, 1850.* The new treaty with the United States was finally concluded in Washington, December 26th, 1849.

A similar just and equitable treaty was concluded with Great Britain July 10th, 1851.

Negotiations with Mr. Perrin, 1851.—Mr. Perrin was again sent to the islands as commissioner of France, in the corvette "Serieuse," which arrived at Honolulu December 13th, 1850, and remained in port three months. He opened a voluminous correspondence with the Hawaiian Government, and on the 1st of February, to the surprise of every one, presented the identical ten demands of Mr. Dillon, although the last claim had been fully paid. He also resumed Mr. Dillon's policy of an annoying diplomatic interference with the internal affairs of the kingdom.

After a month's fruitless discussion of these demands, the king and privy council passed a proclamation, which was duly signed by the king and premier, March 10th, 1851, placing the islands provisionally under the protection of the United States, until their relations with France should be placed "upon a footing compatible with the king's rights as an independent sovereign, and with his treaty engagements with other nations," or, if this should be found to be impracticable, declaring the said protector-

* The princes were much improved by their foreign tour, and made a very favorable impression abroad.

ate to be perpetual. This declaration was communicated to the governments of Great Britain and the United States.

The result of this action was that Mr. Perrin soon discovered that the difficulties with his government were reduced to two points, viz.: "the liberty of Catholic worship and the trade in spirits." A joint declaration, comprising four moderate articles, was agreed upon and signed by both parties, March 25th, the question of indemnity to the king being referred to the decision of the President of the French republic. Nothing more was ever heard of the rest of the ten demands.*

*Mr. Perrin left for Paris May 24th, 1851, to obtain fresh instructions, and did not return until January 8th, 1853. The legislature of 1851 confirmed the action of the privy council.

CHAPTER XXXIII

1851-1854

THE CLOSE OF KAMEHAMEHA III.'S REIGN

The Constitution of 1852.—The legislature of 1850 provided for the appointment of three commissioners to draft a new constitution. The king was represented by Dr. Judd, the nobles by John Ii, and the representatives by Chief-justice Lee. The draft, which had been chiefly prepared by Judge Lee, was submitted to the legislature of 1852, and after having been discussed at length and amended, was finally adopted June 14th, 1852, by both houses, and signed by the king. This constitution was a great advance upon that of 1840, and has formed the basis of those that have succeeded it.

The legislature was to be composed of two houses, to sit in separate chambers. The nobles were to be chosen by the king for life, their number being limited to thirty. The number of representatives was not to be less than twenty-four, who were to be elected by universal suffrage. The privy council was now made distinct from the house of nobles. The singular institution of a *kuhina nui* or vice-king was continued.

The courts were organized very nearly as they now exist, viz.: a Supreme Court, consisting of a chief-justice and two associate justices, and four circuit courts, besides a petty judge for each district. It was an extremely liberal constitution, and together with his gift to the people of lands in fee simple, forms the glory of the reign of Kamehameha III.

Between the years 1850 and 1860 a large part of the government land was sold in small tracts to the natives, at low prices, and great efforts were made to encourage habits of industry and thrift among them. The census taken in 1850 gave a total population of 84,165, showing a decrease of 24,414 in fourteen years. The number of foreigners was only 1,962.

Material Progress.—The rapid settlement of California opened a new market for the productions of the islands, and gave a great stimulus to agriculture. For a short time, sugar brought from eighteen to twenty cents a pound in San Francisco, and large profits were made by raising potatoes in Kula, Maui, and elsewhere for the California market. The culture of wheat also increased, and in June, 1854, a steam flouring mill was started in Honolulu. The next year four hundred and sixty-three barrels of Hawaiian flour were exported. A foundry was started at Honolulu at the same time.

In August, 1850, the Royal Hawaiian Agricultural Society was organized with Judge Lee as president, and existed for more than twenty years.*

The year 1851-52 was noted for one of the severest droughts ever known at the islands, after which the coffee plantations were attacked by blight.

Steam Navigation.—In November, 1853, a California company brought a small steamer called the "S. B. Wheeler" (afterwards the "Akamai"), to run between the islands, and obtained a charter from the government. In 1854 the company added an old, shaky boat called

* It did much to encourage industry and to introduce valuable plants and animals.

the "West Point" or "Kalama," which was wrecked at Koloa in 1856.

Before this a larger boat, the "Sea Bird" or "Kamehameha," had been put on the windward route, but she was withdrawn in a year or two, and the company's charter was annulled in October, 1856.

The Sailors' Riot of 1852.—A serious riot was caused by the death of a seaman named John Burns, who died in the fort from the effects of a blow from a policeman's club, November 9th, 1852. After his funeral, in the afternoon of the 10th, a mob of four or five hundred sailors demanded that the policeman should be delivered up to them, and they threatened to take the fort. Later in the evening they burned the station-house, a two-story building near the foot of Nuuanu Street, and broke open several liquor saloons. The next morning many of the foreign residents assembled in the fort and formed a military organization of two hundred men. Meanwhile Governor Kekuanaoa, keeping his soldiers in reserve, ordered the unarmed multitude of natives looking on to clear the streets, which was soon done without any loss of life, and forty or fifty rioters were locked up in the fort.

Later on, the foreign volunteer companies patrolled the streets, and made some arrests. On the 17th, the first military company of foreigners was formed under the name of "The Hawaiian Guards."

Filibusters.—At that time California was resorted to by lawless adventurers from all parts of the world, and filibustering expeditions were common. One General Walker headed a raid of this kind into Lower California in 1853, another into Nicaragua in 1855, and a third in 1861, in which he was taken and shot. The Hawaiian

Government received many warnings in the fall of 1851, that a band of filibusters was being organized to invade the kingdom. Accordingly, at their request, the U. S. sloop-of-war "Vandalia," Captain Gardner, was kept in readiness to seize any suspicious vessel, and a small body of native soldiers was drilled for several months by his officers. A number of suspicious characters came down by the "Gamecock" in November, 1851, who rifled the mail-bag on the voyage down, and threw the letters overboard. The greater part of them, however, soon returned. For several years the peace of the country was guaranteed by the presence of British and American ships-of-war.

The Small-pox Epidemic.—The year 1853 was one of the darkest in the history of this nation.

In the early part of that year the small-pox was prevalent in San Francisco. The clipper ship "Charles Mallory" from that port touched at Honolulu February 10th, with one case of small-pox on board. It was strictly quarantined, and no harm resulted.*

Three months later, in the month of May, several cases of small-pox were discovered on Mauna Kea Street in Honolulu. It has never been ascertained how it was introduced, but it was generally believed to have been brought from San Francisco in some hundred chests of old clothing, which had been sold at auction.

In spite of all precautions, the pestilence spread rapidly. On the 10th of May, three commissioners of public health, viz., Mr. Parke, Dr. Judd, and Dr. Rooke, were appointed with full powers. Sub-commissioners and

* Three meetings of the resident physicians were held, and their advice was adopted by the privy council. Vaccine matter was imported, and great efforts were made to vaccinate all the people through the voluntary services of medical men, missionaries, and others.

agents were also appointed for every district, and the coasting vessels were forbidden to take any passengers who were not vaccinated — an ineffectual precaution.

On Oahu the ravages of the disease were terrible, especially in Honolulu and in the district of Ewa. A large proportion of those taken with it had been vaccinated. Temporary hospitals were established, and the physicians, missionaries, and many other volunteers were untiring in their efforts to dispense food, medicine, and comforts among the suffering people, and to vaccinate all who had not taken the disease. The amount expended by the commissioners was over $28,000.

There were but few cases on Kauai, and none on Molokai, where a strict policy of non-intercourse was maintained. At Lahaina, effective measures were taken to properly vaccinate all the people, and to isolate those who brought the infection with them, of whom seven died. There were only a few cases in the district of Hana, and a few in Hilo, but a considerable number in Kawaihae and in the district of Kona, Hawaii. The total number of deaths caused directly by this epidemic was between two thousand five hundred and three thousand. It finally ceased in October.

The census taken in December gave a total population of 73,137, showing a decrease of 11,027 in three years.

Political Agitation.—A portion of the foreign community, many of whom had recently come from California, took advantage of this calamity to foment partisan strife. Two members of the cabinet, Messrs. Armstrong and Judd, were selected as scapegoats, and held responsible for the spread of the disease. Great efforts were made to excite the native population against them, but they utterly failed. Indignation meetings were held, and petitions presented to the king for their removal from office. Threats were also used to intimidate the chiefs. An active agitation was commenced at the same time in favor of annexation to the United States. A committee of thirteen was appointed to carry out these objects. On the 29th of August the British and French consuls presented to the king a joint remonstrance against any annexation scheme. A few days later the whole cabinet resigned, but were all reappointed with the exception of Dr. Judd, who was succeeded by Hon. E. H. Allen, whose appointment gave general satisfaction, and caused no change in the policy of the government.

Proposed Annexation. — The history of this reign would be incomplete without a reference to the agitation in favor of annexation to the United States that went on during the years 1853 and 1854.*

Petitions in favor of it were presented to the king in August, 1853, and in January, 1854. There were at that time strong commercial interests in its favor, and the prospect of it stimulated speculation and led to new enterprises. The missionaries, however, of both denominations were generally opposed to the project, believing that its effects would be disastrous to the native race. But it was favored by the king, as a refuge from impending dangers. He was tired of demands made upon him by foreign powers, and of threats by filibusters from abroad and by conspirators at home to overturn the government.†

* Although mostly confined to the foreign residents, it was so great as to lead in 1854 to a general belief of the certainty of the event.

† "His purpose, though it happily fell through, secured to his successors a more peaceful possession of their inheritance."

The fearful decrease of the population, the rapid extinction of the order of chiefs, the relapse of the king into the excesses of his youth, and the perils overhanging the feeble government, disheartened some true friends of the nation, and led them to favor the preliminary steps then taken. On the 6th of February, 1854, in view of danger from filibusters and conspirators, the king commanded Mr. Wyllie to ascertain on what terms a treaty of annexation could be negotiated, to be used as a safeguard to meet any sudden emergency. Every proposition was to be considered by the cabinet and Prince Liholiho, and the treaty as a whole was to be submitted to His Majesty for his approval, modification, or rejection.

The negotiations were carried on between Mr. Wyllie and Mr. Gregg, the American minister, with many delays. On the 11th of November Mr. Wyllie was informed that three hundred filibusters were expected in two vessels from San Francisco, and that there was a formidable armed organization of Californians and others in town, who would compel the king to sign the treaty, although Prince Liholiho was absent on Kauai. By order of the king and cabinet, Mr. Wyllie immediately applied to the representatives of the Great Powers, and was promised the support of the forces on board of the United States ships "Portsmouth" and "St. Mary's," of the British ship "Trincomalee," and of the French frigate "Artémise." The expected filibusters never appeared.

On the 13th of December, a proclamation was published, declaring that the king had accepted the assistance of the naval forces of the three powers named, and that "his independence was more firmly established than ever before."

Death of Kamehameha III.—After a short illness of

five or six days, Kamehameha III. expired at noon on Friday, December 15th, 1854, in the forty-second year of his age. His adopted son and heir, Alexander Liholiho, was immediately proclaimed king, under the title of Kamehameha IV.

The funeral of the late king was celebrated January 10th, 1855, with the most imposing procession ever seen in the islands. The mourning for his death was universal and sincere. His memory will ever be dear to his people for his unselfish patriotism, for the liberal constitution which he granted them, and for the gift of the right to hold lands in fee simple. His reign will also be memorable for the unexampled progress made by the nation, and for its wonderful preservation from the many perils which beset it. While there were grave faults in his character, there were also noble traits. He loved his country and his people. He was true and steadfast in friendship. Duplicity and intrigue were foreign to his nature. He always chose men of tried integrity for responsible offices, and never betrayed secrets of state, even in his most unguarded moments.

CHAPTER XXXIV

1855–1863

THE REIGN OF KAMEHAMEHA IV.

THE brief reign of Kamehameha IV. began with bright hopes, but ended in disappointment and sorrow. He took the oath to maintain the constitution January 11th, 1855, in the old Stone Church, where he delivered an eloquent inaugural address to his people and to the foreigners present. He was then twenty-one years of age, of brilliant talents and winning manners, and his accession to the throne was hailed with high anticipations by the nation at large. A diligent student of English history, he was ambitious to reign as a constitutional king.

KAMEHAMEHA IV.

Foreign Relations.—The negotiations that had been commenced with Mr. Gregg were now broken off, and Chief-justice Lee was sent as ambassador to Washington, where he concluded a treaty of reciprocity July 20th, 1865. By the terms of this treaty, Hawaiian sugar, coffee, wool, hides, etc., were to be admitted into the United States free of duty. It failed, however, to be ratified by the senate.*

An act reducing the duty on brandy to three dollars a gallon was passed by the legislature of 1855, whereupon negotiations were resumed by Mr. Perrin which occupied more than two years, the chief difficulty being in regard to the official use of the French language. The new treaty with France was finally ratified September 7th, 1858, with a clause limiting the duties on wines and brandy for ten years more. On the 19th of February, 1858, Mr. Perrin presented the king with a silver épergne, an ormolu clock, a pair of silver candelabra, and a Sèvres dinner-service from the Emperor Napoleon.

In 1861 Sir John Bowring was commissioned as minister-plenipotentiary to urge the project of a joint guarantee of the independence of the islands by the three great maritime powers, but nothing came of it. In May, 1857, Laysan, Lisiansky, and other islands to the northwest were taken possession of by Captain John Paty, in the name of the Hawaiian Government.

Notable Deaths.—After Judge Lee's return to the islands, he drafted the Penal Code, and was engaged on the Civil Code when he died, May 28th, 1857. His death was mourned by all as a national loss. He was succeeded as chief-justice by Hon. E. H. Allen. In the same year died John Young 2d, and Konia, widow of Paki. Admiral Thomas also died August 22d, 1857, near London.

The King's Marriage.—On the 19th of June, 1856, the king married Emma Rooke, a granddaughter of John Young. She had been adopted in childhood by Dr. Rooke,

* The next year, Hon. E. H. Allen was sent to Washington to urge the ratification of the treaty, but did not succeed, and twenty years more were destined to pass away before this boon was attained.

an English physician who had married Kamaikui, a sister of her mother, Fanny Kekela Young. She had been educated in the Young Chiefs' School, and both by her character and by her talents was worthy of her high station.

QUEEN EMMA

Birth of the Prince of Hawaii.—On the 20th of May, 1858, the queen gave birth to a son, to the great joy of her subjects of all classes. His title was officially declared to be "The Prince of Hawaii," and it now seemed as if the Kamehameha dynasty was firmly established.

The Queen's Hospital.—The crowning act of this reign, by which Kamehameha IV. and Queen Emma will ever be remembered with gratitude, was the founding of the "Queen's Hospital." During the year 1859 the king and queen personally canvassed the town of Honolulu for subscriptions, and met with a generous response.

A board of trustees was organized June 22d, 1859, and a dispensary was established in a hired house.*

The Neilson Tragedy.—During a visit to Lahaina in August, 1859, in a moment of passion the king was led to commit an act for which he ever afterwards suffered

* The king had the satisfaction of laying the corner-stone of the hospital July 17th, 1860, with impressive ceremonies, and of seeing the building completed in December.

in mind and health. While under the influence of liquor, he shot his private secretary, Mr. H. A. Neilson, who died from his wound after lingering many months in suffering. "If," says Mr. Hopkins, "the most heart-felt sorrow and the tenderest care could have availed to avert the catastrophe, Mr. Neilson's life would have been saved." The king's first impulse was to abdicate the throne, but from this he was dissuaded by his advisers. The nobles were then called together at Honolulu, and on the 3d of October, 1859, the Prince of Hawaii was duly proclaimed heir to the throne.

Commencement of the Anglican Mission.—In December, 1859, Mr. Wyllie communicated to the Hawaiian consul in London the desire of the king and queen that a clergyman of the Church of England should be settled in Honolulu, to act as chaplain for the royal family, who offered to guarantee a certain sum toward his support, and to give a site for a church. The king also wrote an autograph letter on the subject to Queen Victoria. This request excited much interest in England, where a committee was formed to organize a mission to the islands. After some further correspondence, the Right Rev. T. N. Staley, D.D., was consecrated as Bishop of Honolulu, December 15th, 1861.

It was expected that his first official act would be the baptism of the Prince of Hawaii, but Providence ordered otherwise.

Death of the Prince of Hawaii.—The little prince, in whom so many hopes were centered, was attacked by brain fever on the 19th of August, 1862, and died on the 27th, amid the universal grief of the nation. The king never recovered from the blow, and was a broken-hearted man during the remainder of his life.

Arrival of the Anglican Mission.—The king now retired to a country residence, where he resumed the work, which he had already commenced, of translating the English Book of Common Prayer into the Hawaiian language. His translation is an excellent one, and the preface written by himself has been justly admired.

Bishop Staley, accompanied by other clergymen, arrived at Honolulu on the 11th of October, 1862, and soon afterwards received the king and queen into the communion of his church. A temporary cathedral was erected, and several schools established, among which were the Iolani College for boys, St. Andrew's Priory for girls, etc.

Death of Kamehameha IV.—During the next year the king was steadily failing in health. He avoided state ceremonials as much as possible, and lived a retired life. At last, on the 30th of November, 1863, he suddenly passed away, at the early age of twenty-nine, having reigned nearly nine years. The building of the present mausoleum was then commenced. The Queen's Hospital is, however, his best monument.

Public Improvements.—Several important public improvements were executed during this reign. The reef belonging to the land of Waikahalulu, on the south side of Honolulu Harbor, had been purchased by the government from the Queen Dowager Kalama for $22,000. The fort was demolished in 1857. The work of filling in the sixteen acres of land known as the "Esplanade" or "Ainahou," and of building up a water-front of two thousand feet, with a depth of water of from twenty to twenty-five feet, occupied several years, from 1856 to 1860, and cost $242,000. The present prison was built in 1856–57, to take the place of the old fort. The new custom-house was completed in 1860. The water-works were much enlarged, and a system of pipes laid down in 1861, at an expense of $45,000. A gas company was chartered in 1859 by Mr. W. H. Tiffany and others, and the pipes for it were laid, but the enterprise failed after a few months' trial from want of patronage. On the night of March 28th, 1858, the old custom-house was entered by burglars, and robbed of $8,573.*

Inter-Island Steamer.—By an act of the legislature passed March 7th, 1859, a charter was granted to C. A. Williams and others, under the title of the Hawaiian Steam Navigation Company, together with extensive privileges. The steamer "Kilauea," of four hundred and fourteen tons, was built for the company in New London, Connecticut, and arrived at Honolulu the following year. She started on her first regular trip to Hawaii July 24th, 1860, and continued to run between the islands, in spite of many casualties, for seventeen years.

Agriculture, etc.—During this period the development of the country was nearly at a stand-still. The cultivation of wheat as well as that of coffee was mostly given up. The exports diminished, and the main dependence of the people continued to be on the whaling fleet. During the year 1859 one hundred and ninety-seven whale ships visited the islands.

Experiments in the culture of rice were commenced by Mr. Holstein in 1858, and in 1860, with seed from South Carolina, they proved to be a decided success. Such an interest was excited in this new industry that in 1862 nine hundred and twenty-three thousand pounds of rice and paddy were exported, and rice has ever since been the crop second in value in the islands.

* Although a reward of $1,000 was offered for any information that would lead to the detection of the guilty persons, they have never been discovered.

Pulu was an important article of export to California from 1860 to 1870. The quantity exported rose at one time to six hundred thousand pounds in a year, but both the demand and the supply soon fell off. The first honey-bees were imported from San José, California, August 20th, 1857, and their number rapidly increased.

The census of 1860 gave a total population of sixty-nine thousand eight hundred, showing a decrease of three thousand three hundred and thirty-eight in seven years.

Schools, etc.—After 1850, the English language was taught more and more in the government schools. The Royal School was opened in its present building December 5th, 1851. The Punahou School was chartered as Oahu College in 1854, under the presidency of the Rev. E. G. Beckwith.*

Partial Withdrawal of the American Board from the Mission to the Hawaiian Islands.—As early as 1848, the American Board had prepared to retire from the Hawaiian Islands as a missionary field, and to organize a self-governing and self-supporting religious community there, to carry on the work which had been begun. The greater part of the property held by the board at the islands was transferred to its missionaries, the government giving them titles to their land in fee simple. No more missionaries were sent out from the United States, but as fast as possible, churches were formed and placed under the charge of native Hawaiian pastors. In 1863 Rev. R. Anderson, D.D., Foreign Secretary of the American Board, visited the islands to assist in the execution of this plan.

* The death of the Rev. R. Armstrong, September 23d, 1860, was a serious blow to the prosperity of the government schools. He was succeeded by Governor M. Kekuanaoa.

Four island associations were organized, besides the "Hawaiian Evangelical Association," for the whole kingdom, which consists of native and foreign clergymen and lay delegates. This latter body elects an executive board called the "Hawaiian Board," which manages both home and foreign missions, and disburses the funds contributed for these objects. Since then the American Board has merely acted the part of an auxiliary, and not that of a controlling body, and the places of the American missionaries have been gradually filled by native Hawaiian pastors.

Eruptions of Mauna Loa.—Two great eruptions of Mauna Loa took place during this period. On the 11th of August, 1855, a stream of lava burst out of the northeastern side of the mountain, at an elevation of twelve thousand feet, and ran directly toward Hilo. In some places it was over two miles wide. After having flowed for fifteen months, on the 22d of November, 1856, it reached a point within eight miles of the town of Hilo, causing great alarm to its inhabitants; but there the flow ceased to advance, and Hilo was saved.

Again, on the 23d of January, 1859, an eruption took place from a fissure on the northern side of the mountain, about ten thousand feet above the sea. The lava stream flowed to the northwest, passing around the eastern and northern sides of Mount Hualalai, and reached the sea at Keawaiki, North Kona, in eight days, filling up a great fish-pond constructed by Kamehameha I. at Kiholo. The lava continued to flow until August, a period of seven months.

CHAPTER XXXV

1863-1872

THE REIGN OF KAMEHAMEHA V.

Character of Kamehameha V.—Immediately after the death of Kamehameha IV., his elder brother, Prince Lot Kamehameha, was proclaimed king under the title of Kamehameha V., on the 30th of November, 1863.

KAMEHAMEHA V.

He had inherited somewhat of the first Kamehameha's strength of will and practical shrewdness, and had shown considerable administrative ability as Minister of the Interior during the previous reign. He had been opposed to some of the liberal reforms of Kamehameha III.'s reign, believing that his countrymen were not yet fitted to enjoy such privileges. His reign, unlike that of his brother, was marked by bitter party contests, which it is not within the plan of this work to discuss. It was his policy to place able men who were in sympathy with his views at the head of affairs, and to give them a steady support.

The Constitutional Convention.—The king retained Mr. Wyllie in the cabinet, with Mr. C. C. Harris, an

American lawyer, and Mr. C. de Varigny, late secretary of the French consul, as his colleagues. In the following year Dr. Hutchinson became Minister of the Interior.

The king had resolved not to take the oath to maintain the constitution of 1852, but to embrace the opportunity to make such changes in it as would increase the power of the crown. Accordingly, a proclamation was issued May 5th, 1864, for the election of a constitutional convention, to be held June 13th. The king himself, attended by Mr. Wyllie, made a tour through the islands, explaining and defending the changes which he desired to make in the constitution. The convention met July 7th, being composed of sixteen nobles and twenty-seven elected delegates, presided over by the king in person. After a week's debate it was decided that the "three estates" should sit together in one chamber. The next question was whether the convention had the right to proceed to make a new constitution, which was finally decided in the affirmative.*

The Constitution of 1864.—On the 20th of August the king promulgated a new constitution upon his own authority, which continued in force for twenty-three years. There were fewer changes in it than had been expected.

The useless office of *kuhina nui* or vice-king was abolished. The right of suffrage was made to depend on a small property qualification, and also, for those born since 1840, on ability to read and write. The nobles and representatives were henceforth to sit and vote together

* After a long discussion of the proposed property qualification for voters, the king's patience broke down, and on the 13th of August, 1864, he declared the constitution of 1852 *abrogated*, and prorogued the convention.

in one chamber. A new legislature was elected October 15th, which passed several important measures.

Immigration.—A Bureau of Immigration was formed, and in April, 1865, Dr. Hillebrand was sent on a mission to China, India, and the Malay Archipelago, to make arrangements for the importation of laborers, to procure valuable plants and birds, and to collect information, especially in regard to leprosy. In July he sent five hundred laborers from China under contracts with the government, who were followed by many others. During his tour he introduced into the islands many kinds of choice plants and trees, and of insectivorous birds, and collected a large fund of useful information.*

Segregation of Lepers.—The dreadful disease of leprosy was first observed in the islands in 1853, and in 1864 it had begun to spread to an alarming extent. Accordingly, an act was passed January 3d, 1865, to isolate the lepers and to provide separate establishments and hospitals for them. A hospital was established at Kalihi in October, 1865, and about the same time Dr. Hutchinson selected the present site of the leper settlement, and purchased lands for it on the north side of Molokai. It is a peninsula, comprising some five thousand acres, surrounded on three sides by the ocean, and on the south side shut in by a steep precipice from two to three thousand feet in height. It includes the fertile valley of Waikolu, besides the villages of Kalawao on the east side and Kalaupapa on the west. About one hundred and forty lepers were sent there in 1866.

The Schools.—By an act which was passed January 10th, 1865, the Board of Education was constituted, and

* In 1868 the first company of Japanese immigrants, one hundred and forty-eight in number, came to the islands on the ship "Scioto."

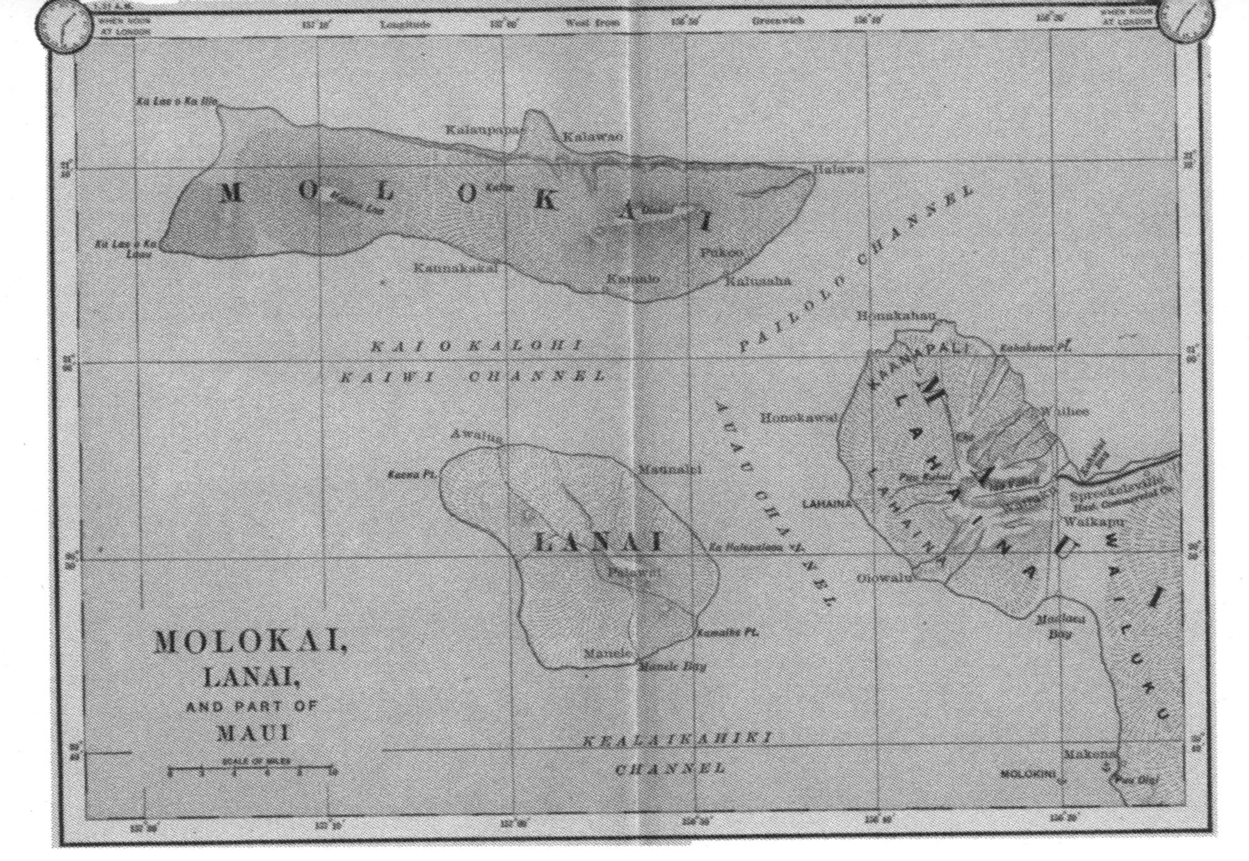
MOLOKAI,
LANAI,
AND PART OF
MAUI
SCALE OF MILES
Longitude
West from
Greenwich
MOLOKAI
Kalaupapa
Kalawao
Halawa
Kaunakakai
Kamalo
Pukoo
Kaluaaha
Ka Lae o Ka Ilio
Ka Lae o Ka Laau
KAI O KALOHI
KAIWI CHANNEL
PAILOLO CHANNEL
AUAU CHANNEL
KEALAIKAHIKI
CHANNEL
LANAI
Awalua
Kaena Pt.
Maunalei
Manele
Manele Bay
Kamaiki Pt.
Honokahau
KAANAPALI
Honokawai
LAHAINA
Olowalu
Waihee
Wailuku
Waikapu
Maalaea
Bay
Makena
MOLOKINI
MAUI
WAILUKU

the office of Inspector-General of Schools was created, which was first held by the late Hon. A. Fornander. The Reformatory School was founded in March, 1865, as well as the Girls' School in Honolulu, which is now located at Pohukaina, on Punch-bowl Street.

Queen Emma's Foreign Tour.—In May, 1865, Queen Emma sailed in H. B. M.'s ship-of-war "Clio," for Panama, on her way to England, accompanied by Mr. and Mrs. Hoapili Kaauwai and Mr. C. G. Hopkins. She spent over a year abroad, mostly in England, where she was treated with much kindness, and returned to Honolulu October 22d, 1866, on the United States ship-of-war "Vanderbilt," Admiral Thatcher.

Burning of Whalers by the "Shenandoah."—Remote as these islands were from the seat of the great civil war then raging in the United States, they did not escape its effects. In April, 1865, the Confederate cruiser "Shenandoah," Captain Waddell, burned four whalers at Bonabe, Caroline Islands, one of which was a Hawaiian vessel, the "Harvest." After this piratical act Captain Waddell sailed north, and burned twenty whalers more in the Arctic Sea in June, 1865. Five vessels were spared to carry the crews of the rest to San Francisco, including several hundred Hawaiian sailors. The bark "Kamehameha V." was sent for the relief of the seamen at Bonabe in August, 1865, and brought them all, ninety-eight in number, safely to Honolulu.

Notable Deaths.—Mr. R. C. Wyllie, the veteran Minister of Foreign Affairs, died October 19th, 1865. His funeral took place October 30th, when his remains were placed in the royal mausoleum, and the following night all the coffins of former kings and chiefs were removed from the old tomb on King Street to the new mausoleum, in an imposing torch-light procession. Victoria Kamamalu, sister of the king and heir-apparent, died May 29th, 1866, at the early age of twenty-seven. Her father, Governor Kekuanaoa, who for nearly forty years had filled so important a place in the history of his country, died November 24th, 1868, at the age of seventy-five.

Treaty of Reciprocity.—In 1867 Mr. C. C. Harris was sent to Washington, as minister-plenipotentiary, to negotiate a treaty of reciprocity with the United States, being accompanied by General McCook, the American minister. In August the treaty was completed and approved by the President and his cabinet. An extra session of the Hawaiian legislature was called, and on the 10th of September a law was passed to change the tariff in case the treaty went into effect.

At Washington, however, it was opposed by Senator Sumner, and failed of ratification by the senate. In 1868 Hon. J. Mott Smith was sent to Washington, to succeed Mr. Harris as minister-resident.

The Great Eruption in Kau.—On the 27th of March, 1868, an eruption began in the summit crater of Mauna Loa, attended by a long series of earthquake shocks. At length, on the 2d of April, a terrific earthquake took place, which shook down every stone wall and nearly every house in Kau, and did more or less damage in every part of Hawaii.

At Kapapala in eastern Kau it caused a destructive land-slip, commonly known as the "mud flow." An enormous mass of marshy clay was detached from the bluff at the head of the valley, and in a few minutes swept down for a distance of three miles, in a stream about half a mile wide and thirty feet deep in the middle. It moved so swiftly that it overtook and buried thirty-one human beings and over five hundred horses, cattle, and goats.

Immediately after this earthquake, a tremendous wave, forty or fifty feet high, rolled in upon the coast of Kau, sweeping away all the villages from Kaalualu to Keauhou, and destroying some cocoanut groves. Over eighty persons perished in a few minutes, and the survivors were left destitute and suffering. At the same time the crater of Kilauea emptied itself of its lava through underground fissures toward the southwest. The central part of the floor of the crater fell in, forming a pit three thousand feet long and five hundred feet deep, with sloping sides.

On the 7th of April, the lava from the central crater of Maunā Loa burst out on the southwest slope of the mountain, in the land of Kahuku, at a point five thousand six hundred feet above the sea. The lava spouted up in great fountains, several hundred feet high, and flowed to the sea, a distance of ten miles, in two hours. This eruption continued only five days. It destroyed several houses and several hundred head of cattle, and overflowed four thousand acres of good land. Three men were imprisoned for several days on a hill surrounded by lava streams, and Captain Robert Brown and his family were obliged to run for their lives.

The government promptly dispatched the steamer "Kilauea" with supplies of provisions, clothing, lumber, etc., for the relief of the sufferers. The king himself, with Mr. and Mrs. Varigny, went on this expedition, and visited the principal landings in Puna and Kau, relieving the pressing wants of the people, and assisting them with materials to rebuild their houses. On their return, the legislature voted a subsidy of nearly $7,000, and about $4,000 was raised by voluntary subscriptions, with which another vessel was sent laden with supplies for the unfortunate people of southern Hawaii. On the 15th of August, 1868, a sudden rising and falling of the sea was observed at all the islands, which was caused by a terrible earthquake in Peru and Ecuador. Another earthquake on February 19th, 1871, was severely felt in Oahu and Maui, but slightly in Hawaii.

The Kaona Insurrection.—In the year 1868, a crazy fanatic by the name of Kaona, who claimed to be a prophet, gathered around him a large number of credulous people in the district of Kona, Hawaii. He was committed to the insane asylum at Honolulu, where he remained for some months, until he was discharged as cured. Returning to Kona, he and his disciples encamped on the land of Honuaino, three miles north of Kealakekua, which had been leased to a Mr. Roy, who brought an action of ejectment against them. On the 19th of October, 1868, the deputy-sheriff, Mr. Richard B. Neville, accompanied by a posse of constables and others, undertook to arrest Kaona and some of his men as trespassers. A fight ensued in which Mr. Neville was killed, and the next day a policeman named Kamai was taken and murdered by the fanatics. A company of troops was immediately sent up from Honolulu, but before it arrived, Mr. Coney, the sheriff of Hawaii, had organized a force, and taken Kaona and his company prisoners without any more bloodshed. About seventy-five of them were taken to Honolulu.*

Visit of the Duke of Edinburgh.—On the 21st of July, 1869, the Duke of Edinburgh, second son of Queen Victoria, in command of the frigate "Galatea," arrived at Honolulu on his way from Tahiti to Japan and China.

*Five of the ringleaders were convicted of manslaughter, and sentenced to imprisonment for terms varying from five to ten years.

He remained in port twelve days, and was entertained in a style befitting his high rank.

The Australian Line of Steamers.—On the 19th of April, 1870, the British steamer "Wonga Wonga" arrived at Honolulu, twenty-three days from Auckland. This was the pioneer of the lines of steamers which have since then continued to ply between the Australian Colonies and San Francisco.

Loss of the Whaling Fleet in the Arctic.—In the autumn of 1871, the whaling fleet in the Arctic Sea was shut in by ice-fields near Point Belcher, and had to be abandoned by the crews on the 14th of September. Thirty-three ships were lost, and over a thousand seamen were brought from Icy Cape to Honolulu in five ships which had escaped, arriving there between October 23d and 25th, 1871. It was estimated that this disaster caused a loss to Honolulu of $200,000 a year.

The Small-pox.—The small-pox was introduced for the second time from San Francisco in May, 1872. Warned by the experience of 1853, the government took energetic measures to prevent its spread. These measures were so successful that on the 6th of September the disease had disappeared, and out of thirty-seven cases only eleven had proved fatal.

Public Improvements.—Several important public improvements date from this reign. The Honolulu lighthouse was first lighted August 2d, 1869. The present substantial post-office was opened in March, 1870. The barracks were built in the same year at an expense of $25,000.

The Hawaiian Hotel was built by the government and opened to the public in 1872, and the new government building known as "Aliiolani Hale" was commenced in

A NATIVE'S HOUSE

March of the same year, and completed in 1874 at a cost of $130,000. The steamer "Kilauea" was taken by the government in 1870, and rebuilt at great expense. The general survey of the kingdom was commenced in 1871.

Agriculture and Trade.—The production of sugar* was greatly increased during this reign, owing to the importation of laborers from abroad, and to the hope of reciprocity with the United States, which, however, was not realized. The whaling fleet steadily fell off to only forty-seven ships in 1871, and continued to decrease after that date. The total exports that year were valued at one million eight hundred thousand dollars. The establishment of regular lines of steamers between Australia and California was of great benefit to the islands in many ways. The census of 1872 gave a total population of 56,897, showing a decrease of 12,900 in twelve years.

Death of Kamehameha V.—The king died suddenly, December 11th, 1872, of dropsy on the chest, in the forty-third year of his age, having reigned nine years. With him ended the line of the Kamehamehas. Unfortunately, no successor had been appointed to the throne.

* The amount produced rose to eleven thousand tons in 1872.

CHAPTER XXXVI

1873–1891

THE REIGNS OF LUNALILO AND KALAKAUA; ACCESSION OF LILIUOKALANI

Election of Lunalilo.— In this chapter the political history of the country to 1891 will be briefly sketched.

As Kamehameha V. had died without appointing a successor, the choice devolved upon the legislature, which was summoned to meet in four weeks, on the 8th of January, 1873. Prince William C. Lunalilo was generally considered to be the highest surviving chief by birth. His mother, Kekauluohi, had succeeded her half-sister, Kinau, in the office of *kuhina nui*, as being a niece of Kaahumanu, and both niece and step-daughter of Kamehameha I. Lunalilo was also universally popular, both with natives and foreigners, from his amiable traits of character and his well-known liberal views. On the 17th of December, 1872, he published an address to the Hawaiian people, requesting them to meet at the different polling-places throughout the kingdom on the 1st of January, 1873, and to cast a vote for the purpose of instructing their representatives as to their

LUNALILO

choice for king. A wave of popular enthusiasm swept over the group, and on New Year's day a larger vote than ever before was cast, almost unanimously, for Lunalilo. The legislature met on the appointed day, and in compliance with the expressed will of the people, elected Lunalilo king amid general rejoicing. The next day, in the Kawaiahao church, he took the oath to maintain the existing constitution of 1864, and delivered addresses to the people and to the legislature.

Amendments to the constitution were then proposed: one to restore the two houses of the legislature and the other to abolish the property qualification for voters, of which only the latter went into effect in 1874.

The Lunalilo Administration.—The Hon. R. Stirling was retained in the new cabinet as Minister of Finance, his colleagues being Hons. C. R. Bishop, Minister of Foreign Affairs, E. O. Hall, Minister of the Interior, and A. F. Judd, Attorney-General.

The new cabinet made a determined effort to carry out the law for the seclusion of lepers, and during that year over five hundred confirmed cases were sent to Molokai. The execution of this painful duty excited a bitter opposition among a large portion of the people. It was considered a favorable juncture to renew negotiations with the government of the United States for a treaty of commercial reciprocity, and it was proposed to offer it the exclusive use of the harbor of Pearl River, Oahu, as a coaling and repair station for its ships-of-war. This proposal gave rise to an extensive agitation, which intensified the suspicion and ill-feeling that already existed. In August, the king's health began to decline rapidly, and at his desire, the negotiations were dropped.

The Mutiny at the Barracks.—On Sunday, September

7th, 1873, the disaffection which had been brewing for some time among the household troops broke out in open mutiny. They assaulted their drill-master, Captain Jajczay, an Austrian, and demanded that both he and the adjutant-general should be dismissed. The following night they dragged two cannons from the palace yard to the barracks, which they loaded with grape-shot. They then bade defiance to the authorities.

A large part of the populace evidently sympathized with the mutineers. On Tuesday, a message having been read to them from the king, who was confined to his bed at Waikiki, thirteen of them surrendered, leaving twenty-four in rebellion. A warrant for their arrest was issued, but not executed. In order to avoid bloodshed and the risk of starting a formidable riot, a siege was resorted to, and guards were posted around the barracks.

On Thursday an autograph letter was sent to the mutineers from the king, ordering them to give up their arms and leave the barracks, and offering them on this condition a free pardon for their crime. They finally left on Friday morning, when the corps was disbanded by order of the king. The result of this affair was a considerable loss of authority on the part of the government, and a further increase of lawlessness and race-hatred throughout the country.

Illness and Death of Lunalilo.—Soon after this affair, the king removed to Kailua, Hawaii, to try the effect of a change of climate. He remained there several months, but nothing availed to stay the progress of the fatal disease. On the 18th of January, 1874, he returned to Honolulu, where he died on the 3d of February of pulmonary consumption, after a reign of only one year and twenty-five days.*

* By his will he left the bulk of his real estate to found a home for aged and poor Hawaiians. It was opened in April, 1881, and will ever keep his memory green.

Election of Kalakaua.—As the late king had failed to nominate a successor, the legislature (which had been elected February 1st) was summoned to meet on the 12th, only nine days after his death.

During this short interval, many mass-meetings were held, and numerous circulars printed in behalf of the two rival candidates, viz.: the Queen Dowager Emma and Colonel David Kalakaua. The legislature, having convened in the old court-house (now occupied by Hackfeld & Co.), elected Kalakaua by thirty-nine votes, only six votes being cast for Queen Emma.

DAVID KALAKAUA

The Court-House Riot.—An immense mob, composed of Queen Emma's partisans, had surrounded the court-house during the election, after which they broke in the back doors and sacked the building. The representatives were savagely assaulted and beaten with clubs. One of them, Lonoaea of Wailuku, afterwards died in consequence of his injuries. As the police proved to be inefficient, and the volunteer troops were divided in their sympathies, the government was compelled to apply to the representatives of the United States and Great Britain for aid. A body of one hundred and fifty marines immediately landed from the United States ships "Tuscarora" and "Portsmouth," and another from H. B. M.'s ship "Tenedos." They quickly dispersed the mob, and took possession of the building. They continued to guard the government buildings, the palace grounds, and the barracks until the 20th. About a hundred of the rioters were arrested and afterwards punished by the courts.

Inauguration of King Kalakaua.—Kalakaua took the oath of office at noon on the 13th of February, 1874, at Kinau Hale, near the palace, and was duly proclaimed king. The next day his younger brother, Prince William Pitt Leleiohoku, was proclaimed heir to the throne.

KAPIOLANI

Kalakaua was born November 16th, 1836, being descended through his father Kapaakea from Kameeiamoku, and through his mother Keohokalole from Keaweaheulu, both distinguished counselors of Kamehameha I. He was married December 19th, 1863, to Kapiolani, a granddaughter of Kaumualii, the last king of Kauai. On the 17th, his first cabinet was formed, consisting of W. L. Green, Minister of Foreign Affairs, H. A. Widemann, Minister of the Interior, P. Nahaolelua, Minister of Finance, and A. S. Hartwell, Attorney-General.

The King's Visit to the United States.—The United States Government having extended an invitation to the king and placed the steamer "Benicia" at his disposal, he embarked November 17th, 1874, for San Francisco, on his way to Washington, accompanied by the

Hon. H. A. Peirce, the American Minister, and other gentlemen. On their arrival they were cordially received, and treated as guests of the nation. After a tour through the northern states the royal party returned to Honolulu February 15th, 1875, having produced a most favorable impression in the United States.

The Reciprocity Treaty.—Negotiations were immediately reopened for a treaty of commercial reciprocity with the United States, which was ratified in June, 1875, and, in spite of strenuous opposition in both countries, the laws necessary to carry it into operation were enacted in September, 1876. This treaty was to remain in force for seven years, and further until twelve months after either government should give notice to the other of its desire to terminate the same. The conclusion of this treaty was the great event of this reign, and perhaps the most important event in Hawaiian history since 1843. It ushered in an era of unexampled prosperity, and set in motion a series of changes of which no man could foresee the end.

Death of the Heir-Apparent.—The following year the nation was called to mourn the untimely death of Prince Leleiohoku, the heir-apparent. He died suddenly, April 10th, 1877, of rheumatic fever, at the early age of twenty-two. His sister, H. R. H. Lydia Kamakaeha Liliuokalani, was proclaimed heir to the throne the next day.

Immigration.—One effect of the reciprocity treaty was to create a pressing demand for labor to carry out the many new enterprises that were projected. Through the agency of Dr. Hillebrand, who was residing in the island of Madeira in 1877, arrangements were made for the immigration of Portuguese from the Azores and Madeira. The pioneer company of one hundred and eighty Portuguese arrived September 30th, 1878, by the ship "Priscilla" from Funchal, and since then over ten thousand more have been added to the population of the islands.

In 1884, the consent of the Japanese Government was obtained for the emigration of its subjects to these islands under certain conditions. The first company of nine hundred and fifty-six Japanese, sent under this agreement, arrived in the "City of Tokio," February 9th, 1885. In six years over ten thousand immigrated to these islands, of whom twelve hundred and sixty returned to Japan. During 1878 and the next six years, about two thousand Polynesians, mainly from the Gilbert Islands, were introduced into this country. These laborers, as a general rule, did not give satisfaction, and nearly all of them have since been returned to their homes.*

The King's Tour around the World.—On the 20th of January, 1881, the king set out on a tour around the world, accompanied by the late Colonel C. H. Judd, his chamberlain, and the Hon. W. N. Armstrong as Commissioner of Immigration. One of the principal objects of this journey was to investigate the whole subject of emigration, and to ascertain the conditions under which foreign governments would sanction it.

After a visit to California, where he received the most flattering attentions, he proceeded to Japan. Here he was received with royal honors, and afterwards had an interview with the famous Chinese statesman Li Hung Chang, in Tientsin.

He was next royally entertained by the king of Siam and the rajah of Johore, after which he crossed British India by rail, and visited the Khedive of Egypt. The

* After 1876 the Chinese came in great numbers until their immigration was checked in 1886.

royal party then made the tour of Europe, visiting the capitals of Italy, Germany, Austria, France, Spain, Portugal, and Great Britain. The king visited Washington on his way home, arriving in Honolulu October 29th, 1881, where a magnificent reception awaited him. He was everywhere received with the utmost courtesy, and afforded every opportunity to collect valuable information for the good of his kingdom.

The Third Small-pox Epidemic.—In the early part of the year 1881 five so-called "tramp steamers" arrived from China in quick succession, bringing nearly seven hundred passengers apiece. Every one of these steamers was infected with small-pox, but the officers of one, the "Quinta," succeeded in concealing the fact. On the 4th of February, a fortnight after she had sailed, several cases of small-pox were discovered on Kukui Place near Nuuanu Street, from which it spread rapidly. All inter-island travel was stopped for a time, and the disease was confined to Honolulu. It was seven months before it had entirely disappeared, during which time there were seven hundred and eighty cases and two hundred and eighty-two deaths.

Volcanic Phenomena.—On the 10th of May, 1877, a great earthquake wave was experienced at all the islands, which washed away the village of Waiakea, Hilo, and drowned five persons. It was caused by a terrible earthquake on the coast of Peru, similar to that of 1868, and was observed throughout the Pacific Ocean.

On the 5th of November, 1880, a light was seen in the summit crater of Mauna Loa. The next day a stream of lava made its appearance at a point eleven thousand one hundred feet above the level of the sea, on the eastern slope of the mountain. It continued to flow for nine months, along the southern edge of the flow of 1855, and finally stopped three quarters of a mile from the town of Hilo, near the Halai hills, August 10th, 1881.

Again, in December, 1886, there were frequent earthquakes in southern Hawaii. At length, January 16th, 1887, fire appeared on the summit of Mauna Loa, and on the 18th an outbreak took place in Kau, north of Kahuku, at an elevation of six thousand five hundred feet, and twenty miles from the sea. The lava stream reached the sea at noon the next day, four miles west of the flow of 1868, and continued to flow until the 24th.

BERNICE PAUAHI BISHOP

The Great Fire of 1886.—The most destructive fire ever known in Honolulu broke out April 18th, 1886, and reduced to ashes nearly the whole of what was known as "Chinatown," which included one third of the city, covering about thirty acres. The loss was estimated at nearly $1,500,000; but like the famous great fire of London, it proved to be a blessing. The streets have been widened, new streets have been opened, and a large part of the burnt district has been solidly rebuilt in brick.

Obituary.—Within the space of four years the nation lost by death four Hawaiian ladies of the highest rank: Ruth Keelikolani, half-sister of Kamehameha V., died May 15th, 1883; Mrs. Bernice Pauahi Bishop, October 16th, 1884; Queen Emma, April 25th, 1885; and the Princess Miriam Likelike Cleghorn, February 2d, 1887.

The Kamehameha Schools will be an enduring monument to the memory of their founder, Mrs. B. P. Bishop, the last descendant of Kamehameha I.

Political Contests.—In the early part of this reign a contest began between two parties, of which the one, headed by the king, aimed at restoring, to a great extent, the ancient system of personal government, while the other sought to limit the sovereign's power, and to make the ministry responsible to the representatives of the people.

In pursuance of the above policy, the king took it upon himself on the 2d of July, 1878, and again on the 14th of August, 1880, to dismiss a ministry without assigning any reason, after it had been approved by a majority vote of the legislature. On the latter occasion his appointment of one Moreno, an Italian adventurer, as premier and Minister of Foreign Affairs, called forth the protest of the diplomatic representatives of Great Britain, France, and the United States, and such a manifestation of public opinion that the king was obliged, after four days of popular excitement, to remove the obnoxious minister.

Systematic efforts were made to turn the constitutional question into a race issue, and to use race jealousy to further party ends. The majority of the members of the legislature, for several sessions, consisted of officeholders, dependent upon the executive. Some of the measures at issue between the two parties were the project of a ten-million-dollar loan, chiefly for military purposes, the removal of restrictions on the sale of liquor to Hawaiians, the licensing of the sale of opium, the chartering of a lottery company, etc. Meanwhile the national debt increased from $389,000 in 1880 to $1,935,000 in 1887.

The Samoan Embassy.—In 1883 two commissioners were sent to the Gilbert Islands and the New Hebrides. to prepare the way for a Hawaiian protectorate over the former group. On the 23d of December, 1886, the king commissioned Mr. J. E. Bush as minister plenipotentiary to the king of Samoa and the king of Tonga, and as high commissioner to the other independent chiefs and peoples of Polynesia. He arrived in Samoa January 3, 1887, and remained there six months, during which time he negotiated an alliance between Hawaii and Samoa. The "Explorer," a small steamer employed in the copra trade, was purchased, fitted up as a man-of-war at great expense, and sent to Samoa March 18, 1887, to strengthen the embassy. It is sufficient to say that the conduct of the representatives of the Hawaiian Government, both on shipboard and on shore, was highly discreditable to their country, and led to their recall in the following July.

The Revolution of 1887.—The dissatisfaction which had long been increasing among the better class of citizens was brought to a crisis in 1887 by gross scandals connected with the sale of a monopoly of the opium traffic to a Chinese firm. On the 30th of June, 1887, an immense mass meeting was held in the armory on Beretania Street, from which a committee was sent to the king with specific demands for radical reforms in the method of carrying on the government. The king, finding himself without support, acceded at once to these demands, dismissed his ministry, and on the 7th of July signed a new constitution. This was a revision of that of 1864, and was intended to put an end to personal government, and to make the cabinet responsible only to the legislature. Officeholders were to be henceforth ineligible to seats in the legislature, and no member of the legislature could be appointed to any civil office under the government, during the term for which he should be elected. The members of the upper house, instead of being appointed by the king, were to be elected for terms of six years by electors possessed of a moderate property qualification.

The Insurrection of 1889.—The execution of the reform measures of 1887 was attended with much opposition on the part of the court and other advocates of the old régime, which came to a head in an insurrection led by R. W. Wilcox, on the 30th of July, 1889. The insurgents, about 150 in number, occupied the grounds of the palace and government building before daylight, and brought over the battery of fieldpieces from the barracks to fortify their position. They then invited the king to come up from his boathouse and proclaim a new constitution, which, however, he did not see fit to do. They were surrounded by the volunteer troops, aided by other citizens, who opened a rifle fire upon them from the neighboring houses, and compelled them to surrender the same afternoon, but not without bloodshed. Seven of the insurgents were killed, and a large number wounded.

The result of this deplorable affair was to intensify the bitter party feeling and race hatred that already existed in the country.

Close of Kalakaua's Reign — Accession of Queen Liliuokalani.—In order to recruit his failing health, the king visited California in the United States cruiser "Charleston," as the guest of Rear-Admiral Brown, in November, 1890. He received the utmost courtesy and hospitality from all classes, both in San Francisco and in southern California.

His health, which seemed at first to have been benefited by the voyage, rapidly failed, in spite of the best medical attendance, and on the 20th of January, 1891, he breathed his last at the Palace Hotel, San Francisco.

IOLANI PALACE

His remains were removed to the "Charleston" with imposing funeral ceremonies, and arrived at Honolulu January 29th, where the decorations for his welcome were suddenly changed into those of mourning. On the same day his sister, the regent, took the oath to maintain the constitution, and was proclaimed queen, under the title of Liliuokalani.

After lying in state for a fortnight, the remains of the late king were laid to rest in the royal mausoleum, on the 15th of February.

KAIULANI

On the 26th of the same month, the queen commissioned a new ministry, consisting of the Hons. S. Parker, Minister of Foreign Affairs, C. N. Spencer, Minister of the Interior, H. A. Widemann, Minister of Finance, and W. A. Whiting, Attorney-General.

On the 9th of March, the Princess Victoria Kaiulani, daughter of the late Princess Likelike, was duly appointed and proclaimed heir-apparent.

Progress of the Country to 1890.—The development of the resources of the islands under the stimulus of reciprocity with the United States surpassed all expectation. The production of the principal staples of the country, sugar and rice, increased to eight times what it was before the treaty. The total value of the domestic exports of the country rose to more than six times, and the total revenues of the government to more than three times what they were before the treaty. Unfortunately, however, the national debt also increased, to nearly $2,600,000.

Much of the wealth thus poured into the country was invested in public and private improvements. The government is spending three times as much for schools and for the health of the people as it did before 1876. In 1896, the use of the English language as the basis and medium of instruction was made by law compulsory in all schools.

Public Improvements.—Among the public improvements made by the government during this period may be mentioned the new palace, built in 1880–81 at a cost of over three hundred and fifty thousand dollars; the marine railway, completed in 1882 at a cost of over ninety thousand dollars; the Kapuaiwa building, built in 1884; and the police-court station, built in 1885. The Honolulu water-works have been greatly enlarged, and the city was lighted by electricity March 23d, 1888. The population of Honolulu has increased to 28,920 (1896). The Molokai light-house was first lighted in 1882, and the Barber's Point light-house, in 1888.

Private enterprise, however, has done still more to develop the resources of the country and to improve the means of communication. A large number of inter-island steamers and sailing vessels have come into existence. The first railway built in the islands was the Wailuku and Kahului Railway, on Maui, which was begun in 1879, and is eleven miles in length. The Kohala Railway was begun in 1881, and was completed the next year. This line is twenty miles in length from Mahukona to Niulii. The year 1889 saw the completion of the Honolulu street tramways, and of the Oahu Railway as far as Waimano, Ewa. The first line of telegraph (afterwards changed to a telephone line) was put up in Maui, between Haiku and Wailuku, in 1878, and telephones were introduced into Honolulu and Hilo in 1882.

In several localities, extensive irrigation canals have been constructed, which have fertilized large tracts of land that were formerly barren.*

The first artesian well in the islands was bored for James Campbell, Esq., at Honoiliuli, Ewa, in July, 1879, and met with unexpected success. The next successful well was bored for the Hon. A. Marques, near Punahou, in the spring of 1880, and gave a fine flow of water. Since then great numbers of artesian wells have been sunk around the island of Oahu, and have added greatly to the resources of the country.

Private generosity has also done much for the educational and charitable institutions of the country.†

* In East Maui the Haiku ditch and the Hawaiian Commercial Company's ditch, which tap the streams flowing down the northern slopes of Haleakala, have brought many thousands of acres into cultivation, and changed the face of the country.

† Among the new institutions founded during this period are the Kamehameha Schools, the Lunalilo Home, the St. Louis College, the Kohala Girls' School, the Lihue Industrial School, and the Bishop Home for Girls at Kalaupapa, Molokai, besides the Honolulu Library and the Young Men's Christian Association Hall.

CHAPTER XXXVII

1892-1898

THE REVOLUTION—ANNEXATION TO THE UNITED STATES

Policy of Queen Liliuokalani.—The troubled reign of Liliuokalani lasted a little less than two years. Its history shows that she was determined to renew the political contest which had been going on during the preceding reign, and to abolish all the restrictions that had been imposed on the power of the crown.

The decision of the supreme court that the term of the last cabinet had expired with the king enabled her to make conditions in advance with the new cabinet, so as to gain control of all appointments. The manner in which this power was exercised caused much dissatisfaction, and grave charges were made against the administration of the police department.

On the 20th of May, 1892, Messrs. R. W. Wilcox, V. V. Ashford, and others were arrested on the charge of conspiring against the government, with the view of establishing a republic, but were finally discharged.

The Legislature of 1892.—The legislative session of 1892 was protracted to eight months by persistent struggles between the opposing parties, during which four changes of ministry took place. During the last week of the session a bill granting a franchise to establish a lottery was passed, as well as an act licensing the sale of opium.

By the same voters an able and upright cabinet was voted out January 12, 1893, two days before the prorogation of the legislature.

The Attempted Coup d'État.— Meanwhile the queen had caused a new constitution to be privately drawn up, by which the principal checks on the power of the crown were to be removed, together with the existing guaranties of the

LILIUOKALANI

independence of the supreme court. Only Hawaiian subjects were to be allowed to vote.

Preparations had been made to proclaim this constitution at the palace on the 14th, shortly after the ceremony of prorogation, in the presence of the legislature, the chief officers of state, and the diplomatic corps. The government troops were drawn up under arms, and a large crowd of sympathizers with the project assembled in and around the palace. Fortunately, however, at the critical moment, the cabinet refused to sign the document, and appealed to leading citizens for advice and support. After a long and exciting contest with her cabinet, the queen partially yielded, and made a speech to the assemblage, stating that with deep regret she had consented to postpone for a few days the execution of her design.

Proceedings of the Committee of Safety.—Meanwhile an informal meeting of residents was held to consider the situation, at which a Committee of Safety was appointed. This committee took steps to form a provisional government, and to reorganize the volunteer military companies, which had been disbanded in 1890.

It also called a mass meeting, which met on the afternoon of the 16th, and ratified its action. On the morning of the same day the queen published a declaration that thenceforth changes in the constitution would be "sought only by methods provided in the constitution itself."

The U. S. S. "Boston," which had unexpectedly arrived from Hilo on the 14th, landed a force on the evening of the 16th, to protect the lives and property of American citizens in case of riot or incendiarism.

Establishment of the Provisional Government.—On the next day, the 17th, the organization of the provisional government was completed by the appointment of an executive council of four members, presided over by Sanford B. Dole, and an advisory council of fourteen members, with general legislative authority.

On the same afternoon the members of the two councils took possession of the government building, and a proclamation by the Committee of Safety was issued, declaring the monarchical system to be abrogated, and establishing the provisional government, to exist "until terms of union with the United States of America have been negotiated and agreed upon." Meanwhile two companies of volunteer troops arrived and occupied the grounds.

By the advice of her ministers, and to avoid bloodshed, the queen surrendered her authority under protest, in view of the landing of United States troops, appealing to the government of the United States to reinstate her in authority. By her orders the station house and the barracks were surrendered the same evening to the provisional government.

Proposed Treaty of Annexation.— On the 19th of January the steamer "Claudine" was dispatched to San Francisco with five commissioners, fully empowered to negotiate a treaty of union with the United States. They arrived in Washington February 3d, and were favorably received by President Harrison. A treaty of annexation was then drawn up by the secretary of state and the Hawaiian commissioners, which was signed on the 14th. It was laid before the senate for its concurrence on the 17th, but was not acted upon before the end of the session. One of the first acts of President Cleveland after his inauguration was to withdraw the treaty from the consideration of the United States senate on the 9th of March.

The Mission of Commissioner Blount.— Two days later President Cleveland dispatched Colonel James H. Blount of Macon, Georgia, as his special commissioner, to investigate the situation in the Hawaiian Islands.

A provisional protectorate of the Hawaiian Islands had been proclaimed, and the flag of the United States had been raised over the government building at Honolulu, on the 1st of February.

Mr. Blount arrived in Honolulu on the 29th of March.

Two days later he gave orders that the flag of the United States should be hauled down, and that the troops on shore should be embarked on board of their respective ships, thus putting an end to the protectorate.

His report, together with the testimony which he had collected, was sent to the Secretary of State July 17th, shortly after which he returned to Washington.

The Attempt to Restore the Queen.—President Cleveland, considering the controversy between the provisional government and the queen to have been submitted to his arbitration, adopted the conclusion of Mr. Blount's report, that the late revolution had been brought about by the aid of the United States minister.

Accordingly, Hon. Albert S. Willis of Louisville, Kentucky, was sent to Honolulu as United States minister, with instructions first to inform the queen of the President's decision, and then, if she would promise to grant a full amnesty to all who had taken part in the revolution, to demand of the president and ministers of the provisional government that they "promptly relinquish to her her constitutional authority."

Mr. Willis arrived in Honolulu November 4th, and, having with difficulty obtained the queen's consent to the amnesty, made a formal demand on the provisional government for her restoration on the 19th of December, 1893. On the 23d President Dole sent the reply of his government to Minister Willis, declining to surrender its authority to the deposed queen.

The Establishment of the Republic.—As all hope of early annexation was now abandoned by the provisional government, steps were immediately taken to establish a republican form of government. A constitutional convention was called to meet May 30th, 1894, for the purpose of framing a constitution for the Republic of Hawaii. The convention finished its labors on the 3d of July, and on the following day the Republic of Hawaii was proclaimed, with Sanford B. Dole as its first president.

The new constitution was in the main modeled after that of the United States. The legislature was divided into two houses, sitting separately, consisting of fifteen members each, a senate and a house of representatives. The qualifications required of voters were similar to those prescribed in the constitution of 1887. The president was to be elected for a term of six years, not being eligible to a second term. No change was made in the national flag. Necker Island was taken possession of on the 27th of May, by Captain J. A. King, in the name of the Hawaiian Government. The first election under the new constitution for members of the legislature was held October 29th, 1894.

SANFORD B. DOLE

The Insurrection of 1895.— Toward the end of the year 1894 a plot was formed to overthrow the existing government and to restore the monarchy. In December of that year a cargo of arms and ammunition was shipped from San Francisco to the islands in the schooner "Wahlberg," and secretly landed at Kaalawai, east of Diamond Head. On Sunday, January 6th, 1895, a body of native royalists was assembled there under the command of Messrs. R. W. Wilcox and S. Nowlein. Their plan was to enter the city after midnight and attack the government headquarters, while their allies in town were expected to seize the electric-light works, telephone offices, and station house. Toward evening, however, a squad of police, which had been sent to search a house at the foot of Diamond Head, was fired upon by an outpost of the insurgents. Mr. C. L. Carter, a leading citizen, was killed, and two native policemen were wounded. The military companies and Citizens' Guard were immediately called out, and all roads leading into town strictly guarded. There was some skirmishing during the night, and Mr. Nowlein and his company intrenched themselves on a rocky hill near the mouth of Palolo valley, from which they were dislodged the next day, and about forty of them taken prisoners. The other band of insurgents under Mr. Wilcox was discovered on the 8th, while crossing the upper part of Manoa valley, and a sharp skirmish took place, in which one of their number was killed and three were taken prisoners, the rest escaping over the ridge into Nuuanu valley. On the 14th Mr. S. Nowlein and his three lieutenants were captured near Moiliili, while Mr. Wilcox was taken in a fishing hut near Kalihi. Liliuokalani was arrested on the 16th, and was confined for nine months in the former palace. On the 24th she formally renounced all her claims to the throne, appealing to the government for clemency toward those who had taken part in the insurrection. In all about 190 persons were brought to trial, 90 of whom pleaded guilty. The ex-queen and 48 others were granted conditional pardons September 7th, 1895, and on the following New Year's Day all the remaining prisoners were set at liberty.

The Cholera Epidemic.— An epidemic of Asiatic cholera prevailed in Honolulu during part of the months of August and September, 1895. It was undoubtedly introduced by a Chinese immigrant, who was landed from the steamer "Belgic," August 10th. The disease made its first appearance among Hawaiians at Iwilei on the 18th, and spread through the Palama quarter and along the Nuuanu stream. By the energetic measures of the board of health and the active coöperation of public-spirited citizens, the epidemic was stamped out in about thirty days. The number of deaths caused by it was 63 out of a total of 88 cases, while the expenses incurred by the board of health amounted to $60,000.

Census of 1896.—On the 24th of September, 1896, an official census of the islands was taken under the superintendency of A. T. Atkinson, Esq. The result showed a total population of 109,020, of whom 39,504 were Hawaiians and part-Hawaiians by descent, and 13,733 were Hawaiian-born "foreigners" (including 4,312 Asiatics, 6,959 Portuguese, and 2,240 other whites).

Of the foreign-born, the Japanese numbered 22,329, the Chinese 19,382, the Portuguese 8,232, and other whites 5,007. (For classification by races, see Appendix A.)

Difficulty with Japan.—During the years 1896 and 1897 certain Japanese emigration companies made strenuous efforts to induce large numbers of their countrymen to emigrate to the Hawaiian Islands. Having ascertained that extensive frauds were being practiced on these people, and that the immigration laws were being evaded, the Hawaiian Government caused a strict examination to be made, and on the 23d of March, 1897, forbade the landing of several hundred Japanese immigrants. In all, about 1,100 immigrants on different occasions were obliged to return to Japan, where this severe action excited intense feeling. The Japanese Government sent the cruiser "Naniwa" in May, with a special commissioner, to investigate the matter. After a lengthy correspondence, the difficulty was amicably compromised the next year by the payment of an indemnity of $75,000 to Japan. This was done at the instance of the United States Government, to remove a possible hindrance to annexation.

Annexation to the United States.—On the accession of President McKinley in March, 1897, negotiations for annexation to the United States were renewed, and on the 16th of June, 1897, a new treaty providing for annexation was signed at Washington. It was ratified by a unanimous vote of the Hawaiian senate on the 8th of the following September, but was not pressed to a vote in the United States senate, as the support of two thirds of the members, required by the United States constitution, could not be counted upon. At last a joint resolution to the same effect, having passed the house of representatives by a vote of 209 to 91, and the senate by a vote of 42 to 21, was signed by President McKinley July 7th, 1898. The news was received with great enthusiasm in Honolulu on the 13th of July, and on the 12th of August, 1898, the formal transfer of sovereignty was made, and the flag of the United States was raised over the executive building with appropriate and impressive ceremonies.

In the exercise of the power conferred upon him by the joint resolution, President McKinley directed that the officers of the Republic of Hawaii should continue to exercise the powers held by them before the transfer of sovereignty, subject to the direction of the President of the United States.

By the terms of the joint resolution, the existing laws of Hawaii are left in force so far as they do not conflict with the constitution of the United States. The public debt of the Republic of Hawaii was assumed by the United

States, not, however, to exceed $4,000,000. It was also provided that there shall be no further immigration of Chinese into the Hawaiian Islands, except upon such conditions as are allowed by the laws of the United States.

In compliance with the joint resolution, the President appointed five commissioners to recommend such further legislation by Congress for the government of the islands as they should deem advisable, namely: from the American Congress, Senators Shelby M. Cullom and John T. Morgan, and Representative Robert R. Hitt; and from the Hawaiian Islands, President S. B. Dole and Judge W. F. Frear. They commenced their labors at Honolulu in September, and submitted their report to Congress in December, 1898.

Thus the Hawaiian Islands enter upon a new era, as an integral part of that great country to which they owe so much in all the lines of human progress. Assured of permanent peace and prosperity, the future of the "Paradise of the Pacific" seems brighter than ever before.

APPENDIX A

POPULATION IN 1896

Nationalities.	Males	Females	Totals
Hawaiians	16,399	14,620	31,019
Part Hawaiians	4,249	4,236	8,485
Americans	1,975	1,111	3,086
British	1,406	844	2,250
Germans	866	566	1,432
French	56	45	101
Norwegians	216	162	378
Portuguese	8,202	6,989	15,191
Japanese	19,212	5,195	24,407
Chinese	19,167	2,449	21,616
S. S. Islanders	321	134	455
Other Nationalities	448	152	600
Totals	72,517	36,503	109,020

AREA AND POPULATION BY ISLANDS

Islands	Area in Square Miles	Population, 1896
Hawaii	4,210	33,285
Maui	760	17,726
Oahu	600	40,205
Kauai	590	15,228
Molokai	270	2,307
Lanai	150	105
Niihau	97	164
Kahoolawe	63	
Totals	6,740	109,020

TABLE TO ILLUSTRATE THE COMMERCIAL PROGRESS OF THE COUNTRY

	1875	1888
Export of Sugar..............	25,080,182 lbs.	235,888,346 lbs.
Export of Rice.........	1,573,739 "	12,878,600 "
Total Domestic Exports........	$1,835,382.00	$11,631,434.88
Total Imports..................	$1,682,471.00	$4,540,887.46
Revenue for two years.........	$877,791.85	$2,817,170.87

	1874-1876	1888-1890
Expended for Schools...............	$95,441.33	$391,438.73
Expended by Board of Health.......	$114,000.00	$316,663.75
	1876	1890
National Debt......................	$459,187.59	$2,599,502.94
Number of Pupils in Schools.......	6,981	10,006

APPENDIX B

PRONUNCIATION OF HAWAIIAN WORDS

The original Hawaiian alphabet, adopted by the first missionaries, contained but twelve letters, five of which were vowels and seven consonants, viz.: *a*, *e*, *i*, *o*, *u*, *h*, *k*, *l*, *m*, *n*, *p*, and *w*. The number of distinct sounds is about sixteen.

No distinction was formerly made between the sounds of *k* and *t*, or between those of *l* and *r*. In poetry, however, the sound of *t* was preferred to that of *k*. The letter *w* generally sounds like *v* between the penult and final syllable of a word.

A is sounded as in f*a*ther, *e* as in th*e*y, *i* as in mar*i*ne, *o* as in n*o*te, *u* as in r*u*le or as *oo* in m*oo*n.

Ai when sounded as a diphthong resembles the English *ay*, and *au*, the English *ou* in l*ou*d.

Besides the sounds mentioned above, there is in many words a guttural break between two vowels, which is represented by an apostrophe in a few common words, to distinguish their meaning, as Kina'u.

Every word and every syllable must end in a vowel, and no two consonants occur without a vowel sound between them.

The accent of about five sixths of the words in the language is on the penult. A few of the proper names are accented on the final syllable, as Paki', Kiwalao', and Namakeha'.

APPENDIX C

HAWAIIAN NAMES OF MONTHS

1. Makalii.	5. Welo.	9. Hilinaehu.
2. Kaelo.	6. Ikiiki.	10. Hilinama.
3. Kaulua.	7. Kaaona.	11. Ikuwa.
4. Nana.	8. Hinaieleele.	12. Welehu.

NAMES OF THE DAYS IN THE MONTH

	1. Hilo.		16. Mahealani.
	2. Hoaka.		17. Kulu.
Kapu Ku	3. Ku-kahi.		18. Laau-ku-kahi.
Kapu Ku	4. Ku-lua.		19. Laau-ku-lua.
Kapu Ku	5. Ku-kolu.		20. Laau-pau.
	6. Ku-pau.		21. Ole-ku-kahi.
	7. Ole-ku-kahi.		22. Ole-ku-lua.
	8. Ole-ku-lua.		23. Ole-pau.
	9. Ole-ku-kolu.	*Kapu Kanaloa or Kaloa*	24. Kaloa-ku-kahi
	10. Ole-ku-pau.	*Kapu Kanaloa or Kaloa*	25. Kaloa-ku-lua
	11. Huna.		26. Kaloa-pau.
	12. Mohalu.	*Kapu Kane*	27. Kane.
Kapu Hua	13. Hua.	*Kapu Kane*	28. Lono.
Kapu Hua	14. Akua. Full Moon.		29. Mauli.
	15. Hoku.		30. Muku.

APPENDIX D

SELECTED GENEALOGIES

CHIEFS OF HAWAII ABOUT THE END OF THE EIGHTEENTH CENTURY

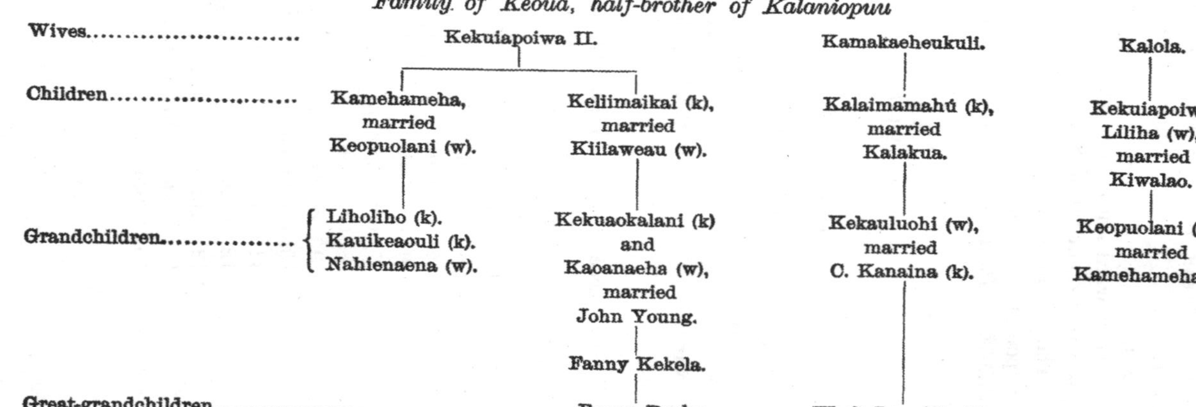

Family of Kalaniopuu, king of Hawaii

Wives	Kalola, sister of Kahekili.	Kanekapolei.
Children	Kiwalaó (k), married to Kekuiapoiwa Liliha (w).	Keoua Kuahuula (k).
Grandchild	Keopuolani (w), married to Kamehameha I.	

Family of Keoua, half-brother of Kalaniopuu

Wives	Kekuiapoiwa II.		Kamakaeheukuli.	Kalola.
Children	Kamehameha, married Keopuolani (w).	Keliimaikai (k), married Kiilaweau (w).	Kalaimamahú (k), married Kalakua.	Kekuiapoiwa Liliha (w), married Kiwalao.
Grandchildren	Liholiho (k). Kauikeaouli (k). Nahienaena (w).	Kekuaokalani (k) and Kaoanaeha (w), married John Young. Fanny Kekela.	Kekauluohi (w), married C. Kanaina (k).	Keopuolani (w), married Kamehameha I.
Great-grandchildren		Emma Rooke.	W. C. Lunalilo (k).	

APPENDIX D—CONTINUED

Family of Kamehameha I.

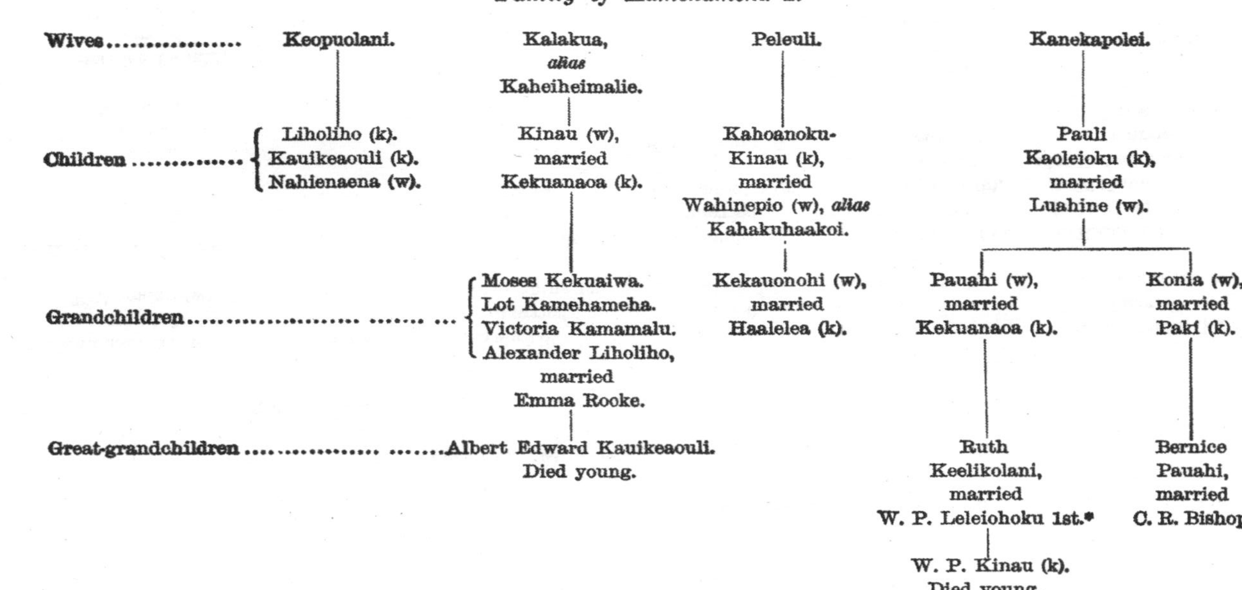

* Son of Kalanimoku (k) and Kuwahine (w).

APPENDIX E

THE MAUI FAMILY OF CHIEFS

Kekaulike, king of Maui until A.D. 1736

Wives............... Kekuiapoiwa I.

- Kamehamehanui (k), married Kukamano (w).
  - Kalanihelemaiiluna (k), married Kawao (w).
    - Pakí (k), married Konia (w).
      - Bernice Pauahi, married C. R. Bishop.
- Kalola (w), married Kalaniopuu. (See No. 1.)
- Kahekili (k), married Kauwahine (w).
  - Kalanikupule (k). Last king of Oahu.

Hoolau.

- Kaeo (k), married Kamakahelei.
  - Kaumualii (k), married Kapuaamohu (w).
    - Kealiiahonui (k).

Haalou.

- Namahana (w), married Keeaumoku (k).
  1. Kaahumanu (w).
  2. Kalakua (w).
  3. Keeaumoku (k), or Gov. Cox.
  4. Piia, *alias* Lydia Namahana.
  5. Kuakini (k), or Gov. Adams, married Keoua (w).
     - Kamanele (w). Died in 1834.
- Kuamanoha (k), married Kamakahukilani (w).
  1. Kalanimoku (k).
  2. Boki (k).
  3. Wahinepio (w), *alias* Kahakuhaakoi (w), married Kahoanoku-Kinau (k).
     - Kahalaia (k) and Kekauonohi (w), married L. Haalelea (k).

APPENDIX E—CONTINUED

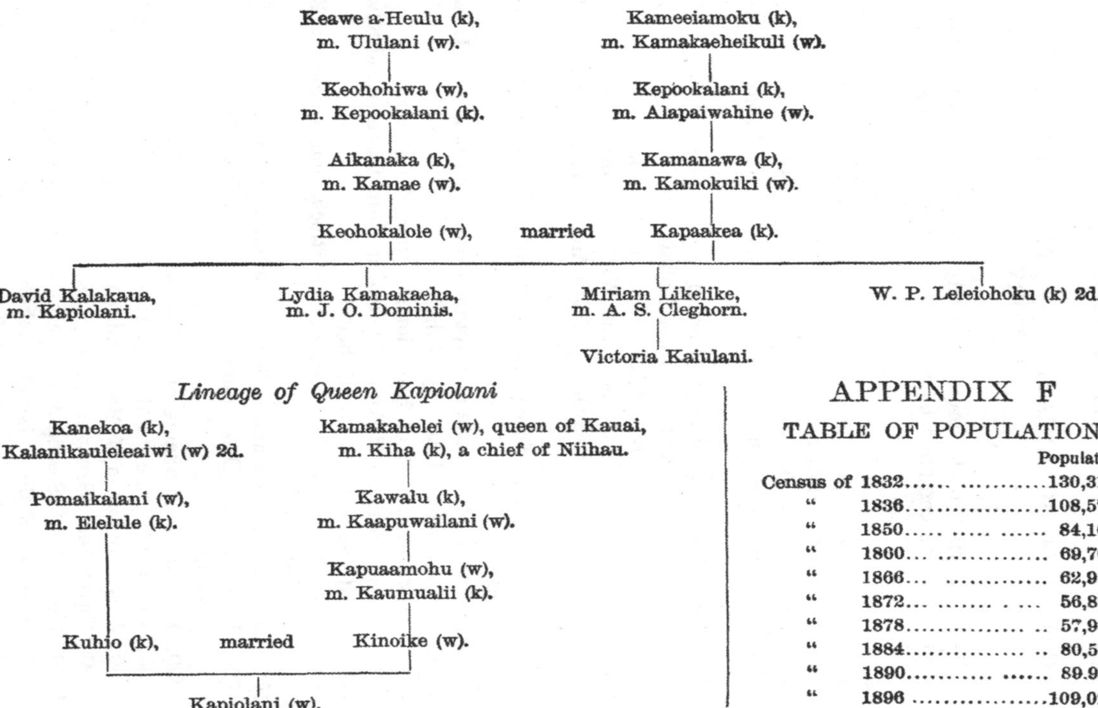

APPENDIX F

TABLE OF POPULATION

	Population
Census of 1832	130,313
" 1836	108,579
" 1850	84,165
" 1860	69,700
" 1866	62,959
" 1872	56,897
" 1878	57,985
" 1884	80,578
" 1890	89.990
" 1896	109,020

APPENDIX G

CHRONOLOGICAL TABLE OF EVENTS IN HAWAIIAN HISTORY

The following table, prepared solely for purposes of reference, is based upon one compiled by the late Hon. A. Fornander:

A.D.

1527, November. Probable arrival of shipwrecked Spaniards at Keei, in Kona, Hawaii.

1555, Discovery of the Hawaiian Islands by Juan Gaetano.

1736, November. Birth of Kamehameha I. at Kokoiki, Kohala, Hawaii.

1737, Great battle at Kawela, Molokai.

1738, Battle of Keawawa, north of Lahaina.

1768, Kaahumanu born at Kauwiki, Hana, Maui.

1776, Kalaniopuu defeated near the Waikapu sand-hills.

1778, January 18. Discovery of Oahu and Kauai by Captain James Cook.

1778, November 26. Discovery of Maui on Captain Cook's second visit.

1779, February 14. Death of Captain Cook at Kealakekua, Hawaii.

1781, Reconquest of Hana by Kahekili.

1782, January. Death of Kalaniopuu, king of Hawaii.

1782, July. Battle of Mokuohai between Kamehameha and Kiwalao.

1783, Conquest of Oahu by Kahekili.

1786, May 26. Arrival of Captains Portlock and Dixon at Kealakekua.

1787, September. Kaiana sailed for China with Captain Meares.

1788, December 29. Reception of Kaiana by Kamehameha at Kealakekua.

1790, February. Massacre of natives at Olowalu by Captain Metcalf.

1790, March 17. The "Fair American" cut off by Kameeiamoku.

1790, July. Invasion of Maui and battle of Kepaniwai at Wailuku.

1790, November. Great eruption of Kilauea.

1790, November. Sea-fight off Waimanu, Hamakua, Hawaii.

1791, Building of the heiau of Puukohola at Kawaihae.

1791, Autumn. Assassination of Keoua Kuahuula at Kawaihae.

1792, March 5. Arrival of Captain Vancouver at Kealakekua.

1792, May 7. Murder of Messrs. Hergest and Gooch at Waimea, Oahu.
1793, February 14. Second visit of Captain Vancouver. First cattle landed.
1794, January 9. Third visit of Vancouver.
1794, February 25. Cession of Hawaii to Great Britain.
1795, January 1. Massacre of Captains Brown and Gardner in Honolulu Harbor.
1795, May. Battle of Nuuanu and conquest of Oahu.
1796, April. Failure of expedition against Kauai.
1796, August. Rebellion of Namakeha in southern Hawaii suppressed.
1796, October 31. Wreck of Captain Barber's ship at Barber's Point.
1797, Liholiho born at Hilo.
1801, Eruption of Hualalai.
1802, Kamehameha sailed with the *peleleu* fleet to Lahaina.
1803, May 24. First horses landed at Kawaihae by Captain Cleveland.
1804, Purchase of the ship "Lelia Byrd" by Kamehameha.
1804, The pestilence called "Mai okuu."
1809, Death of Keliimaikai, brother of Kamehameha I.
1810, Cession of Kauai by Kaumualii to Kamehameha I.
1810, May. Death of Isaac Davis.
1811, Return of Kamehameha I. to Hawaii.
1813, August 11. Birth of Kauikeaouli at Keauhou, Kona, Hawaii.
1815, Fort built by Dr. Scheffer at Waimea, Kauai.
1816, Fort built at Honolulu.
1816, Death of Pauli Kaoleioku, son of Kamehameha I.
1816, November 24. Arrival of Captain Kotzebue at Kailua, Hawaii.
1818, Arrival of Spanish pirates, and their capture by the "Argentina."
1819, May 8. Death of Kamehameha I. at Kailua, Kona, Hawaii.
1819, August. Visit of Captain Freycinet in the "Uranie."
1819, October. Abolition of idolatry.
1820, January. Battle of Kuamoo and death of Kekuaokalani.
1820, March 31. Arrival of First American Missionaries in brig "Thaddeus."
1820, Arrival of first whale-ship at Honolulu, the "Mary," Captain Allen.
1821, July 21. Voyage of Liholiho to Kauai in an open boat.
1821, August 25. First Christian meeting-house built in Honolulu.

1822, January 7. First printing in Hawaiian.

1822, May 1. The schooner "Prince Regent" presented to Liholiho by Captain Kent for the British Government.

1822, August 11. First Christian marriage in Honolulu.

1823, February 4. Arrival of Mr. Ellis from Tahiti.

1823, September 16. Death of Keopuolani at Lahaina.

1823, November 27. Departure of Liholiho and suite for England.

1824, May 26. Death of Kaumualii, ex-king of Kauai.

1824, July 8. Death of Kamehamalu, the queen, in London.

1824, July 14. Death of Liholiho in London.

1824, August 8. Rebellion on Kauai and attack on the Waimea fort.

1824, August 18. Defeat of insurgents at Wahiawa, Kauai.

1824, December. Kapiolani descends into the crater of Kilauea and defies Pele.

1825, May 4. Arrival of the "Blonde" at Lahaina with the remains of Liholiho and his queen.

1825, June 6. Kauikeaouli proclaimed king and Kaahumanu regent.

1825, October 5. Outrage at Lahaina by crew of the "Daniel."

1826, February 26. Outrage in Honolulu by crew of United States schooner "Dolphin."

1826, Mosquitoes introduced at Lahaina by ship "Wellington."

1826, October. Visit of the United States ship "Peacock," Captain Ap Catesby Jones.

1827, February 8. Death of Kalanimoku.

1827, July 7. Arrival of the first Catholic missionaries in the "Comet."

1827, October 27. Outrage at Lahaina by crew of the "John Palmer."

1827, December 8. First laws published.

1829, October 14. Arrival of the United States ship "Vincennes," Captain Finch.

1829, December 2. Departure of Boki on a sandal-wood expedition.

1830, August 3. Return of the "Becket" with news of the loss of the "Kamehameha" with Boki and most of his party.

1830, December 11. Birth of Lot Kamehameha, afterwards Kamehameha V.

1831, September. Commencement of Lahainaluna Seminary.

1831, December 24. Banishment of the Catholic priests to California on the brig "Waverly."

1832, January 31. Birth of Lunalilo.

1832, June 5. Death of Kaahumanu.

1832, December 23. Arrival of Japanese junk at Waialua.
1833, March. Kauikeaouli assumed the power of king.
1833, November 28. Bethel Church opened for worship.
1834, The newspaper "Kumu Hawaii" printed at Honolulu.
1834, February 9. Birth of Alexander Liholiho, afterwards Kamehameha IV.
1835, December 16. Death of John Young, Sr., in Honolulu.
1836, July 30. First English newspaper, the "Sandwich Island Gazette."
1836, September 30. Arrival of Rev. R. Walsh at Honolulu.
1836, November 16. Birth of David Kalakaua.
1836, December 30. Death of Harriet Nahienaena at Honolulu.
1837, February 2. Marriage of Kamehameha III. to Kalama, daughter of Kapihe.
1837, April 17. Return of Messrs. Bachelot and Short on the "Clementine."
1837, July 7. Arrival of H. B. M.'s ship "Sulphur."
1837, July 10. Arrival of the French frigate "Venus."
1837, November 2. Arrival of Rev. M. Maigret on the "Europa."
1837, November 7. Extraordinary earthquake wave.
1837, November 23. Departure of Messrs. Maigret and Bachelot in the "Honolulu."
1838, September 2. Birth of Queen Lydia Kamakaeha Liliuokalani.
1839, April 4. Death of Kinau, the *kuhina nui*.
1839, June 7. Declaration of Rights.
1839, June 17. Edict of Toleration.
1839, July 9. Arrival of French frigate "Artemise," Captain Laplace.
1839, July 25. Treaty signed and $20,000 paid to Captain Laplace.
1840, May. Return of Rev. L. Maigret to Honolulu.
1840, May. Royal School opened.
1840, May 30. Eruption from Kilauea.
1840, October 8. First Constitution proclaimed.
1841, May. Death of Kapiolani.
1841, May 17. Great volcanic wave.
1842, May 15. Treasury Board appointed—Dr. Judd president.
1842, July 8. Departure of Messrs. Haalilio and Richards for United States and Europe as ambassadors.
1842, July 11. Punahou school opened.
1842, August 24. Arrival of the "Embuscade," Captain Mallet.
1842, September 26. Departure of Mr. Charlton for England *via* Mexico.

1842, December 19. Recognition of independence by the United States.

1843, January 10. Eruption of Mauna Loa to the north.

1843, February 10. Arrival of H. B. M.'s ship "Carysfort," Lord George Paulet.

1843, February 25. Provisional cession of the islands to Great Britain.

1843, March 11. Departure of Messrs. Simpson and Marshall for England.

1843, July 31. Restoration of independence by Admiral Thomas.

1843, November 28. Recognition of independence by Great Britain and France.

1844, December 9. Death of Kuakini (Governor Adams).

1845. March 23. Return of Mr. Richards with the remains of Haalilio.

1845, June 7. Death of Kekauluohi.

1846, February 11. Land Commission organized.

1846, March 26. Arrival of French frigate "Virginie," and restoration of the $20,000.

1846, March 26. New treaties with Great Britain and France concluded.

1848, January 27 to March 7. *Mahele* or division of lands.

1848, August. First party left for the gold diggings in California.

1849, June 23. Death of Kealiiahonui.

1849, August 12. Arrival of Admiral Tromelin in the "Poursuivante."

1849, August 25. Occupation of the fort and seizure of the yacht "Kamehameha III."

1849, September 11. Departure of Dr. Judd and Princes Lot and Alexander on a diplomatic mission.

1849, December 26. Treaty concluded with the United States.

1850, September 9. Return of Dr. Judd and the princes from Europe.

1850, December 13. Arrival of Mr. Perrin, French consul, in the "Serieuse."

1851, March 10. Protectorate offered to the United States.

1851, June 2. Death of Keahikuni Kekauonohi.

1851, July 10. New treaty concluded with England.

1852, February 17. Eruption from Mauna Loa on the east.

1853, April 28. Arrival of Mormon missionaries.

1853, May—October. Epidemic of small-pox.

1853, November 12. Arrival of steamer "S. H. Wheeler," afterwards the "Akamai."

1854, December 15. Death of Kamehameha III.
1855, June 13. Death of Paki.
1855, August 11. Great eruption of Mauna Loa toward Hilo.
1855, Introduction of lantana from Chile by Mr. John Ladd.
1856, June 19. Marriage of Kamehameha IV. to Queen Emma.
1857, Demolition of the fort at Honolulu.
1857, May 28. Death of Judge Lee.
1857, July 2. Death of Konia.
1857, August 22. Death of Admiral Thomas.
1857, October 21. Introduction of the first honey-bees.
1858, May 20. Birth of the Prince of Hawaii.
1858, September 8. New treaty with France.
1859, January 23. Eruption of Mauna Loa to the northwest.
1860, July 17. Corner-stone of the Queen's Hospital laid.
1860, July 18. First regular trip of steamer "Kilauea."
1860, September 23. Death of Rev. R. Armstrong.
1862, March 29. Death of Mr. Perrin.
1862, August 19. Death of the Prince of Hawaii.
1862, October 11. Arrival of Bishop Staley.
1863, November 30. Death of Kamehameha IV.
1864, July 7. Meeting of Constitutional Convention.
1864, August 3. The Constitutional Convention dismissed.
1864, August 20. A new constitution decreed.
1865, May 6. Departure of Queen Emma for England on H. B. M.'s ship "Clio."
1865, April 11. Order of Kamehameha founded.
1865, October 19. Death of R. C. Wyllie, Minister of Foreign Affairs.
1865, October 30. Removal of the remains of the kings to the new mausoleum.
1866, May 29. Death of Victoria Kamamalu.
1866, October 22. Return of Queen Emma from England.
1867, March 5. Corner-stone of Anglican Cathedral laid.
1868, April 2. Great eruption of Mauna Loa in Kahuku, Kau, accompanied by earthquakes and a volcanic wave.
1868, March 25. Death of J. P. Parker, Esq.
1868, August 15. Great volcanic wave.
1868, October 19. Kaona insurrection in Kona, Hawaii.
1868, November 24. Death of Governor Kekuanaoa.
1869, July 21. Arrival of the Duke of Edinburgh at Honolulu.
1870, April 19. Arrival of the "Wonga Wonga," first steamer on the Australian route.

1870, September 20. Death of Queen Kalama, widow of Kamehameha III.

1871, February 19. Earthquake at Honolulu and Lahaina.

1871, September 14. Thirty-three whale-ships abandoned in the ice in the Arctic Sea.

1872, March 20. Corner-stone of "Aliiolani Hale" laid.

1872, December 11. Death of Kamehameha V.

1873, January 8. Lunalilo elected king by the legislature.

1873, September 7. Mutiny at the barracks.

1874, February 3. Death of Lunalilo.

1874, February 12. Election of David Kalakaua as king by the legislature.

1874, February 12. Court-house riot.

1874, February 14. Prince W. P. Leleiohoku proclaimed heir-apparent.

1874, November 17. Departure of the king for the United States on the United States ship "Benicia."

1875, February 15. Return of the king on the United States ship "Pensacola."

1875, October 16. Birth of the Princess Kaiulani.

1876, August 15. Reciprocity treaty ratified.

1877, April 10. Death of Prince Leleiohoku.

1877, April 10. Princess Liliuokalani proclaimed heir-apparent.

1877, May 10. Destructive volcanic wave.

1877, July 23. First telegraph line on Maui put in operation.

1879, July 17. Kahului Railway opened.

1879, July. First artesian well in Honouliuli, Ewa.

1879, December 31. Corner-stone of the palace laid.

1880, April 28. First artesian well in Honolulu.

1880, November 6. Great eruption of Mauna Loa, which nearly reached Hilo.

1881, January 20. King Kalakaua set out on his tour around the world.

1881, February. Introduction of small-pox at Honolulu.

1881, April 9. Corner-stone of Lunalilo Home laid.

1881, October 29. Return of the king from his tour around the world.

1883, May 15. Death of Ruth Keelikolani.

1884, October 16. Death of Mrs. Bernice Pauahi Bishop.

1885, April 25. Death of Queen Emma Kaleleonalani.

1886, April 18. Great fire in Honolulu.

1887, January 16. Eruption of Mauna Loa in Kau.

1887, February 2. Death of Princess Likelike.
1887, July 7. New constitution proclaimed.
1889, July 30. Insurrection led by R. W. Wilcox.
1891, January 20. Death of King Kalakaua in San Francisco.
1891, January 29. Accession of Queen Liliuokalani.
1893, January 17. Provisional government begun.
1894, July 4. Establishment of the Republic.
1895, January 6. Insurrection in favor of Liliuokalani.
1898, July 7. American annexation secured.
1898, August 12. United States flag raised at Honolulu.
1899, March 6. Death of Princess Kaiulani.

APPENDIX H

SOVEREIGNS OF THE HAWAIIAN ISLANDS

NAME	BIRTH	ACCESSION	DEATH
Kamehameha I	Nov. 1736	1795	May 8, 1819
Kamehameha II	1797	May 20, 1819	July 14, 1824
Kamehameha III	Aug. 11, 1813	June 6, 1825	Dec. 15, 1854
Kamehameha IV	Feb. 9, 1834	Jan. 11, 1855	Nov. 30, 1863
Kamehameha V	Dec. 11, 1830	Nov. 30, 1863	Dec. 11, 1872
William C. Lunalilo	Jan. 31, 1832	Jan. 8, 1873	Feb. 3, 1874
David Kalakaua	Nov. 16, 1836	Feb. 12, 1874	Jan. 20, 1891
Liliuokalani	Sept. 2, 1838	Jan. 29, 1891	

THE KUHINA NUI'S

Kaahumanu, from May, 1819, until June 5, 1832.
Kinau, until April 4, 1839.
Kekauluohi, until June 7, 1845.
John Young 2d, until January 15, 1855.
Victoria Kamamalu, until August 13, 1864.

APPENDIX I

A LIST OF ALL THE CABINET MINISTERS WHO HAVE HELD OFFICE IN THE HAWAIIAN ISLANDS

REIGN OF KAMEHAMEHA III.

DR. G. P. JUDD	President of Treasury Board.	May 10, 1842.
	Recorder	May 15, 1842.
	Commissioned to correspond with Messrs. Richards and Haalilio	July 18, 1842.
	Minister of Foreign Affairs	November 2, 1843.
	Minister of the Interior	March 30, 1845.
	Minister of Finance	April 15, 1846.
	Resigned	September 5, 1853.
JOHN RICORD	Attorney-General	March 9, 1844.
	Resigned	May 17, 1847.
R. C. WYLLIE	Minister of Foreign Affairs through this reign	March 26, 1845.
JOHN YOUNG 2d	Minister of the Interior through this reign	March 4, 1846.
W. RICHARDS	Minister of Public Instruction	April 13, 1846,
	until his death	November 7, 1847.
R. ARMSTRONG	Minister of Public Instruction through this reign	December 6, 1847.
E. O. HALL	Acting Minister of Finance	September 6, 1849,
	until	September 26, 1850.
E. H. ALLEN	Minister of Finance through this reign	September 6, 1853.

Kamehameha III. died December 15, 1854.

REIGN OF KAMEHAMEHA IV.

R. C. WYLLIE	Minister of Foreign Affairs through this reign	January 15, 1855.
E. H. ALLEN	Minister of Finance	January 15, 1855,
	until appointed Chief-Justice.	June 11, 1857.
JOHN YOUNG 2d	Minister of the Interior	January 15, 1855.
	Died	July 18, 1857.

LOT KAMEHAMEHA...	Minister of the Interior through this reign... ...	June 6, 1857.
R. ARMSTRONG.......	Minister of Public Instruction	January 15, 1855,
	until abolition of the office..	July 1, 1855.
DAVID L. GREGG. ...	Minister of Finance.........	May 26, 1858.
	Resigned....................	August 18, 1862.
C. G. HOPKINS.......	Minister of Finance.........	November 5, 1863.

Kamehameha IV. died November 30, 1863.

REIGN OF KAMEHAMEHA V.

R. C. WYLLIE........	Minister of Foreign Affairs..	December 24, 1863
	until his death..............	October 19, 1865.
C. DE VARIGNY.......	Minister of Finance..... ...	December 24, 1863
C. C. HARRIS........	Attorney-General...........	December 24, 1863.
G. M. ROBERTSON....	Minister of the Interior.....	December 24, 1863,
	until re-appointed first Associate-Justice of the Supreme Court............	February 18, 1864.
C. G. HOPKINS.......	Minister of the Interior.....	February 18, 1864.
	Left for England with Queen Emma............... ...	May 6, 1865.
F. W. HUTCHINSON...	Minister of the Interior through this reign.....	April 26, 1865.
C. DE VARIGNY.......	Minister of Foreign Affairs.	December 21, 1865.
	Returned to France in......	July, 1868.
	Resignation received........	November, 1869.
STEPHEN H. PHILLIPS.	Attorney-General through this reign................	September 12, 1866.
C. C. HARRIS........	Minister of Finance.........	December 21, 1865,
	until.........................	December, 1869.
	Minister of Foreign Affairs.	December 21, 1869.
	Resigned....................	August 25, 1872.
J. MOTT SMITH.......	Minister of Finance.........	December 21, 1869.
	Resigned....................	August 25, 1872.
R. STIRLING..........	Minister of Finance through this reign................	September 10, 1872.
F. W. HUTCHINSON...	Minister of Foreign Affairs *pro tem.* through this reign....................	September 10, 1872.

Kamehameha V. died December 11. 1872.

Reign of Lunalilo

C. R. Bishop	Minister of Foreign Affairs	January 10, 1873.
E. O. Hall	Minister of the Interior	January 10, 1873.
R. Stirling	Minister of Finance	January 10, 1873.
A. F. Judd	Attorney-General	January 10, 1873.

Lunalilo died February 3, 1874.

Reign of Kalakaua

W. L. Green	Minister of Foreign Affairs	February 17, 1874.
H. A. Widemann	Minister of the Interior	February 17, 1874.
P. Nahaolelua	Minister of Finance	February 17, 1874.
A. S. Hartwell	Attorney-General	February 17, 1874.
W. L. Green	Minister of Foreign Affairs	May 28, 1874.
	Minister of Interior *ad interim*	May 28, 1874.
P. Nahaolelua	Minister of Finance	May 28, 1874.
R. H. Stanley	Attorney-General	May 28, 1874.
W. L. Green	Minister of Foreign Affairs	October 31, 1874.
W. L. Moehonua	Minister of the Interior	October 31, 1874.
J. S. Walker	Minister of Finance	October 31, 1874.
R. H. Stanley	Attorney-General	October 31, 1874.
	Died	November 5, 1875.
J. S. Walker	Attorney-General *ad interim*.	November 5, 1875.
W. R. Castle	Attorney-General	February 15, 1876
H. A. P. Carter	Minister of Foreign Affairs	December 5, 1876.
J. Mott Smith	Minister of the Interior	December 5, 1876.
J. M. Kapena	Minister of Finance	December 5, 1876.
A. S. Hartwell	Attorney-General	December 5, 1876.
H. A. Peirce	Minister of Foreign Affairs	March 1, 1878.
J. M. Kapena	Minister of Foreign Affairs	July 3, 1878.
S. G. Wilder	Minister of the Interior	July 3, 1878.
Simon K. Kaai	Minister of Finance	July 3, 1878.
Edward Preston	Attorney-General	July 3, 1878.

CELSO CÆSAR MORENO.	Minister of Foreign Affairs..	August 14, 1880,
	until	August 19, 1880.
J. E. BUSH	Minister of the Interior.	August 14, 1880.
M. KUAEA	Minister of Finance	August 14, 1880.
W. CLAUDE JONES	Attorney-General	August 14, 1880.
J. E. BUSH	Minister of Foreign Affairs *ad interim*	August 19, 1880.
W. L. GREEN	Minister of Foreign Affairs..	September 22, 1880.
W. L. GREEN	Minister of Foreign Affairs..	September 27, 1880.
H. A. P. CARTER	Minister of the Interior	September 27, 1880.
J. S. WALKER	Minister of Finance	September 27, 1880.
	Attorney-General *ad interim*.	September 27, 1880.
W. N. ARMSTRONG	Attorney-General	November 29, 1880.
H. A. P. CARTER	Attorney-General	January 17, 1881.
W. N. ARMSTRONG	Attorney-General	November 5, 1881.
	Minister of the Interior *ad interim*	December 4, 1881.
W. M. GIBSON	Minister of Foreign Affairs.	May 20, 1882.
SIMON K. KAAI	Minister of the Interior	May 20, 1882.
	Minister of Finance	August 8, 1882.
J. E. BUSH	Minister of Finance	May 20, 1882.
	Minister of the Interior	August 8, 1882.
EDWARD PRESTON	Attorney-General	May 20, 1882.
	Resigned	May 9, 1883.
W. M. GIBSON	Minister of Foreign Affairs..	Continued.
J. M. KAPENA	Minister of Finance	February 13, 1883.
W. M. GIBSON	Attorney-General	May 14, 1883.
	Minister of the Interior *ad interim*	July 26, 1883.
C. T. GULICK	Minister of the Interior	August 6, 1883.
PAUL NEUMANN	Attorney-General	December 14, 1883.
W. M. GIBSON	Acting Attorney-General	September 18, 1884.
C. T. GULICK	Acting Minister of Finance.	September 1, 1885.
R. J. CREIGHTON	Minister of Foreign Affairs.	June 30, 1886.
W. M. GIBSON	Minister of the Interior	June 30, 1886.
P. P. KANOA	Minister of Finance	June 30, 1886.
JOHN T. DARE	Attorney-General	June 30, 1886.

W. M. GIBSON	Minister of Foreign Affairs.	October 13, 1886.
L. AHOLO	Minister of the Interior	October 13, 1886.
J. L. KAULUKOU	Attorney-General	October 13, 1886.
L. AHOLO	Attorney-General *ad interim*.	October 22, 1886.
A. ROSA	Attorney-General	November 15, 1886
GODFREY BROWN	Minister of Foreign Affairs.	July 1, 1887.
L. A. THURSTON	Minister of the Interior	July 1, 1887.
W. L. GREEN	Minister of Finance	July 1, 1887.
C. W. ASHFORD	Attorney-General	July 1, 1887.
JONATHAN AUSTIN	Minister of Foreign Affairs.	December 28, 1887
S. M. DAMON	Minister of Finance	July 22, 1889.
JOHN A. CUMMINS	Minister of Foreign Affairs.	June 17, 1890.
C. N. SPENCER	Minister of the Interior	June 17, 1890.
GODFREY BROWN	Minister of Finance	June 17, 1890.
A. P. PETERSON	Attorney-General	June 17, 1890.

REIGN OF LILIUOKALANI

S. PARKER	Minister of Foreign Affairs.	February 26, 1891.
C. N. SPENCER	Minister of the Interior	February 26, 1891.
H. A. WIDEMANN	Minister of Finance	February 26, 1891.
W. A. WHITING	Attorney-General	February 26, 1891.
J. MOTT SMITH	Minister of Finance	July 28, 1891.
H. A. WIDEMANN	Minister of Finance	January 28, 1892.
H. A. WIDEMANN	Attorney-General *ad interim*	July 27, 1892.
PAUL NEUMANN	Attorney-General	August 29, 1892.
SAMUEL PARKER	Minister of Foreign Affairs.	September 12, 1892.
CHARLES T. GULICK	Minister of the Interior	September 12, 1892.
E. C. MACFARLANE	Minister of Finance	September 12, 1892.
PAUL NEUMANN	Attorney-General	September 12, 1892.
JOSEPH NAWAHI	Minister of Foreign Affairs.	November 1, 1892.
CHARLES T. GULICK	Minister of the Interior	November 1, 1892.
W. H. CORNWELL	Minister of Finance	November 1, 1892.
CHARLES CREIGHTON	Attorney-General	November 1, 1892.

MARK P. ROBINSON	Minister of Foreign Affairs	November 8, 1892.
GEORGE N. WILCOX	Minister of the Interior	November 8, 1892.
PETER C. JONES	Minister of Finance	November 8, 1892.
CECIL BROWN	Attorney-General	November 8, 1892.
SAMUEL PARKER	Minister of Foreign Affairs	January 13, 1893.
JOHN F. COLBURN	Minister of the Interior	January 13, 1893.
W. H. CORNWELL	Minister of Finance	January 13, 1893.
A. P. PETERSON	Attorney-General	January 13, 1893.

PROVISIONAL GOVERNMENT

SANFORD B. DOLE	President Minister of Foreign Affairs	January 17, 1893
JAMES A. KING	Minister of the Interior	January 17, 1893.
PETER C. JONES	Minister of Finance	January 17, 1893.
WILLIAM O. SMITH	Attorney-General	January 17, 1893.
T. C. PORTER	Minister of Finance	March 15, 1893.
SAMUEL M. DAMON	Minister of Finance	May 29, 1893.
FRANCIS M. HATCH	Minister of Foreign Affairs	February 15, 1894.

REPUBLIC OF HAWAII

SANFORD B. DOLE	President	July 4, 1894.
FRANCIS M. HATCH	Minister of Foreign Affairs	July 4, 1894.
JAMES A. KING	Minister of the Interior	July 4, 1894.
SAMUEL M. DAMON	Minister of Finance	July 4, 1894.
WILLIAM O. SMITH	Attorney-General	July 4, 1894.
HENRY E. COOPER	Minister of Foreign Affairs	November 6, 1895.
THEO. F. LANSING	Minister of Finance	July 20, 1897.
SAMUEL M. DAMON	Minister of Finance	August 12, 1897.

APPENDIX K

SUPREME BENCH OF THE HAWAIIAN ISLANDS

Superior Court

Established by the act of 1846 to organize the judiciary.

Chief Justice, Hon. William L. Lee, appointed January 15, 1846.
First Associate, Hon. Lorrin Andrews, appointed January 15, 1846.
Second Associate, Hon. John Ii, appointed January 15, 1846.

The above court was abolished by the constitution of 1852, and

The Supreme Court

established in its stead, with the same justices, since which time the changes of incumbents have been as follows:

Chief Justices

Hon. William L. Lee, reappointed June 14, 1852; died May 28, 1857.

Hon. E. H. Allen, appointed June 4, 1857; resigned February 1, 1877, to accept the appointment of Hawaiian minister resident at Washington, at which post he died January 1, 1883.

Hon. C. C. Harris, appointed February 1, 1877; died July 2, 1881.

Hon. A. F. Judd, appointed November 5, 1881.

First Associate Justices

Hon. Lorrin Andrews, reappointed June 14, 1852; resigned January 10, 1855.

Hon. G. M. Robertson, appointed January 10, 1855; resigned December 24, 1863, to accept a cabinet appointment, and reappointed February 18, 1864; died March 12, 1867.

Hon. A. S. Hartwell, appointed September 30, 1868; resigned February 18, 1874, to enter the cabinet.

Hon. C. C. Harris, appointed February 18, 1874; promoted to be Chief Justice February 1, 1877.

Hon. A. F. Judd, appointed February 1, 1877; promoted to be Chief Justice November 5, 1881.

Hon. Lawrence McCully, appointed November 5, 1881; died April 10, 1892.

Hon. R. F. Bickerton, appointed April 11, 1892; died December 10, 1895.

Hon. Walter F. Frear, appointed January 6, 1896.

Second Associate Justices

Hon. John Ii, reappointed June 14, 1852; resigned February 16, 1864.

Hon. R. G. Davis, appointed February 16, 1864; resigned July 8, 1868.

Hon. J. W. Austin, appointed July 10, 1868; resigned July 10, 1869.

Hon. H. A. Widemann, appointed July 10, 1869; resigned to enter the cabinet February 18, 1874.

Hon. A. F. Judd, appointed February 18, 1874; promoted to be First Associate Justice February 1, 1877.

Hon. Lawrence McCully, appointed February 1, 1877; promoted to be First Associate Justice November 5, 1881.

Hon. Benjamin H. Austin, appointed November 7, 1881; died July 5, 1885.

Hon. Edward Preston, appointed November 7, 1885; died January 17, 1890.

Hon. R. F. Bickerton, appointed April 29, 1890; promoted to be First Associate Justice April 11, 1892; died December 10, 1895.

Hon. S. B. Dole, appointed April 11, 1892; resigned January 17, 1893.

Hon. Walter F. Frear, appointed March 7, 1893; promoted to be First Associate Justice January 6, 1896.

Hon. William A. Whiting, appointed January 11, 1896.

Third Associate Justices

Hon. R. F. Bickerton, appointed December 29, 1886; promoted to be Second Associate Justice April 29, 1890; died December 10, 1895.

Hon. S. B. Dole, appointed April 29, 1890; promoted to be Second Associate Justice April 11, 1892.

Fourth Associate Justices

Hon. Abraham Fornander, appointed December 29, 1886; died November 1, 1887.

Hon. S. B. Dole, appointed December 28, 1887; promoted to be Third Associate Justice April 29, 1890.

Note.—In accordance with an act of the legislature of 1886, the supreme court was increased to five members. During the legislative session of 1888 an act was passed which provided that "hereafter, as vacancies occur in the offices of the justices of the supreme court, no new appointments shall be made so as to increase the number above three."

INDEX

L

www.ingramcontent.com/pod-product-compliance
Ingram Content Group UK Ltd.
Pitfield, Milton Keynes, MK11 3LW, UK
UKHW012247290726
14090UKWH00013B/505

9 780898 753240